EFFECTIVE MATH INTERVENTIONS

The Guilford Practical Intervention in the Schools Series

Kenneth W. Merrell, *Founding Editor*
T. Chris Riley-Tillman, *Series Editor*

www.guilford.com/practical

This series presents the most reader-friendly resources available in key areas of evidence-based practice in school settings. Practitioners will find trustworthy guides on effective behavioral, mental health, and academic interventions, and assessment and measurement approaches. Covering all aspects of planning, implementing, and evaluating high-quality services for students, books in the series are carefully crafted for everyday utility. Features include ready-to-use reproducibles, lay-flat binding to facilitate photocopying, appealing visual elements, and an oversized format. Recent titles have Web pages where purchasers can download and print the reproducible materials.

Recent Volumes

Classwide Positive Behavior Interventions and Supports:
A Guide to Proactive Classroom Management
Brandi Simonsen and Diane Myers

Promoting Academic Success with English Language Learners:
Best Practices for RTI
Craig A. Albers and Rebecca S. Martinez

Integrated Multi-Tiered Systems of Support: Blending RTI and PBIS
Kent McIntosh and Steve Goodman

The ABCs of CBM, Second Edition:
A Practical Guide to Curriculum-Based Measurement
Michelle K. Hosp, John L. Hosp, and Kenneth W. Howell

DBT Skills in Schools:
Skills Training for Emotional Problem Solving for Adolescents (DBT STEPS-A)
*James J. Mazza, Elizabeth T. Dexter-Mazza, Alec L. Miller, Jill H. Rathus,
and Heather E. Murphy*

Interventions for Disruptive Behaviors:
Reducing Problems and Building Skills
Gregory A. Fabiano

Promoting Student Happiness:
Positive Psychology Interventions in Schools
Shannon M. Suldo

Effective Math Interventions:
A Guide to Improving Whole-Number Knowledge
Robin S. Codding, Robert J. Volpe, and Brian C. Poncy

Group Interventions in Schools: A Guide for Practitioners
Jennifer P. Keperling, Wendy M. Reinke, Dana Marchese, and Nicholas Ialongo

Emotional and Behavioral Problems of Young Children, Second Edition:
Effective Interventions in the Preschool and Kindergarten Years
Melissa L. Holland, Jessica Malmberg, and Gretchen Gimpel Peacock

Transforming Schools: A Problem-Solving Approach to School Change
Rachel Cohen Losoff and Kelly Broxterman

Effective Math Interventions

A Guide to Improving Whole-Number Knowledge

ROBIN S. CODDING
ROBERT J. VOLPE
BRIAN C. PONCY

THE GUILFORD PRESS
New York   London

Copyright © 2017 The Guilford Press
A Division of Guilford Publications, Inc.
370 Seventh Avenue, Suite 1200, New York, NY 10001
www.guilford.com

Printed in Canada

This book is printed on acid-free paper.

Last digit is print number: 9   8   7   6   5   4   3   2   1

Library of Congress Cataloging-in-Publication Data

Names: Codding, Robin S. | Volpe, Robert J., 1964– | Poncy, Brian C.
Title: Effective math interventions : a guide to improving whole-number
   knowledge / Robin S. Codding, Robert J. Volpe, Brian C. Poncy.
Description: New York : The Guilford Press, [2017] | Series: The Guilford
   practical intervention in the schools series | Includes bibliographical
   references and index.
Identifiers: LCCN 2016047418 | ISBN 9781462528288 (pbk. : alk. paper)
Subjects: LCSH: Mathematics—Remedial teaching. | Response to intervention
   (Learning disabled children) | Mathematics—Study and teaching. | Numeracy.
Classification: LCC QA20.I53 C63 2017 | DDC 372.7/2—dc23
LC record available at *https://lccn.loc.gov/2016047418*

To my parents, reading and mathematics specialists, whose passion for and dedication to teaching inspired my commitment to improve the educational opportunities for all students

And to my husband—thanks for taking this journey with me

—R. S. C.

To my daughter, Sophie

—R. J. V.

To my parents, Paul and Sandy, who have always supported me throughout my career

And to Dr. Chris Skinner, with thanks for his mentorship and instruction on the intricacies of intervention design and evaluation, which are the foundation of the MIND materials

—B. C. P.

About the Authors

Robin S. Codding, PhD, BCBA, is Associate Professor in the Department of Educational Psychology at the University of Minnesota. She has served as Associate Editor of *Journal of Behavioral Education, Journal of School Psychology*, and *School Psychology Review*, and is a recipient of the Lightner Witmer Award from Division 16 (School Psychology) of the American Psychological Association. Dr. Codding's research focuses on the development and evaluation of school-based interventions, the factors that contribute to student responsiveness to intervention, and strategies to support intervention implementation. Her work has emphasized academic interventions and associated assessment for data-based decision making, particularly in the area of mathematics. She has authored more than 50 articles and book chapters.

Robert J. Volpe, PhD, is Associate Professor in the Department of Applied Psychology and Co-Director of the Center for Research in School-based Prevention at Northeastern University. He is 2017 President of the Society for the Study of School Psychology and serves on the editorial advisory boards of *Journal of Attention Disorders, Journal of School Psychology, School Psychology Review*, and *School Mental Health*. Dr. Volpe's research focuses on designing academic and behavioral interventions for students with disruptive behavior disorders, and feasible systems for assessing student behavior in problem-solving models. He has authored over 80 articles, book chapters, and books.

Brian C. Poncy, PhD, is Associate Professor in the College of Education at Oklahoma State University. He is a recipient of the Outstanding Dissertation Award from Division 16 of the American Psychological Association. Dr. Poncy's research focuses on academic interventions and behavioral principles of learning, specifically in the area of mathematics. He teaches classes focusing on the design, selection, implementation, and evaluation of academic interventions and single-case research designs. He has published approximately 20 research articles and book chapters.

Acknowledgments

Many thanks for the supporting work of graduate students Kaitlin Gould, Whitney Kleinert, Leigh Pearrault, and Victoria Sheppard at the University of Massachusetts Boston.

Contents

CHAPTER 1

Introduction

MATH MATTERS

Math principles are embedded in simple daily tasks such as cooking or grocery shopping, and also in more advanced, yet equally important, tasks like paying taxes or balancing a household budget. Mathematical understanding underlies the technological advances that we rely upon hourly such as our smartphones and tablets (National Research Council [NRC], 2001; Patton, Cronin, Bassett, & Koppel, 1997). Math knowledge and reasoning are required to make economically sound decisions such as buying a home or taking out a loan (Crowe, 2010). Math is required for civic engagement: Can we interpret political polling data and critically evaluate the source? Is world population growth really a challenge? Does climate change actually exist (Crowe, 2010)? Numeracy skills are necessary for managing personal health. It is estimated that only 50% of insured adults and 38% of uninsured adults would correctly compute when to take prescribed medication, particularly if one dose is missed (Thompson, 2013). Interpretation of percentages, proportions, and frequencies are necessary when determining the risk–benefit analysis of medical treatments or the risk of acquiring a health condition like diabetes (Ancker & Kaufman, 2007).

In short, individuals with low foundational math knowledge and skills experience challenges effectively participating in society. Adults with poor skills in math are less likely to be involved within their communities, have difficulty managing finances, and encounter various employment challenges (Methe et al., 2011). As we plan for the future experiences of today's schoolchildren, there are high stakes to consider. For example, competence in math is fundamental to science and engineering careers, which are predicted to outpace general job growth 3:1 (National Mathematics Advisory Panel [NMAP], 2008). Students who take higher-level math and science courses in high school are more likely to attend college and earn bachelor's degrees (Adelman, 2006; Attewell & Domina, 2008), and students with higher math competence obtain better-paying jobs (Dowker, 2005; Parsons & Bynner, 1997).

Despite this importance, U.S. math achievement scores demonstrate consistent performance that is below national and international expectations. According to the National Center for Education Statistics (NCES; 2013, 2015), only 40% of fourth graders are at or above proficient levels and these statistics get progressively worse in eighth (33%) and 12th (26%) grades. Also problematic is a persistent gap in achievement experienced by black (19% proficient), Hispanic (28%), and American Indian (23%) fourth-grade students compared with white (51%) and Asian (62%) fourth-graders. Achievement gaps are also observed for students from low-socioeconomic-status households and for students with disabilities. When it comes to the math literacy of adults, only 9% of U.S. adults performed at the highest levels of proficiency as measured by the Program for the International Assessment of Adult Competencies (PIAAC; Goodman, Finnegan, Mohadjer, Krenzke, & Hogan, 2013). The PIAAC assesses practical everyday use of math principles such as computing mileage for reimbursement by an employer and using information on supermarket tags to make purchases. Overall, the United States was outperformed by 18 of the 22 participating countries (Goodman et al., 2013).

These math difficulties begin as early as preschool and persist through the intermediate grades without intervention (e.g., Duncan et al., 2007; Morgan, Farkas, & Wu, 2009). When comparing school entry skills such as early reading, early math, and attention, compelling research has demonstrated that among these three, the strongest predictor of later math *and reading* achievement is early math skills (Claessens, Duncan, & Engel, 2009; Duncan et al., 2007). These data indicate that students with lower numeracy skills in kindergarten will experience smaller gains in math over the course of elementary school and exhibit poorer overall school achievement (Jordan, Kaplan, Ramineni, & Locuniak, 2009; Judge & Watson, 2011).

Only recently has math learning garnered the type of national attention that has long been paid to reading (Fuchs, 2005; Gersten, Jordan, & Flojo, 2005; Grégoire & Desoete, 2009; Kilpatrick, Swafford, & Findell, 2001). Although hard to fathom, math difficulties in preschool and kindergarten have often been overlooked (Dowker, 2005). In our own consultative work with schools, time allocated to daily math instruction is often not provided in kindergarten. A nationally representative survey found that kindergarten teachers spend nearly twice as much instructional time on reading per week as compared with math (Claessens, Engel, & Curran, 2014). Although fewer evidence-based curricula and standardized intervention programs are available in math than reading (Fuchs, Fuchs, Powell, et al., 2008; Gersten, Chard, Jayanthi, Baker, Morphy, et al., 2009; Slavin & Lake, 2008), simple, brief, targeted instructional interventions and strategies can improve foundational whole-number operation skills and competencies (Booth & Siegler, 2008; Codding, Burns, & Lukito, 2011; Codding, Hilt-Panahon, Panahon, & Benson, 2009; Griffin, Case, & Siegler, 1994; Locuniak & Jordan, 2008; Siegler & Ramani, 2008).

WHAT IS MATH PROFICIENCY?

Math is a multifaceted topic that can lead to confusion regarding the relationship among key content areas (Foegen, Jiban, & Deno, 2007). The Common Core State Standards (CCSS) for Mathematics (National Governors Association Center for Best Practices & Council of Chief State School Officers [NGA & CCSSO], 2010) organizes instructional content for grades K–5 across six central domains (see Table 1.1). Although math skills are hierarchical within content strands, new strands are periodically introduced that do not share the same mathematical principles as previously learned (Jordan et al., 2009; Powell, Fuchs, & Fuchs, 2013; Siegler & Pyke, 2013). For example, operations and algebraic thinking in kindergarten requires students to compose and decompose numbers, verbally solve basic addition and subtraction story problems, and automatically solve number combinations within numerals 0–5 (Jordan et al., 2009; NGA & CCSSO, 2010). These skills serve as prerequisites for first grade when students are expected to solve word problems that require addition and subtraction within 20 and fluently solve number combinations within 10. However, fractions are introduced in third grade and the principles that define rational numbers do not overlap those with whole numbers. For example, whole numbers are represented by a single numeral but fractions are represented by a numerator and a denominator (Powell et al., 2013; Siegler & Pyke, 2013). Similarly, multiplying whole numbers always results in a larger product but multiplying fractions results in a smaller product. It is important for teachers and interventionists to keep in mind that math is hierarchical, meaning that key foundational prerequisite skills need to be mastered and the underlying principles that govern these skills need to be well understood when addressing the needs of all students in the classroom (Gersten, Beckmann, Clarke, Foegen, Marsh, et al., 2009; Powell et al., 2013).

The focus on math competency, or proficiency, within education integrates the following five elements (Kilpatrick et al., 2001; NMAP, 2008):

1. Conceptual understanding
2. Procedural fluency

TABLE 1.1. Domains of the CCSS for Mathematics in Grades K–5

Grade	Counting and cardinality	Operations and algebraic thinking	Number and operations in base ten	Measurement and data	Geometry	Number and operations— fractions
K	×	×	×	×	×	
1		×	×	×	×	
2		×	×	×	×	
3		×	×	×	×	×
4		×	×	×	×	×
5		×	×	×	×	×

Note. Adapted from National Governors Association Center for Best Practices and Council of Chief State School Officers (2010). Copyright © 2010. Adapted by permission. All rights reserved.

3. Strategic competence
4. Adaptive reasoning
5. Productive disposition

Conceptual understanding for whole numbers is the knowledge of math concepts, laws, and ideas such as the commutative property (e.g., 2 + 5 = 5 + 2), place value according to the base-ten system, use of estimation, and the ability to compose (200 + 50 + 7 = 257) and decompose (7 + 8 = 7 + 7 + 1) whole numbers (NMAP, 2008; Wu, 2011). Table 1.2 provides definitions for and examples of the basic arithmetic operation laws (also referred to as principles). Conceptual understanding also means that students can use estimation to approximate the precise answer to an equation prior to solving a problem. Students should know that estimation helps inform problem solving and that there are multiple ways to estimate an exact value (NMAP, 2008). Another way of describing conceptual understanding is with number sense, which refers to an understanding of what numbers mean as well as

TABLE 1.2. Basic Arithmetic Operation Laws/Principles

Basic law of operation	Definition	Example
Equal sign	Symbolizes that two collections of numbers connected by an arithmetic operation are the same. *Myth: Is a command to perform an operation to get an answer.*	Check if the numbers on both sides of the equal sign are the same: $1 + 4 = 5$ $3 + 6 = 4 + 5$
Associative law of addition	The sum of any three whole numbers added in any order is equal.	$(2 + 6) + 1 = 2 + (6 + 1)$
Commutative law of addition	The sum of any two whole numbers is the same when the order is changed.	$4 + 3 = 3 + 4$
Associative law of multiplication	The product of any three whole numbers multiplied in any order is equal.	$(3 \times 2)4 = 3 \times (2 \times 4)$
Commutative law of multiplication	The product of any two whole numbers is the same when the order is changed.	$7 \times 8 = 8 \times 7$
Distributive law of multiplication over addition	The same answer is obtained when we (1) multiply a group of numbers added together or (2) multiply first and then add.	$2(5 + 6) = (2 \times 5) + (2 \times 6)$
Distributive law of multiplication over subtraction	The same answer is obtained when we (1) multiply a group of numbers subtracted or (2) multiply first and then subtract.	$3(9 - 7) = (3 \times 9) - (3 \times 7)$

Note. Neither the commutative or associative law apply to division; the distributive law for addition and subtraction is applied to division. Based on information in Stein, Kinder, Silbert, and Carnine (2006) and Wu (2011).

the ability to use numbers fluently and flexibly, make quantity comparisons, and perform mental math (Berch, 2005; Clarke, Baker, Smolkowski, & Chard, 2008; Gersten & Chard, 1999; Gersten, Chard, et al., 2009; Kalchman, Moss, & Case, 2001).

Procedural fluency is the notion that students use algorithms, mnemonics, mental math, and other strategies (e.g., counting on, doubles + 1) appropriately and efficiently. Included is the importance of automatic recall of basic facts (NMAP, 2008). Algorithms, when provided in concert with an underlying conceptual understanding of numbers, are a necessary aspect of math. Algorithms permit students to break down more complex problems into simpler subtasks and offer a shortcut from directly counting a large number of items (Wu, 2011). Effective use of algorithms is also reliant upon automatic recall of basic facts and, in turn, use of algorithms strengthens immediate recall of basic facts (NMAP, 2008).

Automaticity with basic facts, otherwise described as computation fluency, is a prerequisite for solving higher-level math problems (Price, Mazzocco, & Ansari, 2013) and is a necessary goal for all children (NMAP, 2008). Longitudinal studies have demonstrated that solving verbal addition and subtraction problems in kindergarten was more predictive of later math achievement than other aspects of number sense (Jordan, Kaplan, Locuniak, & Ramineni, 2007). Recent neurocognitive studies support the central role of math fluency by demonstrating the connection between basic fact retrieval and more advanced math tasks (DeSmedt, Holloway, & Ansari, 2011; Price et al., 2013). Students without automaticity of basic facts probably direct more cognitive resources to retrieving the solution to basic facts, which may interfere with the higher-order thinking required to engage in more complex problem-solving tasks (Barrouillet & Fayol, 1998; Dehaene, 2011).

Strategic competence refers to mathematical problem solving via visual (e.g., number lines, tally marks, drawings, and ten frames) or mental representation (Gersten, Beckmann, et al., 2009). Strategic use of visual representation along with concrete manipulatives and practice with numerals is an essential element of instructional interventions (Flores, 2009; Gersten, Chard, et al., 2009; Mercer & Miller, 1992b; Miller & Mercer, 1993b; Swanson, 2009). Use of counters, chips, and blocks to illustrate early math concepts along with visual representations and abstract numerical symbols is central to math learning (Baroody, Bajwa, & Eiland, 2009). A critical aspect of this progression is that manipulatives are used briefly and faded in order to advance toward visual representations and then finally to numerals. For example, students with math learning disabilities have been shown to benefit from independent practice of number combinations with manipulatives an average of three times before practicing the same concept using visual displays (Flores, 2010; Mercer & Miller, 1992b). Strategic competence is also required to solve word problems. When faced with a word problem, students are expected to derive mental representations of the relationships among the quantities presented in the problem and determine what is known and unknown (Jitendra, 2007; Kilpatrick et al., 2001). The emphasis is on identifying the structure of the word problem, creating an equation to solve the problem, and locating common features among problem types (Jitendra & Hoff, 1996; Powell, 2011).

Adaptive reasoning reflects the ability to explain, question, or reflect upon problem solving such as through the use of think-alouds (Gersten, Chard, et al., 2009; Kilpatrick et al., 2001). Verbalizing the problem-solving process aloud may facilitate the self-regulation of students who struggle with math (Gersten, Chard, et al., 2009; Swanson, 2009). Verbalization can also be used by students to justify why they chose to solve a problem using a particular strategy. Educators and interventionists are integral for facilitating think-alouds and it is important that they both encourage and model this verbalization, demonstrating for students how to communicate the problem-solving process and explanation of correct answers (Siegler & Booth, 2009). There is also some evidence to suggest that the more specific guidance provided to students, the better the outcomes (Gersten, Chard, et al., 2009).

Finally, productive disposition is the motivation to engage in, provide effort toward, and believe in the value of math learning (Kilpatrick et al., 2001; NMAP, 2008). Quantitative literacy within high school students was found to be a culmination of the ability to use math knowledge in everyday situations, belief in one's own ability to solve math problems, and disposition toward math (Wilkins, 2010). Fortunately, young children have a natural curiosity for numbers that is acquired informally through life experiences (Dehaene, 2011; Kilpatrick et al., 2001) and can be capitalized upon once formal schooling begins—that is, educators need to provide engaging experiences with math learning, encourage persistence with problem solving, and connect the importance of mathematical understanding to life experiences and goals. Evidence also suggests that students with low computation fluency may exhibit greater anxiety and lower self-efficacy for math tasks than students with more fluent skills (Cates & Rhymer, 2003; Throndsen, 2010). This means that educators and interventionists should encourage students' active engagement in math activities (Gersten, Chard, et al., 2009; NMAP, 2008); providing reinforcement for putting effort toward, persisting with, and accurately completing tasks may be particularly relevant (Gersten, Chard, et al., 2009). There is also evidence that specific goal setting and feedback directed at increasing performance is meaningful, although targeting effort instead of performance may be more appropriate for students with math learning disabilities (Codding, Baglici, et al., 2009; Codding, Chan-Iannetta, George, Ferreira, & Volpe, 2011; Fuchs, Fuchs, Karns, et al., 1997; Gersten, Chard, et al., 2009; Schunk, 1985a).

Essential to this definition of math proficiency is that each of these elements is mutually dependent (Kilpatrick et al., 2001; NMAP, 2008). For example, the use of effective procedures permits enhanced conceptual understanding of more complex ideas (Fuchs, Fuchs, Compton, et al., 2006; Geary, Bailey, & Hoard, 2009; Geary, Hoard, Byrd-Craven, & DeSoto, 2004; NMAP, 2008; NRC, 2001). However, knowledge of procedures without conceptual understanding or adaptive reasoning may lead to inefficient problem solving and errors. Finally, students need to persist on problem solving tasks to completion in order to experience success, which in turn is likely to facilitate student beliefs that he or she will be successful in the future (NMAP, 2008). Table 1.3 illustrates how conceptual understanding, procedural fluency, and adaptive reasoning interact to solve a simple arithmetic problem. In order to use the addition algorithm, students must be able to automatically perform single-digit addition facts as well as understand the concept of place value (Wu, 2011). Students can use think-alouds to communicate their understanding of why the algorithm results in the correct answer and could also estimate the possible solution prior to finding the exact answer.

TABLE 1.3. Integrating the Standard Addition Algorithm with a Think-Aloud Explanation

Standard addition algorithm		Think-aloud explanation	
Self-guided instructions	Worked problem	Why does this algorithm work?	Worked problem
1. Work from right to left, beginning with the ones column.	$\begin{array}{r} 654 \\ +\ 74 \\ \hline \end{array}$	1. Break down the numbers into hundreds, tens, and ones.	$654 = 600 + 50 + 4$ $\ 74 = \ \ \ 0 + 70 + 4$
2. Add the digits.	$\begin{array}{r} 654 \\ +\ 74 \\ \hline 8 \end{array}$	2. Add the hundreds together.	$654 = \mathbf{600} + 50 + 4$ $\ 74 = \ \ \ \mathbf{0} + 70 + 4$ $\mathbf{600}$
3. The sum in the tens column is more than 10, so you need to regroup. a. $5 + 7 = 12$ b. Enter 2 in the tens column and carry the 1 to the next column (to the left), in this case, the hundreds column.	$\begin{array}{r} {}^{1}654 \\ +\ 74 \\ \hline 28 \end{array}$	3. Add the tens together. Break down the sum into hundreds and tens.	$654 = 600 + \mathbf{50} + 4$ $\ 74 = \ \ \ 0 + \mathbf{70} + 4$ $\mathbf{100 + 20}$ 120
4. Sum the digits in the hundreds column; be sure to add the 1 that you carried.	$\begin{array}{r} {}^{1}654 \\ +\ 74 \\ \hline \mathbf{728} \end{array}$	4. Add the ones together.	$654 = 600 + 50 + \mathbf{4}$ $\ 74 = \ \ \ 0 + 70 + \mathbf{4}$ $\mathbf{8}$
		5. Add the hundreds, tens, and ones together.	$\begin{array}{r} 654 = 600 + \ \ 50 \ \ + 4 \\ +\ 74 = \ \ \ 0 + \ \ 70 \ \ + 4 \\ \hline 600 + (100 + 20) + 8 \\ 700 + \ \ 20 \ \ + 8 \\ \mathbf{728} \end{array}$

Note. Based on information in Wu (2011).

APPLYING RESPONSE TO INTERVENTION TO MATH

National legislation, such as the Individuals with Disabilities Education Improvement Act (IDEIA) of 2004 (Public Law 108-446), has emphasized that schools apply a prevention-based framework to service delivery in order to avert the onset of academic difficulties and mitigate poor outcomes by intervening early when problems do occur. The outcome of this legislation is the use of a multi-tiered system that emphasizes academic screening of all students, evaluation of the impact of curricula, and provision of small-group and individualized intervention services, as well as progress monitoring of student response to intervention (RTI; Batsche et al., 2006). Response to intervention, the name this multi-tiered system is widely known as, has been fully or partially implemented in 94% of districts participating in a national survey (Spectrum K–12 School Solutions, 2011). The vast majority of these districts report applying RTI to reading with fewer districts adopting the framework for math. The low performance of U.S. students in math (NMAP, 2008), combined with evidence that RTI has reduced the number of special education referrals and improved annual yearly progress (Spectrum K–12 School Solutions, 2011), suggests that implementing RTI with math might be an essential aspect of overall improvements in math learning.

BOX 1.1. Resources for Applying the RTI Framework to Math	
Resource	**Resource type**
Bende, W. N., & Crane, D. (2011). *RTI in math: Practical guidelines for elementary teachers.* Bloomington, IN: Solution Tree Press.	Book
Gersten, R., Newman-Goncher, R., & Vaughn, S. (2011). *Understanding RTI in mathematics: Proven methods and applications.* Baltimore: Brookes.	Book
Riccomini, P. J., & Witzel, B. S. (2010). *Response to intervention in math.* Thousand Oaks, CA: Corwin Press.	Book
Gersten, R., Beckmann, S., Clarke, B., Foegen, A., Marsh, L., Star, J. R., et al. (2009). *Assisting students struggling with mathematics: Response to intervention (RtI) for elementary and middle schools* (NCEE 2009-4060). Washington, DC: National Center for Education Evaluation and Regional Assistance, Institute of Education Sciences, U.S. Department of Education. Retrieved from *http://ies.ed.gov/ncee/wwc/practice_guides/rti_math_pg_042109.pdf*.	IES practice guide
National Mathematics Advisory Panel. (2008, March). *Foundations for success: The final report of the National Mathematics Advisory Panel.* Washington, DC: U.S. Department of Education. Retrieved November 11, 2008, from *www2.ed.gov/about/bdscomm/list/mathpanel/report/final-report.pdf*.	Panel report
National Center on Intensive Intervention *www.intensiveintervention.org*	Website
National Center on Response to Intervention *www.rti4success.org*	Website
RTI Action Network: A Program of the National Center for Learning Disabilities *www.rtinetwork.org*	Website

A panel convened by the Institute of Education Sciences (IES) has developed a practice guide for applying RTI to math (Gersten, Beckmann, et al., 2009). This panel provided eight major recommendations with evidence supporting these recommendations ranging from low to strong. Using this practice guide and other resources, we developed an RTI implementation survey (see Form 1.1) and a corresponding action plan (see Form 1.2) that can help schools identify which of these recommended elements have been adopted. Readers are encouraged to directly access the IES reference. See *http://ies.ed.gov/ncee/wwc/ pdf/practice_guides/rti_math_pg_042109.pdf* for more comprehensive details. A number of books have also been published to guide school professionals in the adoption and implementation of RTI for math and national websites offer further guidance (see Box 1.1). Although the tips and tools described throughout this book could be used regardless of whether the RTI framework is implemented, it is our belief that student outcomes might be enhanced when such a framework is applied (see Fuchs, Fuchs, Craddock, et al., 2008; Fuchs, Fuchs, & Hollenbeck, 2007).

THE INSTRUCTIONAL HIERARCHY

A fundamental component of RTI is data-based decision making. Different types of data need to be used to make various types of decisions (Salvia, Ysseldyke, & Bolt, 2010). For example, screening measures with strong predictive validity should be used to catch all students who are potentially at risk. However, measures that are sensitive to growth over time should be administered to evaluate student response to treatment (Salvia et al., 2010). Generally, school teams have been found to accurately collect screening and progress monitoring data (Burns, Peters, & Noell, 2008) but unfortunately teams have more difficulty interpreting, using, and planning for treatment with data. The success of RTI arguably hinges upon matching each at-risk student with an appropriate research-based intervention that addresses the appropriate target skill. Although the CCSS (NGA & CCSSO, 2010) and the National Council of Teachers of Mathematics (NCTM; 2006) have derived comprehensive scope and sequence recommendations for each grade level, educators and interventionists will also need to identify prerequisite skills and determine mastery of these foundational skills for students who struggle with accessing the curriculum (Gersten, Beckmann, et al., 2009; Powell et al., 2013).

Rather than simply identifying available interventions and providing those to all students experiencing math difficulties, it might be useful to apply a problem-solving approach so that the treatment selection matches students' math knowledge. Selecting treatments according to the match with students' skill level means that educators and interventionists could identify what to teach and how.

The instructional hierarchy is a heuristic that describes one way to conceptualize skill progression and has been applied to math learning (Burns, Codding, Boice, & Lukito, 2010; Haring & Eaton, 1978; Rivera & Bryant, 1992); the hierarchy includes five stages of skill development: (1) acquisition, (2) fluency, (3) maintenance, (4) generalization, and (5) adaptation. These stages of learning have also been described as establishing, remembering, enduring, and applying (Johnson & Layng, 1992).

Acquisition Stage

A student in this stage of learning exhibits slow and inaccurate math performance, suggesting that the student has limited knowledge of the math skill or concept being instructed. In other words, the skill is new to the student. Instructional strategies that are most useful to facilitate accuracy include demonstration or modeling; a narrow curricular scope; instructor-provided cues or prompts; high rates of immediate, corrective, and elaborate feedback with reinforcement; and opportunities for guided practice; as well as explicit and strategy instruction.

Fluency Stage

A student in this stage of learning exhibits accurate but slow performance. The student has been taught the underlying concept of a skill and understands how to use it but requires additional opportunities to practice using the skill to build accurate and fast performance, or automaticity. Instructional strategies that are most useful to facilitate fluency include providing many varied opportunities for practice, performance feedback, goal setting, and performance-based reinforcement contingencies.

Maintenance Stage

A student in this stage of learning exhibits accurate and fluent performance with a skill or concept over time, even when learning a new more advanced skill or concept. Instructional strategies that facilitate maintenance include increasing opportunities for independent practice, goal setting and performance feedback, self-monitoring and regulation, and cumulative review.

Generalization Stage

A student in this stage of learning displays fluency and maintenance with a skill or concept. At this point, the student should also be exhibiting the application of these skills in different settings and situations, across materials and tasks, and with different people. For example, students who have demonstrated automaticity with math facts in a small-group setting with an interventionist should also be able to do so during core instruction taught by the general education teacher within the classroom. Students should be able to apply skills to learning centers or math games. Instructional strategies that promote generalization include providing a range of tasks and activities during which students have to use a skill or concept that includes varied levels of difficulty, providing cues for generalization, and fading adult support.

Adaptation Stage

A student in this stage of learning is able to solve novel problems by adapting previously mastered mathematical concepts and skills to a new situation. This might be evident in daily living skills when a recipe has to be doubled to feed more people or altered because all of the ingredients are not available (Rivera & Bryant, 1992). Students might have to solve a word problem that requires them to describe how to build a table but only a portion of the materials are present. To perform either of these tasks students will have to use and apply a variety of previously learned math concepts and skills in novel ways to solve the current problem. Instructional strategies that facilitate adaptation include the presentation of novel problem-solving tasks that require use and adaptation of previous knowledge, think-alouds, and performance feedback on skill application.

PURPOSE OF THIS BOOK

The emphasis of this book is on how to use data to inform decisions on which instructional interventions to provide to students struggling with math. To do so we emphasize the use of data, such as curriculum-based assessment (CBA) and computer-adaptive testing (CAT), and the application of these data to determine students' placement within the instructional hierarchy. The use of empirically supported interventions is essential to ensure student learning. For an intervention to be effective, procedures must also be appropriately matched to the needs of the student, which we believe can be better determined by using data. For example, if a student displays slow and inaccurate performance (e.g., completes 8 digits correct per minute [DCPM] on a CBA tool with 60% accuracy) when completing addition problems, opportunities for novel practice will not be effective. For students who show this pattern the more appropriate intervention would include demonstration, modeling, guided practice, and immediate feedback. Similarly, if a student displays slow but accurate performance (e.g., completes 25 DCPM on a CBA tool with 98% accuracy), using an intervention with demonstration, modeling, guided practice, and immediate feedback would be less efficient. This is because the student would not need modeling and feedback to respond to the problem. Therefore, the inclusion of these intervention components would drastically reduce opportunities to respond and student growth rates compared with using an intervention that facilitates novel and frequent practice. Even if both interventions are "empirically supported," in order to maximize efficacy it is important for educators to know how to use student data to select and/or transition across different types of interventions.

Table 1.4 describes the correspondence between the stages of the instructional hierarchy, the instructional components recommended for instruction according to each stage, and common student responses. We divided the first two stages of the instructional hierarchy (i.e., acquisition and fluency) into two types of response patterns: initial and functional. In our work, we have learned that students within the acquisition and fluency stages exhibit a wide range of performance patterns that suggest students may benefit from slightly different approaches. In the sections that follow, we describe each stage of the instructional

TABLE 1.4. Using the Instructional Hierarchy for Treatment Selection

Stage	Instructional components	Student response patterns
Adaptation: Transferring skills to new problems and new situations. APPLYING	• Simulations • Problem solving	Student has mastered and maintained skills and now is working on integrating this knowledge and applying skills to novel problems.
Maintenance and generalization: Combining skills and procedures to increase responding across time and problem types. ENDURING	• Discrimination training • Cues for generalization • Self-regulation • Independent practice • Procedural skills/strategies	Although student has mastered skills, he or she is having difficulty accurately and quickly responding when applying learned skills to altered contexts.
Fluency: Once a skill is acquired, practice is needed to increase speed of responding. Fluent responding has been shown to benefit generalization across time and skills. REMEMBERING	• Performance feedback • Goal setting • Reinforcement • Practice (timed, with peers) • Drill	*Functional fluency*: Student is developing automaticity across all items. Skills are becoming memorized. CBM scores range from 30 to 40 DCPM. *Initial fluency*: Student is slow but accurate. Often strategy dependent. CBM scores range from 20 to 30 DCPM.
Acquisition: First stage of learning, emphasis on promoting accurate responding. Necessitates demonstration or model, a narrow curricular scope (limited items), and high rates of feedback with reinforcement. ESTABLISHING	• Performance feedback • Corrective feedback • Prompts and cues • Models • Demonstration • Explicit instruction • Strategy instruction	*Functional acquisition*: Accuracy of target item set ranges from 60 to 100%. CBM scores <20 DCPM. *Initial acquisition*: Student is first learning a skill. Accuracy of target item set ranges from 0 to 60%.

Note. DCPM, digits correct per minute, the type of score yielded from curriculum-based measurement (CBM). The content of this table was adapted with permission from Brian Poncy and Gary Duhon. Copyright © 2015.

hierarchy as well as how the intervention session content can be altered according to the use of data.

ACQUISITION

When students are first introduced to a skill as occurs during general core instruction they are initially working on building accuracy with the skill. In order to improve accuracy, initially a smaller set of numerals, number combinations, or problem types might be presented within teacher-directed activities that contain lots of immediate feedback. Once students' accuracy with these small sets of whole numbers improves to 60%, the instructional components remain the same; however, the intensity of those elements changes. Modeling can shift from teacher directed to student directed; fewer demonstrations need to be provided; prompts and cues can be offered to students for independent use; and feedback might alter from immediate responses provided following the presentation of each numeral, fact, or word problem to reviewing work after a longer interval of time.

Case Example

When given a 2-minute CBA probe in single-digit addition facts sums to 10, Logan, a second-grade student, received a score of 8 DCPM and his accuracy score was 25%. Mrs. Beacon recognized that Logan was performing in the initial acquisition stage of the instructional hierarchy and she decided to initially focus intervention sessions on single-digit addition facts sums to 5. She began each lesson by modeling each addition fact for Logan using base-ten blocks and then provided an opportunity for Logan to practice with the blocks with her assistance. Next, she modeled how to solve each addition fact using worksheets containing pictorial representations of the same facts. Finally, she ended the session by presenting flash cards with each practiced fact. Mrs. Beacon provided Logan with a 2-minute CBA probe in single-digit addition facts sums to 5 at the end of each session to assess his progress. Once he achieved greater than 60% accuracy and more than 10 DCPM, representative of the functional acquisition phase, she provided Logan with practice using flash cards that focused only on the remaining unknown facts and built in opportunities for him to review known facts such that he was presented with known and unknown facts in an alternating order.

FLUENCY

Students who exhibit 100% accuracy with a skill but are slow to perform the skill fall in the fluency stage of the instructional hierarchy. Students in the initial fluency stage benefit from novel, timed opportunities to practice and it is often useful to provide students with feedback on the fluency of their performance and show them how to monitor their own performance with graphs (Codding, Chan-Iannetta, Palmer, & Lukito, 2009). Once students achieve about 30–40 DCPM, those students are entering the functional fluency stage. Students in this stage are beginning to demonstrate automatic retrieval of skills such as numerals or number combinations and increasing the number of opportunities for practice is useful for promoting fluency.

Case Example

Continuing the example of Logan and Mrs. Beacon above, Mrs. Beacon observes a 2-minute CBA probe containing single-digit addition facts sums to 10 on which Logan receives a score of 20 DCPM with 100% accuracy. She is pleased with his progress and alters the intervention sessions to include opportunities for Logan to use a cover–copy–compare (CCC) worksheet that provides a model of the correct problem stem and answer along with identical problem stems without the answer for him to record the answer. During some sessions, Mrs. Beacon provides Logan with headphones and an audiocassette recording with the instructions that he should "beat the tape" by recording his answer to the problems on the worksheet in front of him before the tape provides the answer. Using progress monitoring with single-digit addition facts sums to 10, Mrs. Beacon realizes that this practice has led to improvements in Logan's performance. He is now completing 30 DCPM without any errors, performance indicative of the functional fluency stage. She once again adjusts the intervention sessions to emphasize fast and accurate independent practice. Logan uses a kitchen timer to see how many problems he completes in 1 minute and then graphs his performance. He repeats this procedure three times during each intervention session with the goal of trying to meet or beat 40 DCPM. Mrs. Beacon alters this activity with the opportunity to practice the target skill using a freely available computer software program.

MAINTENANCE AND GENERALIZATION

Once students have achieved fluency to 40 DCPM, their performance is considered to be mastery. However, students may experience difficulty maintaining this performance over time—so they may exhibit inconsistent performance. Alternatively, students may exhibit consistent levels of performance at high rates on the target skill but have difficulty applying that skill to other contexts. Students may benefit from self-monitoring checklists that serve as reminders to apply the skill, cues to apply the skill, or additional opportunities to practice the skill in different contexts. For example, students should be able to retrieve known addition facts whether the facts are presented vertically, horizontally, in the context of worksheets that contain addition and subtraction facts, and when presented in nontraditional formats (e.g., $x + 5 = 9$).

Case Example

Mrs. Beacon realizes that Logan's performance has been variable, sometimes reaching 40 DCPM with addition facts sums to 10 but not consistently. Mrs. Beacon works with Mr. Quincy, Logan's second-grade teacher, to provide additional independent practice activities twice a day in the classroom (once first thing in the morning and once immediately after lunch as the class is settling into the afternoon routine). Now, Logan has the opportunity to practice at least once daily and often twice daily. This strategy worked and he has maintained high rates of performance. Mrs. Beacon now provides Logan with instruction and practice with nontraditional addition equations as well as addition and subtraction fact-family worksheets.

CONCLUSION

In this book we present information on standardized evidence-based math interventions as well as describe a number of low-cost, low-resource, simple intervention strategies from the peer-reviewed literature that can be used in isolation or combined to generate treatment packages. Our math content focus is on whole-number knowledge that aligns with two Common Core areas: (1) number operations in base ten and (2) operations and algebraic thinking. The chapters that follow begin with the importance of supplementing existing math curricula and providing universal screening, and proceed with an emphasis on instructional interventions appropriate for students who are at risk for or are experiencing math difficulties. The book concludes with a discussion of how to evaluate students' progress and make adjustments to interventions accordingly.

RTI Implementation Survey for Math

	0 No skills or knowledge/ not in place	1 Beginning to learn/put in place	2 Partially competent/ in place	3 Fully competent/ in place
School System Capacity and Support				
☐ Principal supports RTI model in math.				
☐ Faculty and staff received an overview of the RTI model as applied to math.				
☐ Majority (80+%) of faculty and staff support the use of an RTI model in math.				
☐ Multidisciplinary problem-solving teams have been formed (e.g., building, grade, combination) in order to evaluate data; establish building, grade, class, individual student goals; select curricula and interventions; select tools for screening and monitoring progress; evaluate outcomes.				
☐ Resources currently available are inventoried (e.g., curricula/programs/interventions, personnel, materials, time).				
☐ Expert(s) in math or math instruction (e.g., math coaches, math teachers, math department heads, university-level mathematicians) are included on district- and building-level problem-solving teams.				
Data-Based Decision Making				
Universal Screening				
☐ Select screening measures reflective of grade-level content standards (e.g., map onto NCTM [2006] focal points, NMAP [2008] recommendations, and Common Core [NGA & CCSSO, 2010]).				
☐ Select screening measures that are reliable, valid (predictive validity), and efficient.				
☐ Same screening measures are used across district.				

(continued)

Note. RTI, response to intervention. Based on information in Gersten, Beckmann, et al. (2009); Shapiro (2012); Slavin and Lake (2008); Slavin, Lake, and Groff (2009); Stein, Kinder, Zapp, and Feuerborn (2010); and Wright (2011).

	0 No skills or knowledge/ not in place	**1** Beginning to learn/put in place	**2** Partially competent/ in place	**3** Fully competent/ in place
☐ Screening is conducted with all students two or three times yearly (fall, winter, spring).				
☐ Screening data are used in combination with state testing results (recommended for grades 4–8).				
Progress Monitoring				
☐ Students receiving Tiers 2 and 3 services are monitored weekly, biweekly, or monthly using grade-level general outcome measures.				
☐ Students slightly above cutoff score are monitored (recommendation: one standard error of measurement above cutoff score) monthly.				
☐ Use progress monitoring measures that are reliable, valid, and designed to measure growth.				
☐ Monitor progress for students receiving Tiers 2 and 3 services using curriculum-embedded or mastery measures daily or weekly to evaluate response to treatment.				
☐ Use progress monitoring to determine when instructional changes or regrouping are needed.				
High-Quality Instruction; Aligned with Standards				
☐ Designated block of time is assigned for core math instruction (recommendation 45–60 minutes).				
☐ Select core curricula reflective of grade-level content standards (e.g., map onto NCTM [2006] focal points, NMAP [2008] recommendations, and Common Core [NGA & CCSSO, 2010]).				
☐ Include instructional process components like peer tutoring or cooperative learning activities.				
☐ Independent practice activities (classwork and homework) are provided for content that can be completed with a minimum of 80% accuracy.				
Tiered Interventions				
☐ Tiered instruction/intervention, in addition to core instruction, is provided for enrichment (students at or above expectations on screening measures), support (small-group Tier 2 intervention), and intensive support (individualized/smaller-group Tier 3 intervention).				

(continued)

	0 No skills or knowledge/ not in place	1 Beginning to learn/put in place	2 Partially competent/ in place	3 Fully competent/ in place
☐ 20–40 minutes is scheduled four to five times weekly for tiered instruction/intervention (more may be designated for Tier 3).				
☐ Range of professionals, staff, and volunteers are identified as interventionists (e.g., professionals with specialized training often reserved for Tier 3 services).				
☐ Tiers 2 and 3 interventions should include instruction that is explicit and systematic (e.g., modeling, demonstration, verbalization of thought process [think-aloud], guided practice, corrective feedback, and frequent cumulative review).				
☐ Tiers 2 and 3 interventions emphasize foundation and prerequisite skills.				
☐ Tiers 2 and 3 interventions focus on deep understanding of and proficiency with whole numbers (grades K–5).				
☐ Tiers 2 and 3 intervention materials should include visual representation of math concepts.				
☐ Tiers 2 and 3 interventions should include 10 minutes of math facts fluency building.				
☐ Tiers 2 and 3 interventions should include motivational strategies.				
☐ Scripted protocols are used or developed to enhance treatment integrity.				
Professional Development and Support				
☐ Coaches or consultants are identified to provide training to interventionists, continuous feedback and support, and evaluate treatment integrity.				
☐ Interventionists are trained in specific intervention protocols with added emphasis on using multiple types of visual representations to illustrate math concepts (especially problem solving).				
☐ Inservice and ongoing training (coaching/consulting) and support for classroom teachers on core curricula is identified, developed, and scheduled.				

FORM 1.2

RTI Action Plan for Math

School System Capacity and Support	
☐ Multidisciplinary problem-solving teams have been formed to establish building, grade, class, and individual student goals; select curricula and interventions; select screening and monitoring tools; evaluate outcomes.	List team members:
☐ Resources currently available are inventoried (e.g., curricula/programs/interventions, personnel, materials, time).	List known resources:
☐ Expert(s) in math or math instruction included on district- and/or building-level problem-solving teams.	List math experts:
Data-Based Decision Making	
Universal Screening	
☐ Screening measures should be: • Reliable, valid (predictive validity), efficient. • Consistent across district. • Combined with state testing results (grades 4–8).	Selected screening tool:
Progress Monitoring	
☐ Progress monitoring measures need to be reliable, valid, and designed to measure overall growth (usually grade level).	Selected general progress monitoring tool:
☐ Monitor progress for Tiers 2 and 3 students using curriculum-embedded or mastery measures daily or weekly to evaluate response to treatment.	Selected mastery measure/embedded tool:
High-Quality Instruction; Aligned with Standards	
☐ Designated block of time is assigned for core math instruction (recommendation 45–60 minutes).	Identify time for math instructional block:

(continued)

Note. RTI, response to intervention.

☐ Select core curricula reflective of grade-level content standards (e.g., map onto NCTM [2006] focal points, NMAP [2008] recommendations, and Common Core [NGA & CCSSO, 2010]).	Select appropriate core curricula:
☐ Include instructional process components like peer tutoring or cooperative learning activities.	Select supplemental activities:
Tiered Interventions	
☐ Tiers 2 and 3 interventions should: • Include instruction that is explicit and systematic. • Cover foundation and prerequisite skills. • Focus on deep understanding of whole numbers. • Provide 10 minutes of fact fluency practice. • Incorporate visual representation. • Include motivational strategies. • Offer scripted protocols.	Identify potential interventions:

CHAPTER 2

Effective Core Math Curriculum and Instruction

Math curriculum and instruction has been undergoing various reform efforts over the last two decades to facilitate deeper understanding of mathematical principles. The purpose of this chapter is to capture the most recent efforts for improving math education in the United States. We begin the chapter by discussing the evidence available for guiding the selection of an effective math curriculum and then briefly describe the CCSS for Mathematics (NGA & CCSSO, 2010). Next, we discuss recommendations for providing effective core instructional content and practices. Finally, we describe supplemental programs that can be used alongside general math instruction.

CURRICULAR CONTENT

A unique problem with math instruction in the United States has been the poor performance of the general education curricula. In a review of available curricular programs at the elementary level only a weak effect (median effect size = 0.10) on student outcomes was found (Slavin & Lake, 2008). Unfortunately, there were also a limited number of quality studies that examined curricula. This lack of quality studies regarding math curricula persists according to recent evaluations from the What Works Clearinghouse (WWC; *http://ies. ed.gov/ncee/wwc*), which has found only four primary-level curricula as providing evidence of potentially positive outcomes on math achievement (see Table 2.1). The Best Evidence Encyclopedia (*www.bestevidence.org/math/elem/top.htm*), another reputable website that evaluates various math programs (created by the Johns Hopkins University School of Education's Center for Data-Driven Reform in Education [CDDRE]), did not identify *any* traditional math curriculum as having either strong or moderate evidence according to their rat-

TABLE 2.1. Elementary-Level Math Curricula Receiving a Potentially Positive Effectiveness Rating from the WWC

Curricula	Number of empirical studies meeting WWC evidence standards[a]	Number of empirical studies not meeting WWC evidence standards[c]	Effectiveness rating[b]	Explanation of rating
Everyday Mathematics®	1	33	Potentially positive	One study showed a statistically significant positive effect on math achievement.
Investigations in Number, Data, and Space®	2	6	Potentially positive	One study showed an unclear effect and one study showed a statistically significant positive effect on math achievement.
Saxon Math	2	12	Potentially positive	One study showed an unclear effect and one study showed a statistically significant positive effect on math achievement.

[a]Includes studies meeting standards with and without reservations.
[b]WWC defines the potentially positive effectiveness rating as a positive effect without contrary evidence.
[c]Studies that did not meet evidence standards (those ineligible for review are not included in this count).

ing criteria. When considering these findings it is important to keep in mind the challenges affiliated with the effective evaluation of math curriculum:

1. It is difficult (e.g., cost, feasibility) to conduct highly controlled randomized studies to accurately evaluate curriculum.
2. The impact of a curriculum on student outcomes may take several years (Fuchs, Fuchs, & Compton, 2012; Slavin & Lake, 2008).

Nationwide, only a small number of curricula are used at the elementary level—for example, seven curricula represent 91% of all programs used by teachers in grades K–2 (Resnick, Sanislo, & Oda, 2010). A comparison of four common curricula provided to students in grades 1 and 2 showed that some curricular comparisons produced different outcomes for first and second graders, whereas for other comparisons no differences were found (Agodini et al., 2010). The curricula compared were Investigations in Number, Data, and Space (Russell et al., 2008), Math Expressions (Fuson, 2009), Saxon Math (Larson, 2008), and Scott Foremen-Addison Wesley Mathematics (SFAW; Charles et al., 2005). First graders who were instructed with *Math Expressions* outperformed students who were instructed with Investigations and SFAW. No differences in math achievement were found between first graders taught by Math Expressions as compared with those taught by Saxon Math. Second graders who were instructed with Math Expressions and Saxon Math outperformed students who were instructed with SFAW. Only small nonsignificant differences among the other curriculum comparisons were found.

These findings help support recommendations from the NMAP (2008) that a blend of student-centered and teacher-directed instructional approaches is important. Investigations is considered a student-centered approach, whereas SFAW and Saxon are both teacher-directed approaches. Math Expressions represented the only blended approach, comprising both teacher-directed and student-centered activities. Interestingly, these four curricula differed in the amount of teacher training embedded, amount of time spent on instruction, and number of lessons taught within each content area. For example, teachers using Saxon reported providing 1 more hour of instruction per week than teachers using the other three curricula (Agodini et al., 2010). These other aspects of instruction may be important for educators to consider when evaluating the success of the core curriculum.

The NMAP (2008) also reported that traditional U.S. math curricula have favored breadth over depth, and provided a weak conceptual emphasis and insufficient opportunities to build procedural fluency. Note that curricular gaps are related to *both* conceptual understanding and procedural fluency. Conceptual knowledge refers to math concepts, laws, and ideas (Doabler & Fein, 2103; NRC, 2001; Wu, 1999). Procedural knowledge refers to students' ability to use algorithms, mnemonics, mental math, and other strategies (e.g., counting on, doubles + 1) appropriately and efficiently (NRC, 2001). Furthermore, the NMAP suggests that conceptual understanding, computational fluency, factual knowledge, and problem solving are *equally important* and serve as foundational skills necessary for algebra.

The emphasis in the NMAP report on the importance of all aspects of foundational skills is noteworthy because it reflects an end to the math curricular wars that have been operating over the past two decades. The two opposing central viewpoints that have historically shaped math curriculum discussions include an emphasis on either (1) mastering basic facts and standard algorithms, or (2) the math problem-solving process (Schmidt, Wang, & McKnight, 2005). The former tends to be teacher directed and the latter tends to be student centered. These approaches differ with respect to how much and when guidance is provided during instruction. The current consensus is that *both viewpoints are important* for math learning and represent essential aspects of math proficiency, as described in Chapter 1 (Kilpatrick et al., 2001; NMAP, 2008).

Concerted efforts to make national improvements to math achievement have been commissioned through the NRC (2001), the NCTM (2006), and the NMAP (2008). Readers are encouraged to access *Adding It Up* (*www.nap.edu/catalog/9822/adding-it-up-helping-children-learn-mathematics*), the seminal publication produced by the NRC, and visit the NCTM website (*www.nctm.org*) for more information. We briefly review the report provided by the NMAP (see the comprehensive document at *www2.ed.gov/about/bdscomm/list/mathpanel/report/final-report.pdf*). The NMAP provided 45 findings and recommendations across the seven areas of math instruction and learning including (1) curricular content, (2) learning process, (3) teachers and teacher education, (4) instructional practices, (5) instructional materials, (6) assessment, and (7) research policies and mechanisms. Table 2.2 lists selected NMAP recommendations in four of these areas that are most relevant to the purposes of our book. The most recent of these efforts, which builds upon these previous recommendations, is the CCSS for Mathematics (NGA & CCSSO, 2010).

As noted in Chapter 1, math performance in the United States lags behind other countries. Although the reasons for this are likely multidimensional, one area of investigation has been to identify what "very successful" countries do differently in terms of the curricular content. In every successful country there is only one national curriculum (Schmidt, Houang, & Cogan, 2002). It also turns out that successful countries have a more demanding, more focused, and more coherent curriculum (Schmidt & Houang, 2012). Focused means that the number of topics covered at each grade level is smaller than traditionally occurring in the United States, and coherent means that topics are sequenced across grades in a manner that is sequential and hierarchical.

The number of math topics covered by successful international countries begins small and gradually increases, ranging from five (grade 1) to 21 (grade 5; Schmidt & Houang, 2012). However, a sample of state standards across the United States from 2000 to 2009 revealed that on average the number of math topics covered ranged from 13 (grade 1) to 21 (grade 5), reflecting the "mile-wide and inch-deep" descriptor that has historically characterized the U.S. curriculum. Although by grade 5 the number of topics taught in the United States (on average) compares with international standards, far more content areas are included in U.S. standards across grades 1–4 (Schmidt & Houang, 2012; Schmidt et al., 2002). The CCSS for Mathematics (NGA & CCSSO, 2010) attempt to address this problem and include standards ranging from eight (grade 1) to 21 (grade 5). A potential outcome of the adoption of the CCSS is to alter curricular content to be more focused and coherent, potentially facilitating a more common national focus, which is similar to the highly effective international approaches to curriculum development.

It is an understandable finding that the U.S. curriculum has been ineffective given the challenge to ensure that textbooks adequately cover all content areas according to these traditional standards (NMAP, 2008; Schmidt et al., 2002). In fact, traditional U.S. textbooks have covered three times the content that a textbook in Japan does, which is an important factor to consider given that Japan represents one of the top-performing countries in math in the world (Schmidt et al., 2002). Some experts argue that U.S. curricula has actually *complicated* math learning by covering so many topics when in actuality, math comprises a small number of central ideas (Schmidt et al., 2002; Wu, 2011). Despite acknowledgment that prerequisite skills should be mastered before more complex material is introduced, U.S. students historically have learned composite (sequences of component skills) and component (basic foundational skills) skills simultaneously (Daly, Martens, Barnett, Witt, & Olson, 2007; Gersten, Beckmann, et al., 2009; Johnson & Layng, 1992; Mayfield & Chase, 2002). Many math topics continue to be reviewed or covered across multiple grades and analyses have demonstrated there is little consensus among states regarding what content ought to be covered (e.g., Porter, Polikoff, & Smithson, 2009; Schmidt, Cogan, Houang, & McKnight, 2011).

TABLE 2.2. Selected Sample of Key Recommendations from the NMAP (2008) Final Report

Content area	Recommendations
Curricular content	1. Math curricula in elementary and middle school should be focused, with an emphasis on key areas, and progress coherently.
	2. A central goal for K–8 math education programming should be to cultivate proficiency with whole numbers, fractions, and essential elements of geometry and measurement. These three areas are thought to be critical foundations of algebra.
Learning processes	1. Integration of conceptual understanding, computation fluency, and problem-solving skills is necessary to prepare students for algebra.
	2. Computational proficiency requires automatic recall of whole-number operations, fluency with standard algorithms, and understanding of core math laws of operations. Sufficient opportunities for practice with whole-number operations are necessary to develop automatic recall of addition, subtraction, multiplication, and division facts.
	3. Math learning of all students can be improved by interventions that address social, affective, and motivational factors.
	4. Educational professionals should emphasize the importance of effort and persistence during math learning.
Instructional practices	1. Exclusive use of either student-centered or teacher-directed instructional approaches is not supported by research.
	2. A cooperative learning approach, Team Assisted Individualization (TAI), has been shown to improve students' computation skills but not conceptual understanding or problem solving.
	3. Formative assessment should be used on a regular basis to assess student learning during the elementary grades.
	4. Mathematical ideas instructed using "real-world" contexts only improves performance on similar real-world problems but does not improve computation, simple word problems, or equation learning.
	5. Students with mathematical difficulties (i.e., students with learning disabilities as well as nonidentified students performing in the lowest third of the general education class) should be provided with some explicit math instruction on a regular basis directed toward ensuring these students have foundational skills and conceptual knowledge.
Instructional materials	1. Educational publishers should produce shorter and more focused textbooks.
	2. States and districts should reach an agreement on common topics to be emphasized and addressed at each grade level. Textbook publishers should use these common topics on the material that is emphasized in the textbooks.
	3. Publishers of math textbooks should include math experts in the development of their materials to ensure accuracy.

Note. Based on information in National Mathematics Advisory Panel (2008).

Some evidence exists to support the notion of common math standards. For example, states with standards more aligned with the CCSS had higher National Assessment of Educational Progress (NAEP) scores, on average, after accounting for low socioeconomic indicators (Schmidt & Houang, 2012). That being said, there is agreement among experts that the idea of CCSS for Mathematics may be helpful, but until the states that have officially adopted the CCSS observe changes in students' math achievement, evidence supporting this potential remains ambiguous (Lee, 2011; Porter, McMaken, Hwang, & Yang, 2011; Powell et al., 2013; Schmidt & Houang, 2012).

Some experts also suggest that the transition to using the CCSS will be more challenging for some states than others due to the wide variability in current state alignment with the Common Core, which averages about 25% (Porter et al., 2011). According to others, the CCSS may emphasize more cognitively demanding mathematical material with less emphasis on math procedures and foundational understanding, which is inconsistent with the NMAP (2008) recommendations and the curricular focus of some of the top-performing countries (Porter et al., 2011; Powell et al., 2013; Russell, 2012). Therefore, it is important that educators balance the more focused, coherent, demanding curriculum that may come with the adoption of the CCSS with ensuring deep understanding of foundational skills and concepts.

CORE INSTRUCTION

The lack of curricula that meets evidence-based standards along with limited consensus on what characteristics comprise effective math instruction (Gersten, Beckmann, et al., 2009) means that little guidance is available for implementing high-quality instruction. This is problematic because the IDEIA of 2004 requires the use of evidence-based approaches within general instruction as well as intervention. Core instruction refers to the primary instruction provided to all students in the general education classroom. Within an RTI framework, core instruction is also considered to have a central role in preventing future academic challenges (Batsche et al., 2006). Put another way, the hope is that by providing evidence-based curricula and effective instructional practices, the needs of 80–90% of students within a school will be met (Batsche et al., 2006). Focusing resources on improving core instruction is cost-effective because such efforts will hopefully result in helping the vast majority of school-age students. Form 2.1 provides a checklist of ways to promote effective math instruction in light of the current challenges the ideas for which are discussed throughout the remainder of this chapter.

It is clear that providing *all students*, regardless of learning disability status, access to core math instruction within the general education classroom during an established block of instructional time is essential for math learning (Bryant, Kethley, Kim, Pool, et al., 2008; Fuchs et al., 2012). Preliminary research has shown that at-risk students who receive both validated core math instruction in the general education classroom and small-group tutoring outperform students who only receive small-group tutoring (Fuchs et al., 2012; Fuchs, Fuchs, Craddock, et al., 2008). Therefore, small-group tutoring for at-risk students should not replace access to core instruction. Ensuring that a block of time is designated daily to math instruction is also critical, with some experts recommending 45–60 minutes of core instruction be provided (Riccomini & Witzel, 2010). This does not include time for additional tutoring or individual supports provided to advanced students, at-risk students, or students with disabilities. Additional time (e.g., 20–40 minutes extra) should also be allocated for those activities (Fuchs et al., 2012).

Instructional Content

Instructional content for primary grades should be sure to cover the key aspects necessary for building math proficiency with whole numbers. According to the NMAP (2008), math proficiency means that students should (1) understand key mathematical concepts; (2) know basic facts automatically; (3) use standard algorithms accurately, fluently, and flexibly; and (4) apply the previous three elements when solving math problems. Both the NMAP (2008) and the CCSS (NGA & CCSSO, 2010) consider proficiency with whole numbers as the central student outcome achieved by the end of fifth grade. In order to display proficiency with whole numbers, the following should be achieved by students at the end of elementary school (NMAP, 2008; Wu, 2011):

- Understand place value.
- Be able to compose and decompose numbers.
- Know the meaning of the four basic operations (i.e., addition, subtraction, multiplication, and division).
  - Know and fluently use the standard algorithms for the four operations.
  - Know the basic laws of operations (i.e., associative, commutative, and distributive properties).
- Apply the basic operations to problem solving.
- Automatically recall basic facts for the four operations.
- Use and understand estimation.

Educators should consider several different approaches to identifying research-supported curricula. First, websites such as the WWC (*http://ies.ed.gov/ncee/wwc*) and the Best Evidence Encyclopedia (*www.bestevidence.org*), which evaluate and identify evidence-based curricula, can be reviewed. Second, educators can independently evaluate curricula using the Common Core grade-level standards (*www.corestandards.org/Math*) and the NMAP (2008) recommendations. The focal points generated by the NCTM (2006) can also be used to guide instructional content (Lembke, Hampton, & Beyers, 2012); however, some of the topics differ from those recommended via the CCSS and the NMAP. Third, textbooks could be evaluated for research-supported instructional design principles. Form 2.2 provides a checklist for evaluating curricula using 11 instructional design principles based on previous math textbook reviews conducted by researchers (Bryant, Bryant, Kethley, et al., 2008; Doabler, Cary, et al., 2012). These instructional design principles were empirically derived and appear to be important for both typically performing students as well as those students struggling in math (e.g., Baker, Gersten, & Lee, 2002; Gersten, Chard, et al., 2009; NMAP, 2008); however, most of this evidence has focused on students at risk for or with math learning disabilities.

Regardless of the curriculum selected, it is also important to determine that the curriculum is delivered as intended by measuring procedural fidelity (Lembke et al., 2012). Procedural fidelity can be assessed by school psychologists, principals, teacher leaders, RTI coordinators, math coaches, or other designated school professionals using checklists. Checklists may come with some curriculum or could be constructed using teacher manuals (Doabler et al., 2014; Lembke et al., 2012). Using this format, core math instructional time is observed to ensure that all central content areas are delivered the way the instructional manual suggests. If the curriculum is not being implemented with fidelity, this may signal that one or more of the following could be considered: (1) provide additional professional development opportunities, (2) hold booster training sessions, (3) implement a supplemental program, (4) revisit the curriculum choice, (5) use a math coach to support teachers, or (6) reorganize math instruction to utilize a central math instructor at each grade level (NMAP, 2008; Riccomini & Witzel, 2010).

Instructional Practices

As we have discussed, both teacher-directed and student-centered approaches to instruction are important to include in the classroom (NMAP, 2008). Other essential instructional practices to consider are the provision of differentiated instruction, explicit instruction, classroom management, and formative assessment.

Differentiated instruction serves to meet the needs of all students as well as provide any necessary accommodations to ensure that all students can access the curriculum (Fuchs et al., 2012; Gersten, Beckmann, et al., 2009; Lembke et al., 2012). Because the expectation is that students who struggle with grade-level math will be included in general instruction it is important to ensure all students' participation. Differentiation of instruction can be imbedded into independent work times as well as small-group or peer-pair-based activities.

Explicit instruction provided to the whole class daily, for at least a portion of the time allocated to core instructional activities, facilitates struggling students' ability to access the curriculum and even reduces the achievement gap with their typical classroom peers (Clarke, Smolkowski, Baker, Fien, Doabler, et al., 2011; Doabler & Fein, 2013; Doabler et al., 2014; Fuchs et al., 2012; Gersten, Beckmann, et al., 2009; NMAP, 2008; Riccomini & Wetzel, 2010). Explicit instruction is characterized as a systematic and structured instructional approach that has extensive support for use with students struggling to learn math (e.g., Baker et al., 2002; Gersten, Chard, et al., 2009; Swanson, 2009). The emphasis on explicit instruction is on mastery learning and establishing concrete roles for teachers and students (Doabler & Fein, 2013; Fuchs, Fuchs, Powell, et al., 2008; Swanson & Sachse-Lee, 2000). Box 2.1 provides a list of explicit instruction characteristics.

Incorporating appropriate classroom management strategies can also improve math outcomes (Slavin & Lake, 2008). Research has demonstrated that in-class attentive behavior, often as rated by teachers, contributes to math achievement (e.g., Claessens et al., 2009;

BOX 2.1. Aspects of Explicit Instruction

1. Break tasks into small, sequential steps.
2. Provide a wide range of examples and non-examples of the math topic being described.
3. Provide repeated practice and cumulative review of math concepts.
4. Provide frequent and immediate corrective feedback.
5. Present an advance organizer to the class prior to beginning the lesson.
6. Demonstrate and model the skill or strategy that students will learn about.
7. Provide guided practice opportunities with a gradual shift to more independent practice activities.
8. Provide independent practice opportunities.
9. Monitor student progress toward mastery using frequent assessment.
10. Provide periodic checks to ensure that students are maintaining mastered skills.

Duncan et al., 2007; Fuchs et al., 2012; Fuchs, Geary, Fuchs, Compton, & Hamlett, 2014; Geary, Hoard, & Nugent, 2012). Attentive behavior refers to task engagement, persistence, eagerness to learn, organization, and independence; however, it is unclear which aspects of attention are important for math learning (Claessens et al., 2009; Geary, Hoard, & Nugent, 2012). Establishing a positive, consistent, and cooperative learning environment through the use of (1) classroom and instructional organization and planning (e.g., seating arrangements, routines, transitions; see Kern & Clemens, 2007, for more information on classroom management), (2) teacher and student cooperatively developed discipline components (e.g., co-constructed classroom constitution), and (3) parent/community involvement appears to influence math outcomes (Friedberg, n.d.; Slavin & Lake, 2008).

Finally, universal screening can be used to identify all students' performance levels on grade-appropriate math measures (see Chapter 3). These data are typically collected two or three times during the course of the academic year during the fall, winter, and spring and can be used to guide instruction and instructional groupings (Gersten, Beckmann, et al., 2009). Screening can also be used to designate whether performance below expected levels is specific to a child or a classroom of children (Ardoin, Witt, Connell, & Koenig, 2005; Burns, Deno, & Jimerson, 2007; VanDerHeyden, Witt, & Naquin, 2003). If it appears that specific classrooms of children are experiencing difficulties, then interventions directed toward classroom needs can be developed. Furthermore, the current IES practice guideline for applying RTI to math (Gersten, Beckmann, et al., 2009) suggests that monthly progress monitoring be conducted with students close to, but still above, the locally or national determined performance cutoff point (often perceived of as the 25th percentile) on the screening measure.

SUPPLEMENTAL INSTRUCTIONAL PRACTICES

Given the transition in curricular focus brought on by adoption of the Common Core as well as the limited availability of evidence-based curriculum (Gersten, Beckmann, et al., 2009), it might be useful to supplement core instruction with effective instructional practices (Slavin & Lake, 2008). When we have consulted with districts that just purchased a curriculum *not identified* as one of the evidence-based options, we often recommend to curriculum directors and principals that core instruction be supplemented. Therefore, supplemental programs can be considered as a way to ensure that core math instruction is well-rounded, uses recommended instructional practices, and addresses all key grade-level content areas. Another way the term *supplemental instruction* has been used is to assist students struggling with math, including those with math learning disabilities, to participate in core instructional activities (e.g., Gersten & Newman-Gonchar, 2011). For our purposes we refer to supplemental instruction as programs or strategies used within the general education instructional time to address *all students'* needs rather than providing a separate program to specifically support at-risk learners (i.e., we refer to this type of support as targeted or Tier 2 intervention supports), although the programs below may also be useful for this alternative purpose as well.

Computer-Assisted Instruction

One of the most widely used supplements to general instruction is computer-assisted instruction (CAI; Slavin & Lake, 2008). We cover the uses of CAI in Chapter 5 and therefore only briefly describe this option now. Currently, CAI programs represent integrated learning systems that incorporate math instruction with placement tests to identify appropriate instructional matches for individual students. The NMAP (2008) suggests that high-quality CAI implemented with fidelity is a useful tool for building students' automaticity with math skills, particularly computation skills. However, it is important that educators carefully evaluate the quality of software packages and ensure that the purpose for using CAI matches the needs of the student users. Slavin and Lake's (2008) review found a medium effect size (0.19) for CAI, with better outcomes for computation than problem solving or conceptual learning. However, Xin and Jitendra (1999) found that CAI that contained representation and strategy training was highly effective for word problem solving, and outcomes were more positive for simple as compared with complex word problems. An added benefit of CAI is the brevity of the sessions required to see student improvement (e.g., maximum of 30-minute sessions, three times weekly; Slavin & Lake, 2008). Unfortunately, most of these reviewed programs are no longer available, which prompted us to include a separate chapter (Chapter 5) on recent programs.

Instructional Process

Another avenue for supplementing the curriculum is not to add another type of instruction but to change the instructional format for using curricular content, also referred to as instructional process strategies. Examples of effective instructional process strategies include cooperative learning (learning in teams or groups), pair learning strategies (otherwise known as peer tutoring), mastery learning, and professional development programs emphasizing math content, classroom management, or student motivation (Slavin & Lake, 2008). According to Slavin and Lake's (2008) review of the research on instructional process strategies, a medium effect size (0.33) on student achievement was found *and* the research was of high quality. Use of these instructional process strategies may assist with differentiating math instruction (Lembke et al., 2012) and also addresses the NMAP recommendation to include social, affective, and motivational strategies within math instruction.

Most of these instructional process strategies provide some form of cooperative learning whether in pairs (i.e., peer tutoring) or teams of four. Cooperative learning may be particularly effective when included within general math instruction because working with other students may encourage persistence on tasks, which is required when solving math problems (Baker et al., 2002; NMAP, 2008). Benefits of cooperative learning includes modest increases in (1) social skills such as conflict resolution, helping behaviors, and attitudes toward others; (2) self-concept about one's self, academics, and competence with targeted skill areas; and (3) learning behaviors such as on task, effort, participation, rule compliance, and frustration tolerance (Ginsburg-Block, Rohrbeck, & Fantuzzo, 2006; Robinson, Schofield, & Steers-Wentzell, 2005).

Programs that are rated as having strong evidence of effectiveness and require students to work in teams of four include (1) PowerTeaching: Mathematics (*www.sfapowerteaching.org*), formerly known as Student Teams-Achievement Divisions, and (2) Team Assisted Individualization: Mathematics (TAI). Both of these programs are designed for intermediate elementary and middle school students, and TAI may be more appropriate for improving computation than applied skills (Slavin & Lake, 2008). Peer tutoring programs have been used with all primary grade levels. Common programs include ClassWide Peer Tutoring (CWPT; Greenwood, Delquadri, & Carta, 1997) and Peer Assisted Learning Strategies (PALS; *http://kc.vanderbilt.edu/pals/index.html*; Fuchs, Fuchs, Hamlett, Phillips, Karns, et al., 1997).

Peer-Assisted Learning

Several meta-analyses have been conducted evaluating the impact of peer tutoring (students work in pairs) or the broader conceptualization of peer-assisted learning (students work in small groups, also described as cooperative or team-based learning). Table 2.3 provides a sample of some of these meta-analyses and the outcomes for math (Baker et al., 2002; Bowman-Perrott et al., 2013; Gersten, Chard, et al., 2009; Kroesbergen & Van Luit, 2003; Kunsch, Jitendra, & Sood, 2007; Rohrbeck, Ginsburg-Block, Fantuzzo, & Miller, 2003). Average effect sizes for peer tutoring or peer-assisted/mediated learning range from small (0.14) to large (0.89) with smaller gains often found when isolating outcomes for students with learning disabilities (Gersten, Chard, et al., 2009; Kunsch et al., 2007) and larger gains often found when used with students struggling in math but without identified disabilities (Baker et al., 2002; Kroesbergen & Van Luit, 2003; Kunsch et al., 2007).

Most of the research examining peer tutoring has focused on computation. A meta-analysis conducted by Kunsch and colleagues (2007) compared the effects of computation versus the conceptual and problem-solving aspects of math, confirming that greater benefits for peer tutoring are found with computation skills. Another important finding, given U.S. achievement gaps identified for students from low-income families, minority students, and

TABLE 2.3. Summary of Selected Meta-Analyses That Included Evaluation of Peer Tutoring and Peer-Assisted Instruction on Math Outcomes for Elementary School Grades

Authors	Total number of studies reviewed	Number of math studies reviewed	Type of peer learning	Grades included	Type of math content	Setting	Treatment duration	Overall mean effect size for math
Baker, Gersten, & Lee (2002)	15	6	Peer tutoring	2–5	Computation	Not reported	10–32 weeks	0.62[a]
Bowman-Perrott et al. (2013)	26	6	Peer tutoring	1–12	Multiplying decimals, changing decimals to fractions, computing %, adding/subtracting time	General education; special education	280–1,137.5 minutes[b]	0.89[a]
Gersten, Beckmann, et al. (2009)	44	6[d]	Peer tutoring	Not reported	Not reported	Not reported	Not reported	0.14[f]
Kroesbergen & Van Luit (2003)	58	10	Peer tutoring	K–6	Computation; problem solving	Not reported	1–52 weeks	0.87[e]
Kunsch, Jitendra, & Sood (2007)	17	17	Peer tutoring	K–5; 7–12	Computation; computation with concepts and application	General education; special education	4–25 weeks	0.53[c,e]
Rohrbeck, Ginsburg-Block, Fantuzzo, & Miller (2003)	90	33	Peer assisted	1–6	Not reported	Not reported	1–144 weeks	0.22[a]

[a]Includes students at risk for math failure.
[b]Duration in terms of weeks was not available; rather dose here refers to a calculation of total weeks of peer tutoring × number of minutes per week × number of sessions per week.
[c]K–5 (elementary) effect size only.
[d]Cross-age peer tutoring data not included.
[e]Includes students at risk for and with disabilities.
[f]Includes students with disabilities only.

students attending urban schools, is that these are the very students who appear to benefit *most* from peer-assisted/mediated learning (Ginsburg-Block et al., 2006; NMAP, 2008; Robinson et al., 2005; Rohrbeck et al., 2003). Some evidence suggests that students in younger elementary grades (e.g., first, second, and third) may benefit from peer-assisted learning more than students in later elementary grades (e.g., fourth and fifth; Ginsberg-Block et al., 2006; Rohrbeck et al., 2003). An implication of these findings for classroom practices is that peer tutoring has the potential to be effective as a general education activity to enhance the computation skills of all students, including struggling students and those students experiencing other environmental risk factors.

Within the classroom setting, same-age peer tutoring can be incorporated with students who have similar or different math skills—that is, both low and typically achieving students benefit from peer tutoring (Bowman-Perrott et al., 2013; Kunsch et al., 2007; Robinson et al., 2005). Peer tutoring offered in general education settings is more effective than when provided in special education settings (Kunsch et al., 2007). Most of the time peer tutoring is reciprocal (Robinson et al., 2005; Rohrbeck et al., 2003), meaning that all students serve as both the tutor (e.g., guiding the instructional activity) and tutee (e.g., practicing the instructional activity in response to the tutor's instructions). However, nonreciprocal tutoring (cross-ability groupings) during which one student is designated as the tutor and a different lower-performing student is identified as the tutee, produces similarly effective outcomes for both tutors and tutees (Menesses & Gresham, 2009). This finding means that peer pairings do not need to include a higher-performing student with a lower-performing student for successful outcomes.

Other factors that are important to consider when developing a peer tutoring intervention are (1) use of rewards, (2) self-management, and (3) use of individualized evaluation procedures. Two meta-analyses demonstrated that general achievement outcomes (i.e., not specific to any subject area) were substantially higher when rewards were incorporated into peer-assisted learning (Bowman-Perrott et al., 2013; Rohrbeck et al., 2003). These studies found that social (e.g., applause, praise) and tangible (e.g., stickers, pencils, certificate of achievement) rewards, along with privileges (e.g., line leader, teacher helper, messenger), were the most commonly used reward types. Interdependent group contingencies were the most commonly used reward format. Interdependent group contingencies are when the whole class is given the same reward after meeting a classwide goal (see Greenwood, Terry, Utley, Montagna, & Walker, 1993; Hawkins, Musti-Rao, Hughes, Berry, & McGuire, 2009). Box 2.2 provides instructions for how to construct a group contingency—for example, students could have extra computer time if the class earned more points during peer tutoring than the previous week.

Rohrbeck and colleagues (2003) also demonstrated that when students participated *in more than half* of the following tasks: (1) set their own performance goals, (2) monitored and (3) evaluated their own performance, (4) selected potential rewards, and (5) administered their own rewards—peer-assisted learning had greater outcomes on student achievement. Finally, even though students are working in pairs or small groups it is essential that evaluation of the skills targeted for use with peer-assisted learning is conducted individually (Rohrbeck et al., 2003). Meeting individual students' needs is a natural part of peer-assisted

BOX 2.2. How to Design a Group Contingency

Interdependent Group Contingency: The entire class is rewarded depending on the class's performance as a group. The target behavior, criteria, and reward are the *same* for all students.

	Components
Target behaviors	• Appropriate responding (e.g., saying the correct answer and correcting your own mistakes). • Listening. • Being respectful (e.g., waiting your turn, using kind words). • Staying on task. • Number of completed problems.
Criteria	• Assign point values to the target behaviors (e.g., 2 points for correct response; 1 point for staying on task). • Set reasonable criteria that can be achieved by the whole class (criteria can be increased over time). • Class beats the previous session point total, tickets earned, or number of problems completed.
Rewards	• Tangibles: certificates, pencils, erasers, stickers, silly bands, stamps, mechanical pencils, highlighters, crayons, markers. • Activities: extra recess time, computer time, games. • Edibles: popcorn party, candy.
Format	• Divide class into two teams, sum points for each team, and compare with criteria selected or reward team with highest points. • Sum total points earned across the whole class and compare with criteria. • Teacher distributes lottery tickets or cards to individual students and class aspires to earn an established number of lottery tickets.

Steps

1. Identify and define target behaviors. Usually task engagement and math performance behaviors are chosen.

2. Select and define criteria. Make sure the criteria can be attained by the class. Criteria can be randomly selected each week or changed to improve student performance over time.

3. Identify rewards that are acceptable and available for your classroom and school. Survey students to gauge their interest in the rewards. Create a menu of options. Rewards can be provided in order according to the menu or can be randomly selected from the list. Mystery prizes can also be used, meaning that the reward is not revealed to students until the class earns the criteria.

4. Determine how points will be awarded. Will lottery tickets be distributed by the teacher? Will each student have a point card that is stamped by the teacher? Will students allocate points on a card for their peer partner? Will points be determined by scoring their own papers and counting the number of completed problems?

5. Select the format that is preferred.

learning when students are encouraged to monitor their own progress, set their own performance goals, and are involved with their own reward selection and administration. This is true as long as an evaluation tool is being administered during or immediately following one or more peer tutoring sessions each week. Peer-assisted learning activities can be implemented for as little as 1 week or as long as 144 weeks (Bowman-Perrott et al., 2013; Kunsch et al., 2007; Robinson et al., 2005; Rohrbeck et al., 2003). Of course, neither of the extreme options (1 week or 144 weeks) is generally recommended.

It is important that peer tutoring be implemented accurately so that achievement gains can be observed. Accurate implementation of peer tutoring steps can be facilitated by procedures already built into the peer tutoring script (see Appendix 2.1 for the Peer Tutoring Intervention Brief): teachers circulate around the classroom and monitor each peer pair at least once per session following training, and teachers review and reinforce peer tutoring steps and rules for partner work. When students experience difficulties grasping the peer tutoring procedures, teachers can provide (1) booster training sessions to the whole class or to specific peer pairs, (2) specific performance feedback on the steps that were missed and those executed correctly immediately prior to or after peer tutoring sessions, or (3) prompt the whole class or specific peer pairs on the peer tutoring steps that are frequently missed (Dufrene, Noell, Gilbertson, & Duhon, 2005).

CONCLUSION

This chapter described four ways to provide core math instruction that is accessible to all students: (1) select empirically supported curriculum, (2) evaluate curriculum according to evidence-based content recommendations, (3) use research-based instructional design principles, and (4) incorporate supplemental instructional strategies such as peer-assisted learning. Table 2.4 provides a summarized list of action steps associated with each of these four ways to make core math instruction accessible to all students. In addition, Form 2.1 provides a checklist for promoting effective classwide math instruction and Form 2.2 provides a checklist for reviewing textbook content for recommended instructional design principles.

TABLE 2.4. Making Core Instruction Accessible to All Students

Options	Examples of action steps
Select, use, and integrate empirically supported curriculum during daily instructional blocks	1. Periodically visit clearinghouse websites, the purpose of which is to evaluate math curriculum such as the WWC website, *http://ies.ed.gov/ncee/wwc*. These websites provide occasional updates on the curricula that are reviewed and the evidence supporting these curricula. Note: Publisher claims that a curriculum is evidence based needs to be verified by other sources. 2. Be sure that 45–60 minutes of core instruction is provided to all students (regardless of disability status) daily. 3. Encourage administrators to plan for a 30-minute intervention block *in addition to* the core instruction block that can be used to provide enrichment, target interventions for at-risk students, and more intensive interventions for students with disabilities. 4. Identify a math coach, instructional or RTI coordinator, or math teacher leader to collaborate with teachers on curriculum implementation. Period reviews of teachers' implementation of the curriculum can be used to facilitate discussion, training, and support of curriculum components.
Evaluate curriculum according to evidence-based content recommendations	1. Educators can review the curriculum in use according to whether it aligns with the Common Core grade-level standards (*www.corestandards.org/Math*). 2. Educators can review the curriculum in use according to whether it aligns with the curriculum focal points generated by the NCTM (2006). 3. Conduct a textbook analysis to ensure that effective instructional design principles are used (see Form 2.2 for a checklist).
Use research-based instructional design principles	1. Embed a blend of teacher-directed and student-centered activities daily. 2. Use differentiated instruction during at least one portion of each math lesson (e.g., independent seatwork, peer-pair activities, and/or small-group work). 3. Provide explicit instruction to explain primary concepts and skills introduced in each lesson. 4. Incorporate classroom management and motivation strategies to encourage students' effort, engagement, and persistence. 5. Use formative assessment (e.g., universal screening three times each year) to guide instruction and instructional grouping.
Incorporate supplemental instructional strategies to enhance core instruction	1. Use CAI to support students' fluency of computation and word-problem-solving skills. 2. Embed the use of cooperative learning groups. 3. Use peer-assisted learning/tutoring within the classroom including same-age groupings during which each student has a turn as the tutor and tutee or facilitate cross-age tutoring with classes from higher grade levels.

APPENDIX 2.1. Peer Tutoring Intervention Brief

CCSS Domain Areas Addressed:			
Counting and Cardinality (K)	Operations and Algebraic Thinking (K–5)	Numbers and Operations in Base Ten (K–5)	Measurement and Data (K–5)
☑	☑	☑	☑

Instructional Hierarchy:

Acquisition	Fluency	Maintenance	Generalization	Adaptation
☐	☑	☑	☑	☐

Setting:			Tier of Support within RTI Framework:		
Whole Class	Small Group	Individual	Universal Prevention	Targeted Intervention	Individualized Intervention
☑	☐	☐	☑	☐	☐

Mediator: ☑ Teacher or Interventionist   ☑ Student (with teacher oversight)   ☐ Parent

Effectiveness: Small (effect size = 0.14) to large (effect size = 0.89) across typical, struggling but not identified students, and students with math disabilities.	**Amount of Evidence:** Six meta-analyses between 2002 and 2013.

Acceptability: Although infrequently collected (Bowman-Perrott et al., 2013; Rohrbeck et al., 2003), when acceptability of peer tutoring is assessed satisfaction ratings are high among teachers, students, and parents, and with teacher reporting it is easy to implement (Bowman-Perrott et al., 2013).

Brief Description: Peer tutoring is a teacher-monitored student-centered instructional approach where students are paired with peers and engage in a specific math problem-solving task. One student serves as the tutor and directs the task while the second student completes the task. Tutor–tutee roles are often interchanged within peer tutoring sessions. Goal setting and rewards are provided for effectively working together as well as for academic performance.

Materials Required: Tutoring script, peer tutoring rules poster, task-specific math materials, goal or score cards, goal charts or graphs, reward menu and reward items, kitchen timer or stopwatch.

Training Required: Students need to be trained in interpersonal skills (e.g., how to be helpful and positive when working in pairs), management skills (e.g., how to keep each other on task), content skills (e.g., what the math task is being performed), and roles (e.g., what behaviors do students engage in when they are a tutor and tutee; Robinson et al., 2005). Training can be conducted with the whole class using the following steps: (1) the teacher passes out the necessary materials and a tutoring script that students can follow; (2) the teacher describes the tutor and tutee roles; (3) the teacher models the procedures described in the tutoring script demonstrating both the tutor and tutee roles separately; (4) two students are selected to role-play the script with prompting and praise from the teacher, and (5) students proceed to their pairings and engage in a practice session (Hawkins et al., 2009).

Duration: A wide range of minutes per session is reported in the literature with one review reporting a mean of approximately 45 minutes about three times weekly (Rohrbeck et al., 2003). Anecdotal sampling of the literature indicates 10–45 minutes per session is common. Total duration in weeks ranges across meta-analyses from 1 to 144 and one study demonstrated a mean of 15 weeks (Rohrbeck et al., 2003). There is no evidence that length of treatment (in weeks) impacts student outcomes.

Active Treatment Components: Modeling, opportunities to practice, error correction, feedback, prompting, goal setting and charting, and rewards.

Procedures:

1. The teacher pairs students through random assignment, same ability, or cross-ability (higher-performing students with lower-performing students). Periodically changing peer pairs is recommended (e.g., weekly, semiweekly, or monthly).
2. The teacher establishes a set amount of time for the peer tutoring session (e.g., 5–20 minutes).
3. The teacher provides an overview of the skill to be targeted (e.g., addition facts) and procedures to be used (e.g., flash cards and number lines) as well as the responsibilities of the tutor and tutee.

The format of these intervention briefs was based on the Evidence-Based Intervention (EBI) Network at the University of Missouri (*http://ebi.missouri.edu/*).

4. The teacher identifies three to five rules for working together (prior to the first peer tutoring session the teacher provides a lesson on these rules). The teacher reminds students of these rules at the start of each session.

5. Peer tutoring rules (e.g., listening to your partner, following directions, helping your partner) are publicly posted and reinforced by the teacher throughout peer tutoring sessions. To make reinforcement of the rules easier, individual score cards can be created by or for each student that includes three to five rules and space for a sticker or stamp. The teacher can visit each peer pair once or twice during each session to provide a sticker or stamp.

6. Goals can also be established for academic performance (e.g., number of problems correctly completed, number of flash cards practiced). Often, goals are established for both academic performance and behavior, and rewarded.

7. Goals and rewards for each pair or for the whole class are established. This can be done by having the teacher choose or randomly select goals and rewards for each session. Or, each student pair can select their own goals and rewards from a short menu developed by the teacher. Or, the teacher and class can discuss possible goals and rewards as a whole class.

8. The teacher establishes a set amount of time for the peer tutoring session (e.g., 10–20 minutes).

9. The teacher identifies for the students who will begin as a tutor or tutee (this can be done once pairs are seated together or collectively as a group before students disperse). If nonreciprocal peer tutoring will be used, then students are simply informed if they are the tutor or the tutee. Sometimes the words *coach* or *teacher* are substituted for the word *tutor*, and the words *player* or *student* are substituted for the word *tutee*.

10. If using reciprocal tutoring, the teacher sets a kitchen timer or stopwatch for the halfway point of the total session, at which time the students will switch roles so that the tutee becomes the tutor.

11. The tutor begins the activity with the tutee. The tutor praises correct responses. Incorrect responses are pointed out by the tutor to the tutee. The tutee is asked to try again. If wrong twice, the tutor provides the answer to the tutee.

12. The teacher walks around the room to monitor student participation, engagement, and accurate implementation of the task. The teacher provides praise to students for effectively working together and task engagement. The teacher provides prompting and assistance to students as needed to facilitate accurate task completion and for following the peer tutoring rules.

13. At the end of each session (or at least once weekly) all students are administered a brief assessment (e.g., CBM, oral flash cards, worksheet, unit test) that is completed individually.

14. Students should be permitted to score their own or their partner's assessment using a provided answer key or teacher-constructed model.

15. Academic and/or behavioral performance should be recorded by each student on his or her own chart or graph and compared with the preset goals (e.g., using a score card, performance on the weekly assessment). If goals are met, then students should be able to select the predetermined or randomly presented rewards.

Treatment Variations:

• Parents provide rewards for goal attainment at home (e.g., reward certificate sent from teacher with student indicating a home reward earned and parents offered a parent–child activity, special event).

Selected References:

1. Bowman-Perrott, L. Davis, H., Vannest, K., Williams, L., Greenwood, C., & Parker, R. (2013). Academic benefits of peer tutoring: A meta-analytic review of single-case research. *School Psychology Review, 42,* 39–55.

2. Hawkins, R. O., Musti-Rao, S., Hughes, C., Berry, L., & McGuire, S. (2009). Applying a randomized interdependent group contingency component to classwide peer tutoring for multiplication fact fluency. *Journal of Behavioral Education, 18,* 300–318.

3. Heller, L. R., & Fantuzzo, J. W. (1993). Reciprocal peer tutoring and parent partnership: Does parent involvement make a difference? *School Psychology Review, 22,* 517–534.

4. Fantuzzo, J. W., King, J. A., & Heller, L. R. (1992). Effects of reciprocal peer tutoring on mathematics and school adjustment: A component analysis. *Journal of Educational Psychology, 84,* 331–339.

5. Robinson, D. R., Schofield, J. W., & Steers-Wentzell, K. L. (2005). Peer and cross-age tutoring in math: Outcomes and their design implications. *Educational Psychology Review, 17,* 327–362.

6. Rohrbeck, C. A., Ginsburg-Block, M. D., Fantuzzo, J. W., & Miller, T. R. (2003). Peer-assisted learning interventions with elementary school students: A meta-analytic review. *Journal of Educational Psychology, 95,* 240–257.

Checklist for Promoting Effective Classroom Instruction in Math

	Occurs	Sometimes Occurs	Not in Place
1. Designate 45–60 minutes of core instruction daily.			
2. Select an evidence-based curriculum or evaluate options using the CCSS for Mathematics (NGA & CCSSO, 2010) and the NMAP (2008) recommendations.			
3. Ensure that sufficient opportunities to practice math concepts, standard algorithms, problem solving, and automatic recall of basic facts are provided.			
4. Assess implementation of the selected core curriculum using a procedural fidelity checklist.			
5. Use a blended instructional approach combining teacher-directed and student-centered activities.			
6. Use differentiated instruction to ensure all students can access the curriculum.			
7. Provide some explicit instruction during lessons daily.			
8. Incorporate motivation strategies that encourage students' effort, engagement, participation, and persistence in math activities.			
9. Consider incorporating supplemental instructional activities such as computer assisted instruction, peer tutoring, and/or team-based instruction.			
10. Conduct schoolwide formative assessment (also referred to as universal screening) two or three times annually.			

Textbook Analysis of Effective Instructional Design Principles

Present	Instructional Design Principle	Description of Instructional Design Principle
☐ Yes ☐ No ☐ Partially	Specific observable and measurable learning objectives are provided.	Lessons include learning objectives that provide specific student behavior expected and the criteria for determining student mastery of the objective.
☐ Yes ☐ No ☐ Partially	Low number of skills/concepts are described in learning objectives.	The lesson's learning objectives introduce only one or two skills or concepts.
☐ Yes ☐ No ☐ Partially	Math models: Manipulatives and representations are used within each lesson.	Manipulatives refer to concrete objects that can be touched and moved, and representations refer to number lines, symbols, drawings, or pictures. All forms of math models are used during teacher instruction and student practice.
☐ Yes ☐ No ☐ Partially	Explicit instruction was to explain the lesson's concept or skill.	Explicit instruction refers to a structured and systematic step-by-step approach that emphasizes student mastery of each skill or concept.
☐ Yes ☐ No ☐ Partially	Many instructional examples are provided.	Multiple examples for illustrating the lesson objective are provided by teachers before and during each lesson. Examples are similar in complexity as student practice examples.
☐ Yes ☐ No ☐ Partially	Adequate practice opportunities and cumulative review are present.	At least four opportunities for students to practice the target skill or concept are provided using verbalizations, written exercises, and discrimination practice (i.e., opportunities to determine when and when not to apply the skill or concept) during the lesson.
☐ Yes ☐ No ☐ Partially	Prerequisite mathematical skills are reviewed.	During each lesson one or more prerequisite skills are reviewed using warm-up activities prior to introducing the new skill or concept.
☐ Yes ☐ No ☐ Partially	Instructions for providing immediate error correction and corrective feedback are incorporated.	Each lesson includes directions for teachers to address student errors and to provide feedback such as specific steps, rules, or prompts to facilitate correct student responses. Hints for anticipating errors are provided to students and reteaching is offered when needed.

(continued)

Note. Based on information in B. R. Bryant, Bryant, Kethley, et al. (2008) and Doabler, Fien, Nelson-Walker, and Baker (2012).

Textbook Analysis of Effective Instructional Design Principles *(page 2 of 2)*

Present	Instructional Design Principle	Description of Instructional Design Principle
☐ Yes ☐ No ☐ Partially	Math vocabulary is addressed.	Each lesson includes key vocabulary terms necessary for mastering the skill or concept as well as provides instruction on their definitions and opportunities for students to use the vocabulary terms.
☐ Yes ☐ No ☐ Partially	Strategy instruction and self-regulatory cues are included.	Self-instructional cues and strategies are listed, described, and applied during each lesson.
☐ Yes ☐ No ☐ Partially	Formative assessment is embedded.	Individual student understanding is checked frequently and compared with a criterion for mastery of the lesson objective. Guidelines are provided for how to make decisions with student assessment data (e.g., such as moving to the next lesson or reteaching).

CHAPTER 3

Math Screening and Determining Student Groups

The use of formative assessment in schools, periodic assessments administered to inform as well as alter learning and instruction, has extensive support among policymakers and researchers (Black & Wiliam, 1998; Hosp, 2012; Kingston & Nash, 2011; NMAP, 2008; Stecker & Fuchs, 2000; Wesson, 1991). One type of formative assessment that can be used schoolwide is universal screening of all students' skill proficiency three times annually during the fall, winter, and spring (Batsche et al., 2006; Riccomini & Witzel, 2010). The benefit of universal screening is to determine which students are at risk for or experiencing math difficulties and who would benefit from additional math supports (Salvia et al., 2011). Universal screening data can be used to identify classes of students who also appear to be at risk so that classroom adjustments to curriculum and instruction can be made (e.g., Lembke et al., 2012; VanDerHeyden, McLaughlin, Algina, & Snyder, 2012). The use of universal screening is highly recommended for math, but only a modest amount of information is available to support its use (Gersten, Beckmann, et al., 2009; NMAP, 2008).

This chapter describes universal screening procedures and tools, according to what is known for elementary school applications. In addition, we discuss follow-up assessment procedures that can be used to assist with homogeneous skill groupings in order to form intervention groups for students determined to be at risk for or experiencing difficulties with math.

Figure 3.1 describes a multistep framework that can guide instructional decision making. The Center on Response to Intervention (*www.rti4success.org*) also describes a multigating process for universal screening containing two steps. The first step, as illustrated in Figure 3.1, is to use a brief, reliable, valid, sensitive measure that is highly predictive of important math outcomes, such as state or national high-stakes exams (Shapiro, 2011). The

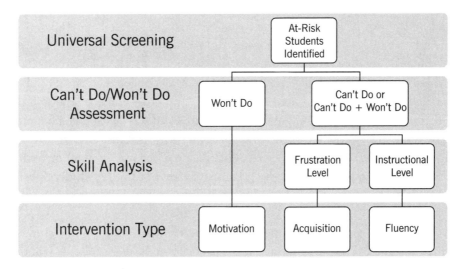

FIGURE 3.1. Instructional decision-making framework for students at risk for math difficulties.

second step is to administer additional measures to refine students' risk for math failure (Fuchs et al., 2011; Gersten, Beckmann, et al., 2009; Lembke et al., 2012). We discuss two types of assessment techniques that can be used to refine the understanding of students' math needs: (1) the can't do/won't do (CD/WD) assessment technique and (2) skill analysis. We propose using the CD/WD assessment technique in order to rule out students experiencing motivation-only difficulties, determine whether students experience both skill- and performance-related math deficits, and identify students experiencing skill deficits in isolation (VanDerHeyden, Witt, & Gilbertson, 2007; VanDerHeyden et al., 2003). After the CD/WD assessment has been administered and skill deficits have been hypothesized as the reason why students exhibited poor math performance during universal screening, a skill analysis assessment can be used to further identify specific strengths and weaknesses. Finally, we describe how this multistage screening process links to the instructional hierarchy (Haring & Eaton, 1978) and intervention selection.

UNIVERSAL SCREENING PROCEDURES AND TOOLS

A number of different types of measures can be used for universal screening. The Center on Response to Intervention provides a comprehensive list of tools that have been evaluated across many psychometric properties to assist school professionals with deciding which measures to apply in their schools and districts (*www.rti4success.org/resources/tools-charts/screening-tools-chart*). It is highly recommended that districts use the same instrument for screening across schools and, if possible, grade levels so that student comparisons can be made over time (Fuchs & Fuchs, 2004; Gersten, Beckmann, et al., 2009). Universal screening tools should also be brief, reliable, valid, and sensitive. The time allocated to universal screening needs to be carefully considered such that the balance of assessment to instruction should be in favor of instruction (e.g., Hosp & Ardoin, 2008). Unfortunately, we have seen many schools make the mistake of selecting screening measures that take 40 or more minutes to be individually administered.

There are numerous efficient screening tools that also meet the criteria of being reliable, valid, and sensitive, as illustrated in Table 3.1. A practice guide by the IES regarding effective RTI practices for math recommends that universal screening take no more than 20 minutes (Gersten, Beckmann, et al., 2009). Reliability means that a measure is consistent. The IES practice guide recommends that reliability coefficients be 0.80 or higher. For a universal screening tool to be valid it should correspond to or predict student performance on important high-stakes math assessments or outcomes. The IES practice guide recommends that predictive validity coefficients be 0.60 or higher.

Universal screening tools are not perfect. These tools will identify some students as *not at risk* for math difficulties when they actually *are* at risk, and some students will be flagged as at risk when they do not need to be. This is referred to as the sensitivity and specificity of a measure. Sensitivity means that the universal screening tool correctly identifies students who are *at risk* for math difficulties (high rates of true positives). Sensitivity is described with the term *specificity*, which means that the universal screening tool correctly identifies students' *not at risk* (high rates of true negatives). Screening tools with a sensitivity level of 0.90 are preferred; however, this benchmark may be too high given the psychometric status of the currently available math tools (Johnson, Jenkins, & Petscher, 2010; Shapiro & Gebhardt, 2012).

Universal screening tools also need to be selected according to the match between the math concepts and skills that are evaluated by the measure and the adopted school/district curriculum standards. Screening tools should align with key curriculum content areas as defined by the Common Core (NGA & CCSSO, 2010), the NMAP (2008) recommendations, or the NCTM (2006) focal points. For early elementary grades these measures should focus on concepts and skills pertaining to whole-number proficiency and also include rational numbers as students enter the intermediate elementary grades (e.g., Gersten, Beckmann, et al., 2009). Box 3.1 provides recommendations for what curriculum-based measurement (CBM) tools to administer according to grade level. Students in kindergarten and grade 1 might be assessed on measures of early numeracy such as number identification, quantity discrimination, and mental number-line skills. Students in grades 2–5 might be assessed in computation and application measures. More than one measure may be required due

BOX 3.1. Content Areas to Assess during Universal Screening for Grades K–5			
Grade	Early Numeracy	Computation	Concepts Application
K	×		
1	×	×	
2–5		×	×

to the multitopic nature of math and the lack of one overall performance indicator of math proficiency (Foegen et al., 2007; Fuchs, Fuchs, Compton, et al., 2007; Fuchs, Fuchs, & Hollenbeck, 2007). For students in grade 4 and above, year-end high-stakes test performance should be considered with universal screening tools when determining students' risk status (e.g., Gersten, Beckmann, et al., 2009). In grades 4 and 5, one of the best predictors of students' performance on future high-stakes tests is their performance on previous high-stakes tests (VanDerHeyden, Codding, & Martin, 2014).

Curriculum-Based Measurement

CBM was designed as a general outcome measure to assess long-term growth across expected year-end objectives (Deno, 1985; Fuchs & Deno, 1991; Shinn, 1989). Therefore, each CBM test contains problems representative of skills and concepts expected to be learned at the beginning, middle, and end of the school year. CBM is intended to evaluate performance within a brief, predetermined amount of time and a unique feature is the ability of CBM to detect small changes in student learning (e.g., Fuchs & Fuchs, 2004). Administration and scoring procedures are standardized, which permits comparison of scores among students and within individual students over time (Hintze, Christ, & Methe, 2006). These features, along with more than 30 years of research confirming the tool's reliability, validity, and utility (e.g., Foegen et al., 2007), have made CBM a popular choice for universal screening (Lembke et al., 2012).

CBMs are paper-and-pencil tasks that can be administered to groups of students or to individual students and each measure takes anywhere from 1 to 8 minutes to administer (Lembke et al., 2012; VanDerHeyden et al., 2003; Witt, Daly, & Noell, 2000). CBM tools assess math knowledge in many ways including place value understanding, application to problem solving, whole-number operations, basic fact fluency, magnitude, mental number line, and strategic counting. These aspects of math knowledge are often grouped into three types of CBMs: (1) early numeracy, (2) computation, and (3) application. The most researched early-numeracy CBM measures for screening evaluate a single component of math knowledge and include oral counting, number identification, missing number, and quantity discrimination (Baglici, Codding, & Tryon, 2010; Chard et al., 2005; Clarke & Shinn, 2004). These measures (see Table 3.1) have strong reliability and validity, and are efficient. CBM computation for early elementary grades tends to evaluate several aspects of math knowledge including basic fact fluency, place value understanding, and whole-number operations. These efficient measures have strong reliability but only modest validity when predicting high-stakes outcomes (Christ, Scullin, Tolbize, & Jiban, 2008; Foegen et al., 2007). CBM application measures are also efficient and evaluate the application of math knowledge to problem solving and place value, as well as whole-number operations. These measures have strong reliability and range from moderate to strong validity with high-stakes outcomes.

The data acquired from the CBM computation and application tools provide a general indication of whether students are at risk for greater math failure but cannot identify specific skill strengths and weaknesses. There are many commercial applications of CBM that can be purchased such as via aimsweb, iSTEEP, and easyCBM (which also offers a free

TABLE 3.1. Universal Screening Measures Selected from the Center on Response to Intervention at the American Institutes for Research

Tool	Website	Cost	Measures	Reliability	Validity	Administration format	Administration and scoring time
aimsweb	*aimsweb.com*	$3.00–$5.00/student/year for all necessary materials	Math CBM	Alternate form (above 0.80)	Below 0.60 (range 0.35–0.54)	Group	2–8 minutes
			Math concepts and applications	Alternate and interrater (both above 0.80)	Construct and predictive (range 0.57–0.67)	Individual and group	11 minutes
			Number identification	Internal consistency and test–retest (both above 0.80)	Construct and predictive (both above 0.60)	Individual	2 minutes
			Missing number	Internal consistency and test–retest (both above 0.80)	Concurrent and predictive (both above 0.60)		
			Quantity discrimination	Alternate form and test–retest (both above 0.80)	Concurrent and predictive (both above 0.60)		
DIBELS Math	*https://dibels.org/pubs.html#math*	Free for 2016–2017 academic year; see website for future years	Early numeracy (beginning quantity discrimination, number identification, next number fluency, advanced quantity discrimination, missing number fluency)	See website for technical reports.	See website for technical reports.	Individual and group	Early numeracy: 1 minute each
			Computation				Computation: 2–6 minutes

46

Name	Website	Cost	Skills	Reliability	Validity	Administration	Time
easyCBM	http://easycbm.com	Teacher version is free; school district version is $1/year	Concepts and application	Internal consistency (above 0.80)	Construct, concurrent, and predictive (all above 0.60)	Individual and group	Concepts and application: 8–16 minutes; 30 minutes
Formative Assessment System for Teachers™ (FAST) Early Numeracy	www.fastbridge.org/earlymath	$5/student for all materials	Grouping and place values	Internal consistency and alternate form (above 0.80); test–retest (above 0.70)	Concurrent (above 0.40); predictive (above 0.50)	Individual	5 minutes
			Match quantity	Test–retest (above 0.70); internal (above 0.90); alternate form (above 0.60)	Concurrent (above 0.40); predictive (above 0.30)		
			Number sequence	Test–retest and internal (both above 0.80); alternate form (above 0.70)	Concurrent (above 0.50); predictive (above 0.40)		
			Decomposing	Test–retest, internal, and alternate form (all above 0.80)	Concurrent (above 0.50); predictive (above 0.50)		
mCLASS: Computation and Math Concepts	www.amplify.com	$13/student annually, $35/complete kit, $200–$300/teacher for handheld computer, $1,400/on-site installation or $400/remote installation	Computation	Test–retest with alternate form (above 0.50)	Predictive (above 0.20)	Group	12 minutes
			Math concepts	Test–retest with alternate form (above 0.40)	Predictive and concurrent (both above 0.40)		

(continued)

TABLE 3.1. *(continued)*

Tool	Website	Cost	Measures	Reliability	Validity	Administration format	Administration and scoring time
mCLASS: Early Numeracy	*www.amplify.com*	$13/student annually, $35/complete kit, $200–$300/teacher for handheld computer, $1,400/on-site installation or $400/remote installation	Missing numbers	Test–retest with alternate form (above 0.70)	Predictive (above 0.30); concurrent (above 0.50)	Individual and group	11–12 minutes
			Next number	Test–retest with alternate form (above 0.60)	Predictive (above 0.50); concurrent (above 0.40)	Individual	5 minutes
			Number identification	Test–retest with alternate form and alternate form (both above 0.80)	Predictive (above 0.40); concurrent (above 0.50)		
			Quantity discrimination	Test–retest with alternate form (above 0.30); alternate form (above 0.60)	Predictive (above 0.10); concurrent (above 0.40)	Individual and group	11–12 minutes
			Number facts	Test–retest with alternate form (above 0.70); alternate form (above 0.60)	Predictive (above 0.30); concurrent (above 0.50)	Individual	11–12 minutes

Monitoring Basic Skills Progress	www.proedinc. com	$79 for one license	Basic math computation	Internal (above 0.90)	Criterion and predictive (both above 0.60)	Individual and group	5–15 minutes
			Basic math concepts and applications	Internal (above 0.90)	Criterion and predictive (both above 0.60)		
STAR	www.renaissance. com	Setup fee and cost depend on number of schools and students	Math computation, math application, and math concepts	Alternate form and split-half (above 0.80)	Concurrent and predictive (both above 0.60)	Individual and group	10 minutes
Yearly Progress Pro: Math	www.ctb.com	$9.25/student annually, $1,700/ technology fee	Basic math computation	Alpha (above 0.80)	Predictive (above 0.60); concurrent (above 0.70)	Individual	15 minutes

Data from Dewey, Rice, Wheeler, Kaminski, and Good (2014).

version). CBM probes can also be constructed from websites such as Intervention Central (*www.interventioncentral.org*) or downloaded from others such as Oklahoma Tiered Intervention System of Support (OTISS; *www.otiss.net*). The downside of constructing your own CBMs is that the psychometric properties of these measures will not have been evaluated—therefore, you do not know how consistent the measures are or whether they are measuring the intended aspects of math knowledge.

Computer-Adaptive Testing

CAT is a relatively new computer-based approach to universal screening that has promise when used for math. CAT measurement systems are capable of assessing a wide range of math skills and the selection of items administered is individually adapted according to students' responses. Overall scores reflecting general performance on specific domains are provided, similar to CBM. However, CAT also provides a more detailed analysis of students' specific skill mastery (Shapiro & Gebhardt, 2012). There are several CAT systems available commercially including the FastBridge Learning (*www.fastbridge.org*) and Renaissance Learning's™ STAR™ (*www.renaissance.com/products/assessments/star-360*) that have excellent reliability and validity evidence, and are relatively efficient. One comparison study of aimsweb CBM computation and application measures with STAR demonstrated that STAR had stronger predictive validity and slightly better reliability than either CBM measure (Shapiro & Gebhardt, 2012). STAR displayed more sensitivity (ability to detect students who are at risk for math failure) than both CBM tools (CBM application in particular). However, neither CBM nor STAR measures reflected the level of sensitivity expected for universal screening. STAR measures correlated modestly with CBM computation and application measures, suggesting that these measures all describe different aspects of math knowledge. This means that more than one measure may be needed to capture at-risk students and/or that school professionals should consider the strengths and limitations of the screening tool selected.

DETERMINING RISK STATUS

Once the screening data are collected and analyzed, school teams are able to evaluate whether the core curriculum is effective for most students by selecting one of three decision-making frameworks: (1) norm referenced, (2), resource allocation, or (3) standards based. The first option, norm referenced, compares the assessment scores with the local or national norms using percentile ranks and determining cutoff scores. Cutoff scores can be determined by school professionals keeping in mind that high cutoff scores, such as the 50th percentile (i.e., all students below the 50th percentile on the screener are considered at risk), are likely to capture nearly all at-risk students as well as many nonrisk students (Gersten, Beckmann, et al., 2009). If the cutoff score is too low, such as the 16th percentile, then nonrisk students will probably not be identified, but it is likely that some students in need of math assistance will be missed. General recommendations indicate that students who fall below the 25th percentile are considered to be at risk (Fuchs, 2003) and those performing below the 16th percentile are likely to be in need of more intensive services (VanDerHeyden et al., 2003).

The second option is a resource allocation model (Burns et al., 2007; VanDerHeyden & Burns, 2005). Within this framework the emphasis is on enhancing the learning of all students—therefore, screening data are aggregated across grade and class. Aggregating these data permits schools to look at class- and grade-level math knowledge rather than just individuals. Grades or classes that fall below a criterion, such as the 25th percentile, are then provided with a specific intervention that addresses a specific skill deficit such as fact fluency or word-problem solving through the use of supplemental instruction or another specific classwide intervention. Grade- or classwide performance is then monitored over time to ensure progress. Once the average class performance improves, then specific individuals who did not respond to the additional core instructional supports are identified and provided with small-group or individualized tutoring (e.g., Ardoin et al., 2005; VanDer-Heyden et al., 2007). If no classwide or grade-level problems are identified, then the lowest-performing 20% of students within each grade are selected for targeted supports.

The third model is a standards-based framework (Hintze, 2008; Silberglitt & Hintze, 2005). In this case, school professionals identify benchmarks that are generated from statistical analyses. The purpose of this approach is to identify specific cutoff scores that are relevant for the local school or district and are highly predictive of performance on high-stakes tests. Students who fall below the designated benchmark would be considered at risk for math difficulties and possibly need additional intervention supports.

STUDENT RISK IS DETERMINED—NOW WHAT?

Once students are identified as being at risk, another set of decisions will need to be made. First, consider whether some classes of students are performing less well than others. If the answer is yes, then you might determine that a classwide intervention should be implemented targeting the specific skills that most students still need to acquire (see Chapter 4 for details). Second, consider whether the individual students determined to be at risk will (1) be monitored periodically, or (2) receive additional instructional support through interventions (Codding & Connell, 2008; Gersten, Beckmann, et al., 2009; Hintze, 2007; Shapiro, 2011). It is possible that schools will find that a very high percentage of students are determined to be at risk. When this happens, school professionals will have to make decisions given the available resources. Theoretically, it is anticipated that approximately 20% of students will need support in addition to the core instruction, presuming that instruction is conducted using scientifically validated curricula and instructional practices (Batsche et al., 2006). A high percentage of low-performing students across the school may suggest that educators first need to determine whether the core instructional materials are adequately addressing all students' needs and make any necessary adjustments (see Chapter 2). Using a resources allocation framework of decision making may be necessary when this occurs—that is, the lowest-performing students at each grade might be identified for further intervention supports while core instructional materials are enhanced (Gersten, Beckmann, et al., 2009). Educators might also combine the universal screening results with other previously collected and available data such as performance on state assessments, other standardized measures (e.g., Iowa Tests of Basic Skills; Hoover, Hieronymus, Frisbie, & Dunbar, 1993), and/or teacher ratings to determine which students should receive additional instructional support and which students' performance should be monitored.

Individual students exhibiting risk can be grouped into three categories: (1) borderline risk, (2) at risk, and (3) high risk following universal screening. We describe the performance of students exhibiting borderline risk as those students scoring between the 25th and 30th percentiles (Codding & Connell, 2008; Hintze, 2007; Shapiro, 2011). Students falling in the borderline risk category do not initially receive small-group or individual interventions, but their performance is monitored weekly or semiweekly using CBM or CAT tools for 4–8 weeks. Often a cutoff score for determining students who are at risk for math difficulties is defined at the 25th percentile. This group of students might be best served by receiving interventions in small groups (one interventionist for four to six students). Finally, students exhibiting high risk are often described as those students whose scores fall below the 10th percentile. This group of students might benefit from receiving interventions that are provided individually or in smaller groups (one interventionist for two to three students). The next task is to group students according to similar skill and conceptual gaps, called homogeneous groupings, and match interventions to students' skill level and potential reasons for math difficulties.

REFINING ASSESSMENT TO MATCH INSTRUCTIONAL INTERVENTIONS

Universal screening is used as a gauge to determine the health of the core instructional curriculum on student outcomes as well as identify students who may need additional instructional intervention supports. Once students are identified as at risk through universal screening, school professionals need to focus on forming homogeneous skill groupings and selecting empirically supported or evidence-based interventions that are designed to address students' skill gaps (American Psychological Association, 2006; Burns, Appleton, & Stehouwer, 2005; Hosp & Ardoin, 2008; Kratochwill & Shernoff, 2003, 2004).

Considering that multiple screening measures are recommended in math (Gersten, Beckmann, et al., 2009), it is useful to generate initial groupings according to how students appear to be performing on these screening tools. Three examples follow. First, let's say a second-grade student is performing between the 10th and 25th percentiles according to national norms on a computation CBM tool but in the 50th percentile on a concepts/application CBM tool. These data might suggest that this student would benefit from intervention supports that target computation skills, and so further information about this student's computation skill strengths and weaknesses would be collected in order to target the appropriate intervention and area. Second, if a third-grade student performed in the 50th percentile on the computation screening tool but between the 10th and 25th percentiles on the concepts/application tool, the intervention target would be in the area of math applications, but further skills analysis of what application areas are difficult for the student would be conducted. Third, if a kindergarten student's screening data suggested that scores were below the 25th percentile in number identification, strategic counting, and magnitude discrimination tasks, the target for intervention supports might begin with number identification, as this skill is required in order to engage in the other two tasks (Clarke et al., 2008). Because early number screening measures are often constructed as separate tools, further skill analysis might not be needed.

Skill-by-Treatment Interaction

Of paramount importance when selecting groupings of students and determining the intervention to be provided, is to ensure that the intervention is functionally related to student performance (Ardoin & Daly, 2007; Christ, 2008; Daly, Hintze, & Hamler, 2000; VanDerHeyden, Witt, & Barnett, 2005; Yell, Shriner, & Katsiyannis, 2006). This means that several possible reasons for a student's math difficulties are analyzed and then an intervention is explicitly matched to address the student's skill gaps and the reasons for those gaps (Christ, 2008; Daly et al., 2000; Fuchs, Fuchs, & Speece, 2002; Hosp & Ardoin, 2008).

Two steps are required to determine skill-by-treatment matches. First, as we described above, administer additional assessments designed to identify students' specific skill strengths and weaknesses. Second, generate and test potential reasons for students' math performance difficulties. Before student groups are determined and interventions are selected it is important to determine *what to teach* students and *how to* teach it (Hosp & Ardoin, 2008). Assessments used to further define students' skill strengths and weaknesses need to have treatment validity (Fuchs et al., 2002)—that is, assessments should provide information to math coaches, teachers, school psychologists, and school-based building teams that align with instructional planning. When making decisions on students' math skills it might be most useful to administer assessments that permit educators to directly observe students' math performance (Christ, 2008; Hosp & Ardoin, 2008).

There are many reasons why students experience academic difficulties and exhibit low performance on the universal screeners (Daly, Witt, Martens, & Dool, 1997; see Box 3.2):

- Students many not be motivated to engage in the task (motivation or performance deficit).
- Students have not had enough practice with the skill or concept being assessed (skill deficit: fluency).
- Students may need more direct assistance to understand the skill or concept (skill deficit: acquisition).
- Instructional materials may be too difficult because students have not mastered prerequisite skills (instructional match).

It is important to first rule out whether students are experiencing a performance deficit, because the appropriate course of intervention is not to address their math skills but

---

BOX 3.2. Why Students Perform Poorly

Skill or Motivation Deficit?
- Can't do (skill), won't do (motivation), or both

What Type of Skill Deficit?
- Acquisition (does not possess)
- Fluency (accurate but slow)

Poor Instructional Match?
- Missing prerequisite skills

---

to address their motivation to engage in math tasks. It is possible, however, that students identified as needing supports in math exhibit both skill and motivation deficits (Reinke, Herman, Petras, & Ialongo, 2008; see Box 3.2). In order to determine whether students are experiencing a skill, motivation, or combined skill and motivation deficit, school-based teams can implement a CD/WD assessment (VanDerHeyden, 2014).

CD/WD Assessment

CD/WD assessment is a very brief and simple technique that can be conducted by school psychologists, math coaches, interventionists, or teachers. The CD/WD assessment is intended to capture whether students' low math performance is the result of a skill deficit, a motivation deficit, or a combined skill and motivation deficit. The procedure can be conducted with unit tests or other placement tests but is often conceptualized for use with CBM (VanDerHeyden et al., 2003, 2007). The materials required for a CD/WD assessment include (1) two alternate forms of grade-level CBM probes in the same content area, (2) CBM administration and scoring instructions, (3) a stopwatch to time administration of the CBM probe, and (4) a treasure chest containing a variety of age- and school-appropriate rewards. The first CBM probe is administered according to standardized instructions. The second CBM probe also follows standardized instructions, but the student is provided with the opportunity to earn a reward following a performance that exceeds the first CBM probe by 20% (see Box 3.3 for procedures). Three outcomes from this assessment can occur:

1. The student's performance was similar during both test administrations, indicating that the student is probably displaying a skill deficit and further analysis of his or her skills is needed.
2. The student's performance was 20% or better when provided with a goal and reward, *and* the score obtained was above the expected performance standard or screening cutoff score, indicating that the student is probably displaying a motivation deficit (Ardoin et al., 2005; Noell, Freeland, Witt, & Gansle, 2001). A behavior plan targeting academic engagement, task initiation, or task completion might be the most appropriate course of action following additional evaluation of the student's motivation within the classroom situation.

BOX 3.3. Procedures for Conducting a CD/WD Assessment

1. Administer a CBM probe using standardized instructions.

2. Score the probe according to digits correct and record the score on the top of the page.

3. Calculate a goal 20% higher than the score obtained on the original probe. For example, if the student scored 10 digits correct on the first probe, the goal score would be 12.

4. Show the original and the goal scores to the student. Let the student know that if he or she meets the goal score, he or she can earn a prize from the treasure chest.

5. Administer a second CBM probe using standardized instructions. Score the probe according to digits correct, record the score at the top of the page, and determine if the goal score was met.

6. If the goal score was met, permit the student to select a prize from the treasure chest.

7. If the goal score was not met, praise the student for effort and offer him or her a sticker or another token reward not provided in the treasure chest.

Note. Adapted from VanDerHeyden (2014). Copyright © 2014 the National Association of School Psychologists. Adapted by permission.

---

3. The student's performance on the second CBM probe matched or exceeded the 20% goal score but the score is below the expected standard of performance or cutoff score for the screening measure. It would be hypothesized that this student is experiencing both skill- and performance-related math deficits. For this student, the nature of the skill deficits needs to be further defined and this student might also benefit from including a motivation component in his or her intervention plan.

Below we provide two different examples of how the CD/WD assessment can be used to identify whether a student might be exhibiting a skill deficit, a motivation deficit, or a combined skill and motivation deficit.

Case Examples: Using the CD/WD Assessment to Evaluate Potential Reasons for Math Difficulties

Case Example 1 (Figure 3.2): Hadley, a second grader, performed below the 25th percentile on the grade-level CBM tool during schoolwide universal screening conducted in the winter. As a result, Hadley was included on a list of students in need of intervention supports. The building school psychologist, Mr. Owen, conducted a CD/WD assessment to determine whether her difficulties were the result of a skill or motivational deficit, or combination of both. Hadley's score on the grade-level CBM probe using standardized instructions was 15. Mr. Owen determined that Hadley's goal score would be 18, which was 20% higher than her original score. Mr. Owen showed Hadley a graph displaying the score she received during universal screening (15 DCPM) and informed her that if she reached the goal score of 18, or better, she could earn a prize. Mr. Owen also showed Hadley the treasure chest of prize options. Mr. Owen then administered the alternative form of the CBM grade-level probe following the standardized instructions. Hadley received a score of 20, which exceeded the goal score of 18, and she was able to choose a prize from the treasure chest. However, when Mr. Owen compared this score with the publisher norms, he noted that Hadley's score still

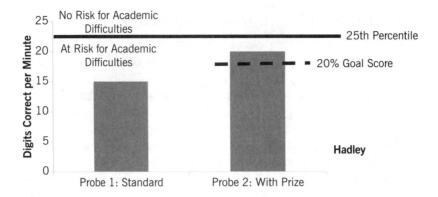

FIGURE 3.2. CD/WD assessment: Case Example 1.

fell below the 25th percentile. Therefore, he hypothesized that Hadley's math difficulties likely stemmed from both a skill and a motivational deficit. As a result, Mr. Owen suggested to the intervention team that a treatment program that targeted Hadley's math skill deficits, as well as incorporated motivational strategies, would likely be successful.

Case Example 2 (Figure 3.3): Following the same procedures, Mr. Owen conducted a CD/WD assessment with Gavin, a third grader whose performance also fell below the 25th percentile during schoolwide universal screening. Gavin received a score of 20 on the grade-level CBM tool so Mr. Owen was able to determine that Gavin's goal score would be 24 (a score 20% higher than he achieved during the universal screening). Gavin was presented with a graph displaying his original score (i.e., 20) and his goal score (i.e., 24), and told he could earn a prize from the treasure chest for meeting or exceeding the goal score. Mr. Owen then administered an alternative form of the grade-level CBM tool following standardized instructions. Gavin received a score of 35, which not only exceeded his goal score but also exceeded the 25th percentile that the school used to determine whether students required additional intervention services. Gavin was able to choose a prize and Mr. Owen presented the results to the

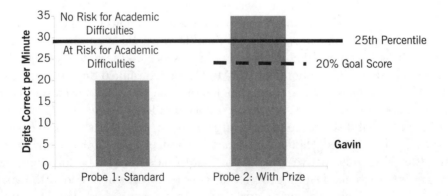

FIGURE 3.3. CD/WD assessment: Case Example 2.

intervention team. The intervention team decided not to include Gavin on the list of students who required additional math supports, and instead decided to investigate whether motivation difficulties were interfering with classroom work in general, potentially requiring that a behavior support plan be generated.

Survey-Level Assessment of Skills

The reasons for skill deficits (acquisition, fluency, instructional match) can be further analyzed by determining which skills students have mastered, not mastered (frustration level), and are in the instructional range (Gickling & Havertape, 1981; Shapiro, 2011). When evaluating these skills it is important to identify all missing prerequisite skills and determine whether students are in the acquisition or fluency stages of skill or concept development (Burns et al., 2010; Powell et al., 2013). We advocate that two steps be used to assist with determining the *what* and *how* of intervention planning: (1) identify specific math strengths and weaknesses, and (2) use a decision-making heuristic to match skill level with an intervention strategy (Burns et al., 2010; Codding et al., 2007; Daly et al., 2000).

A skills analysis is a process whereby performance on any one skill is analyzed to determine skill proficiency, monitor progress, and guide instruction (Codding & Connell, 2008; Fuchs, Fuchs, & Stecker, 1990). We have previously discussed CBM as a general measure of grade-level skills useful for universal screening. CBM is a form of direct assessment that falls under the umbrella of CBA. CBA is any direct, usually production-based, method of measuring student performance according to skills defined by local or national curriculum sequences (Hintze et al., 2006). CBA consists of general outcome measures such as CBM, which assess long-term grade-level outcomes and subskill mastery measures. Subskill mastery measures are particularly useful for instructional intervention planning, because these measures represent a subdivision of broad grade-level skills and/or concepts into smaller slices of the curriculum (Hintze et al., 2006; Hosp & Ardoin, 2008; Shapiro, 2011). For example, the CCSS for Mathematics (NGA & CCSSO, 2010) indicates that students add and subtract numerals within 20 automatically by the end of second grade (i.e., the long-term objective). However, for students who are struggling to meet that standard, it might be useful to identify whether they can add to 5 by using a measure that includes addition problems with numerals 0–5 (Powell et al., 2013). This specific subskill serves as a short-term instructional objective and starting point for the intervention selected. For each subskill, a student's mastery of the skill or concept is evaluated. Once mastery is achieved, a new subskill serves as the target for instruction (Fuchs & Deno, 1991; Hintze et al., 2006).

There are three types of subskill mastery measurement: (1) criterion-referenced CBA (CBA-CR; Blankenship, 1985), (2) CBA for instructional design (CBA-ID; Gickling & Havertape, 1981), and (3) curriculum-based evaluation (CBE; Howell & Nolet, 1999). Distinguishing among these types of subskill mastery extends beyond the purpose of this book (see Hintze et al., 2006, for further explanation). Each of these procedures has in common the idea that student performance on specific math subskills should be measured and compared to a criterion from which it can be determined if the skills represent an appropriate instructional match, whether the skills fall in the frustration range, and which skills a student has mastered. An instructional match represents the skills or concepts that students can work on independently or with teacher support, depending on the planned instructional or intervention activity. An appropriate instructional match for math is represented by a criterion of 70–85% accuracy, when teacher support is provided (Burns et al., 2010; Gickling & Thompson, 1985). Students could be expected to work independently on tasks that represent skills for which students perform with greater than 85% accuracy. However, empirical evidence suggests that how accurate a student is able to perform math tasks may not be as useful an indicator as fluency (Burns, VanDerHeyden, & Jiban, 2006). CBA represents a fluency indicator for math, because these tools provide a measure of accuracy and speed (e.g., the number of digits or problems completed correctly within the 2 minutes allocated for testing).

A survey-level assessment consists of two phases (Hosp, Hosp, & Howell, 2007): (1) administer CBM probes from sequentially lower grade levels to determine instructional placement, and (2) administer subskill mastery probes on isolated skills that match the skill scope and sequence for that grade level. The scores (often recorded as digits correct per 2 minutes) obtained from administration of the subskill mastery measures can then be compared with criteria to determine whether performance falls within the frustration, instructional, or mastery level of skill performance (Burns et al., 2006; Deno & Mirkin, 1977; Howell & Nolet, 1999). The lowest skill in the sequence that is not mastered (falling within either the frustration or instructional range) should be considered the first target skill addressed by the intervention.

Although a survey-level assessment is frequently administered individually, we have conducted survey-level assessments in groups with students' identified as at risk within the same grade. We have done so by creating a packet of single-skill mastery measures (2 minutes each) addressing the isolated skills according to the grade-level scope and sequence chart, and then administering the packet to all at-risk students simultaneously. When computation has been the target concern we have not conducted lower grade-level CBMs, but instead immediately administered single-skill measures using the subskill mastery model.

For CBM application tools, it may be particularly important to administer probes below grade level since there is not a similar set of subskill mastery measures available for these skill types other than word problems (Fuchs, Fuchs, & Zumeta, 2008). A commonly used progress monitoring system, Monitoring Basic Skills Progress (Fuchs, Hamlett, & Fuchs, 1999), includes a CBM concepts and application (CBM-APP) measure. The CBM-APP includes a skills analysis profile that permits the evaluation of students' skill proficiency on a range of topics: number concepts; number naming; vocabulary; measurement; charts, graphs, and grid reading; word problems; area and perimeter; fractions; and decimals. Each of these areas can be determined for instructional match using a coding system containing five levels of proficiency ranging from cold (*not attempted*) to hot (*you've got it*).

It should be reiterated that if CAT is used for universal screening, a profile analysis of skill strengths and weaknesses can often be generated, possibly precluding the need to conduct a survey-level assessment. Early numeracy skills also represent a special case since these skills are often isolated into separate CBM tools—such as oral counting, number identification, magnitude comparison, and strategic counting—which are typically constructed for kindergarten and first-grade students (see Clarke et al., 2008).

Applying the Instructional Hierarchy

Once a survey-level assessment (i.e., skill analysis) has been conducted with students determined to be at risk, the type of skill deficit can be determined with the use of the instructional hierarchy. For computation skills (grades 1–5), there is evidence to support specific ranges of performance at the mastery, instructional, and frustration levels using CBA (Burns et al., 2006; Deno & Mirkin, 1977; Howell & Nolet, 1999). Table 3.2 illustrates performance ranges according to DCPM across three different recommendations. For ease of interpretation throughout the book, we applied the criterion from Howell and Nolet (1999). As an example, let's assume we are conducting a skills analysis for the second-grade student described above who received a score between the 10th and 25th percentiles on the computation screener. According to the Common Core (NGA & CCSSO, 2010), by the end of second grade students should automatically be able to add all single-digit numbers that have sums within 20 and should be able to subtract fluently within 20. In order to assess a student's strengths and weaknesses toward this goal, six different single-skill CBA probes are administered (see Table 3.3). The results indicate that this student has scores (i.e., DCPM) that fall within the mastery range for adding and subtracting within 5 and therefore the student could work independently practicing those skills perhaps within the context of multidigit problems without regrouping (generalization), word-problem solving (generalization), or other novel tasks (adaption). This student's scores suggested that adding

TABLE 3.2. Skill-by-Treatment Interaction: Combining CBA and the Instructional Hierarchy for Treatment Selection

| Performance level | CBA criterion | | | Stage of instructional hierarchy |
	Deno & Mirkin (1977)	Howell & Nolet (1999)	Burns, VanDerHeyden, & Jiban (2006)	
Frustration	Grades 1–3 <10 DCPM	<20 DCPM	Grades 2–3 <14 DCPM	Acquisition
	Grades 4+ <20 DCPM		Grades 4–5 <24 DCPM	
Instructional	Grades 1–3 10–19 DCPM	20–30 DCPM	Grades 2–3 14–31 DCPM	Fluency
	Grades 4+ 20–39 DCPM		Grades 4–5 24–49 DCPM	
Mastery	Grades 1–3 20+ DCPM	40+ DCPM	Grades 2–3 32+ DCPM	Maintenance; generalization; adaptation
	Grades 4+ 40+ DCPM		Grades 4–5 50+ DCPM	

TABLE 3.3. Sample Survey-Level Assessment Sequence

CBA probe administered	DCPM	Performance level	Stage of instructional hierarchy
Addition within 5	50	Mastery	Generalization/adaptation
Addition within 10	23	Instructional	Fluency
Addition within 20	10	Frustration	Acquisition
Subtraction within 5	40	Mastery	Generalization/adaptation
Subtraction within 10	20	Instructional	Fluency
Subtraction within 20	5	Frustration	Acquisition

and subtracting within 10 falls within the student's instructional range, indicating that the student would benefit from more opportunities to practice these skills (fluency) in various ways such as with goal setting, graphing, or peer practice. Finally, scores for adding and subtracting within 20 suggest that skill development is within the acquisition range, indicating that teacher demonstration and guided practice with concrete models or visual representation is needed.

As a second example, for a third-grade student who received a score below the 25th percentile on a universal screening measure assessing math concepts and applications, a second-grade CBM-APP measure might be administered. If the student performs in the 50th percentile within the second-grade CBM-APP measure, this skill would be considered within the instructional range, indicating that application of math concepts within the second-grade curriculum should be further analyzed. (If the student continued to perform below the 25th percentile on the second-grade CBM-APP measure, then the first-grade measure might be administered.) If using the skills analysis profile from the CBM-APP on the Monitoring Basic Skills Progress assessment system (Fuchs et al., 1999), then the level of proficiency within the second-grade content areas could be determined—that is, the student might receive a proficient rating of 5 (*Hot, you've got it*) for number concepts and names of numbers, as well as vocabulary, but receive a 4 (*Very warm, almost have it*) on geometry, and a 2 (*Cool, trying these*) on word problems. These data might suggest that for number concepts and names of numbers/vocabulary the student should practice applying these skills to generalization tasks. For geometry, the student requires more opportunities to practice to build fluency, whereas for word-problem solving (acquisition stage of skill development), the student would benefit from teacher modeling, demonstration, and guided practice.

The following vignette describes a case where a practitioner used CBA data to isolate addition facts that the student was unable to complete fluently. This case illustrates how assessment results were used to differentiate target items and show how student response patterns were used to inform intervention selection using the instructional hierarchy.

Case Example: Using the Instructional Hierarchy to Guide Intervention Selection

Avery was referred for deficiencies in math. To verify the referral, CBA procedures were used with a single-skill addition probe (single-digit addends, sums to 18). Avery scored 23 DCPM. Although Avery's performance fell within the fluency level, she was quick to skip the more difficult problems. To increase the specificity of assessment, the practitioner, Mrs. Howard, created two sets of subskill probes. One set of probes included problems made up of two single-digit addends with sums to 9, and the second set of probes included problems made up of two single-digit addends with sums ranging from 10 to 18. Mrs. Howard assessed Avery on both probe sets and found that while Avery scored 40 DCPM on problems with sums to 9, she only scored 6 DCPM on the probe containing sums from 10 to 18 (acquisition level). In this case, Avery showed she could accurately employ counting strategies with the larger problems, but it took her a lot of time. Given Avery's response pattern of 6 DCPM, it was decided that guided practice with two cover–copy–compare (CCC) worksheets would be completed each day with the 48 problems containing sums 10–18 (each worksheet contained 24 exclusive problems). The CCC intervention was successful because an accurate model was included in the instructional sequence (e.g., $8 + 7 = 15$) that emphasized errorless learning and automatic recall. After Avery finished the CCC worksheets, a probe containing addition problems with sums 10–18 was used to monitor progress. To strengthen results, goal setting, self-graphing, and reinforcement were also included in an effort to enhance Avery's learning rates.

Mrs. Howard implemented the intervention package for eight sessions across 2 weeks, with each intervention session lasting approximately 15 minutes. Daily progress monitoring across the eight sessions on probes with addition facts, sums 10–18, showed an increase of 34 DCPM (4.25-digit increase per session). To measure whether these problems generalized to probes consisting of problems with sums from 0 to 18 (a combination of one- and two-digit addends) a posttest was given to estimate growth. Prior to intervention, Avery scored 23 DCPM. After the eight intervention sessions, Avery scored 51 DCPM (an increase of 28 DCPM), providing evidence that she was performing at the mastery level for basic addition problems.

This case highlights two important facets of intervention selection: (1) understand the strengths and weaknesses of the assessment scope (i.e., item set size), and (2) match student response patterns with the correct intervention. Although multiskill probes are used for screening, they often do little to inform intervention. Even in the current case, if Mrs. Howard would have failed to closely observe Avery's performance, she may have prescribed a fluency-based strategy as the needed intervention. This would have made sense given Avery's score of 23 DCPM. Unfortunately, the fluency-based strategy would have prompted Avery to use inefficient counting strategies on problems with sums 10–18 and reduced rates of responding. As a result, Avery's learning rate would have been reduced. In addition, instructional time would have been poorly spent on problems with sums 0–9, as these items were already mastered. This case example highlights the importance of understanding the scope of the assessment and that student performance across items is not always consistent.

Student variation in responding across items becomes increasingly relevant as the scope of the assessment broadens (e.g., mixed-math probes). Since Mrs. Howard understood this facet of assessment, she appropriately segregated items and matched student responding to the correct intervention.

CONCLUSION

Measures selected for universal screening need to be reliable, valid, sensitive, predictive of high-stakes outcomes, and efficient so that the maximum amount of information is attained within the minimum amount of time. Universal screening can be used to identify classes of students and/or individual students who would benefit from further intervention. Once individual students are determined to be at risk for math difficulties, then a second stage of screening is used to identify the reason for math difficulties. The CD/WD assessment can determine whether students are experiencing skill deficits, performance deficits, or a combination of the two. A skill analysis, otherwise referred to as a survey-level assessment, can be conducted with students exhibiting skill deficits to determine which skills and concepts are in the acquisition, fluency, or generalization stages of skill development. Following this additional stage of assessment, students can be organized into homogeneous groups and an intervention that addresses common conceptual and/or procedural gaps can be implemented.

CHAPTER 4

Classwide Math Interventions

One of the benefits of instituting universal screening of all students' math performance within a school is that it can be determined whether low performance is the result of individual students or classes of students (e.g., Batsche et al., 2006; Burns et al., 2007). We have already discussed several ways to potentially improve core instruction provided to all students: (1) select empirically supported curriculum and textbooks; (2) use research-based instructional design principles; and (3) incorporate supplemental instructional strategies such as peer-assisted learning, CAI, or improve general classroom and instructional management procedures. Another approach is to provide brief interventions to classrooms that are low performing, as indicated by schoolwide screening (Ardoin et al., 2005; VanDerHeyden & Burns, 2005; VanDerHeyden et al., 2007, 2012). Evidence supports benefits to all students, including and especially those at risk for greater math difficulties, when classwide interventions are provided directly targeting word-problem solving or computation skills and concepts (Fuchs, Fuchs, Craddock, et al., 2008; Fuchs, Powell, et al., 2010; Fuchs, Powell, et al., 2014).

Low-performing classrooms can be identified using nationally or locally normed criteria. Classes of students for whom the average (i.e., median or mean) performance falls at or below the 25th percentile on a screening measure that is already being used by a school or district might benefit from an intervention targeting the whole class (Ardoin et al., 2005; Codding, Chan-Iannetta, et al., 2009; Hawkins et al., 2009; VanDerHeyden et al., 2012). Once classrooms are identified, the specific skills that the class, as a group, are missing needs to be identified. The emphasis at the classroom level is on the average performance of all students in the class, as opposed to individual student performance, when determining which areas should be the focus of classwide interventions. Students' skill needs can be identified through use of universal screening data (see Chapter 3). For example, many commercially available CBM applications (e.g., aimsweb, mCLASS, iSTEEP) provide separate tests of computation and concepts/application skills that can help school psychologists, RTI coordinators, math coaches, and/or problem-solving teams determine whether a classwide intervention should focus on one or both areas. CAT (e.g., FAST earlyMath, STAR) can also be used to pinpoint target areas for classwide focus.

Once the general content area is identified (computation, application, or both), then further assessment can be conducted to identify which skill to target first. For example, after interviewing the teacher on skill gaps that are observed from the class and reviewing the scope and sequence chart (or the Common Core standards; NGA & CCSSO, 2010) for grade-level expectations, single-skill CBAs (e.g., basic addition facts; 2 × 2 digit subtraction with and/or without regrouping) can be administered to determine what grade level and/or prerequisite skills students have mastered to criterion and those that have not been mastered according to mean or median classroom performance levels. There are few standardized options for providing additional isolated assessment of math application skills. However, an error analysis could be conducted with a universal screening tool documenting the types of questions that are missed by most students in the classroom.

ENHANCING COMPUTATION FLUENCY AND WORD-PROBLEM-SOLVING SKILLS CLASSWIDE

If school resources prohibit the possibility of collecting additional assessment data to identify specific missing foundational skills, universal screening data can be examined to determine whether weaknesses are in computation, applied problem solving, or both areas. Subsequently, implementing a classwide intervention to facilitate automaticity with basic facts or word-problem solving is an appropriate course of action. Research has illustrated that word-problem solving and calculation represent distinct but related aspects of math knowledge, both of which need to be directly and explicitly instructed (Fuchs, Powell, et al., 2014). Compared with their international peers, U.S. students exhibit less fluency with all four number operations (NMAP, 2008). One study with a relatively large sample of students estimated that only about 50% of third graders and 36% of second graders mastered basic addition facts, and only 26% of third graders mastered basic subtraction facts (Stickney, Sharp, & Keynon, 2012). If this sample is representative of the experience of most second and third graders, these data could suggest that U.S. students are struggling to meet the goals of the NMAP (2008), the Common Core (NGA & CCSSO, 2010), and the NCTM (2006), which all recommend that every student is fluent in basic addition and subtraction facts by the end of third grade. Unfortunately, students who do not master basic computation skills experience difficulty solving more advanced math problems compared with same-age peers (Powell et al., 2013; VanDerHeyden & Burns, 2009), exhibit lower math achievement scores (DeSmedt et al., 2011; Price et al., 2013; Stickney et al., 2012), and are less likely to generalize basic skills to more complex math tasks (Codding, Chan-Iannetta, et al., 2009; Fuchs, Powell, et al., 2010). Several studies have illustrated that providing classroom interventions targeting computation fluency improves the performance of most students and can also raise year-end accountability scores (Ardoin et al., 2005; VanDerHeyden et al., 2007, 2012).

Similarly, traditional math instruction has provided limited opportunities for directly teaching word-problem solving, and when instruction is provided it tends to be limited in scope (Woodward et al., 2012). For example, word-problem-solving instruction has overemphasized surface features such as keywords or phrases instead of teaching the underlying structures of word problems. A survey of Algebra I teachers indicated that word-problem solving represented a substantial area of weakness for students and requested greater preparation be provided at the primary levels (NMAP, 2008). In particular, students experience difficulties translating word problems into numerical expressions. Research illustrates that all students, including those at risk for math difficulties, display better outcomes when word-problem solving is first targeted at the class level (Fuchs, Fuchs, Craddock, et al., 2008; Fuchs, Seethaler, et al., 2008).

Reasons for this lack of proficiency with basic computation facts and word-problem solving could be attributed to problems with core math instruction and textbook activities (Daly et al., 2007; Doabler, Fien, Nelson-Walker, & Baker, 2012; NMAP, 2008). An evaluation of math textbooks in grades 2 and 4 demonstrated a lack of opportunities to (1) review prerequisite skills and concepts before new skills/concepts were introduced, (2) practice skills/concepts in order to achieve mastery, (3) engage in discrimination training whereby students learn the differences between new and previously learned problems (such as when to rename or switch operations), and (4) receive frequent and meaningful feedback on errors or fluent performance (Doabler, Fien, et al., 2012; Woodward et al., 2012). Unfortunately, traditional instructional practices similarly do not appear to provide enough opportunities for individual or group practice or responding during core math instruction; both of which are needed to facilitate positive student-teacher interactions and ensure that teachers are consistently evaluating student learning needs (Bryant, Bryant, Kethley, et al., 2008; Doabler, Cary, et al., 2012, 2014; Johnson & Layng, 1992; NRC, 2001). Notably, one of the best predictors of math competence in adulthood is the quantity and quality of school-based opportunities to practice math skills and concepts (Bahrick, Hall, & Baker, 2013).

Teachers may be able to improve core foundational math skills simply by increasing (1) the number of opportunities to practice math skills (e.g., math facts, multidigit number combinations, and word-problem solving) provided in the classroom, and (2) the amount and type of feedback provided to students depending on students' level of skill development. The instructional hierarchy is useful for constructing practice and feedback activities. Table 4.1 illustrates how practice type, content, activity, and performance feedback can vary across the acquisition, fluency, and generalization phases of skill proficiency.

Opportunities for practice along with feedback that is provided by teachers and/or directed by students themselves (i.e., such as scoring, recording, and comparing their own scores to mastery criterion) should be offered daily during core instruction (Daly et al., 2007; Doabler, Fien, et al., 2012; NMAP, 2008). Taking advantage of downtime by programming in opportunities to practice computation facts in brief spurts even twice daily can improve performance over time and may be better than arranging one longer practice session (Schutte et al., 2015). Progress monitoring should also be employed for classes that are lower performing to determine whether students are benefiting from focused interventions

TABLE 4.1. Generating Opportunities for Practice across the Instructional Hierarchy

	Acquisition: ESTABLISHING	Fluency: REMEMBERING	Generalization: ENDURING
Type of practice	Teacher guided; fully or partially worked examples.	Student-directed nonworked examples.	Student-directed nonworked examples.
Practice content	Narrow content and discrete tasks that are sequentially presented according to mastery criteria (e.g., begin with small sets of number combinations or one-word problem type).	Narrow content and discrete tasks that are sequentially presented according to mastery criteria (e.g., begin with small sets of number combinations or one-word problem type).	Combination of established with new skills/content (discrimination practice) and broad tasks.
Feedback provided during and after practice	Elaborate, immediate, teacher-directed feedback on prerequisite and conceptually relevant principles to improve accuracy.	Student/teacher-directed feedback emphasizing fast and accurate performance.	Student/teacher-directed feedback on selecting correct strategies to solve various types of problems.
Practice activities	• Teachers work several full examples applying the concrete–representation–abstract sequence while class follows along. • Teacher works a partially complete example while class follows along. • Students practice partially worked examples in pairs and teacher provides immediate error correction. • Response cards or whiteboards used during group instruction for teachers to assess understanding of each student and immediately address learning gaps. • Teacher asks for class to answer simultaneously using choral responding so that all students have the opportunity to answer.	• 10 minutes of daily independent or peer practice on word problems or math facts that were previously instructed. • Peer correcting and scoring. • Students score, record, and track their own performance on graphs until mastery is achieved. • Teachers acknowledge and reward improved performance (accurate and fast).	• Classwide games requiring students to apply previously instructed or practiced skills. • Application of recently acquired and fluent skills to solve real-world problems. • Team-based problem-solving activities requiring the use of prerequisite, current, and previously learned knowledge. • Self-monitoring and peer correcting.

and to make adjustments in instructional strategies as needed. In particular, if subskills or concepts are being instructed sequentially, then teachers will need to monitor average class performance to determine when to move to the next subskill or concept (Hattie, 2009). The goal is to ensure that most students in the class are demonstrating conceptual understanding while solving math problems fluently and flexibly across contexts. Moving too quickly through the identified instructional sequences can result in errors that prohibit solving more complex problems (Mayfield & Chase, 2002).

We consulted with one math coach who taught the teachers in her district to differentiate practice activities across students and skill proficiency. The curriculum that the school used already included daily guided practice on new instructional targets. The math coach organized a meeting with teachers to construct and/or identify already existing independent practice activities, generalization activities (e.g., games or application tasks), and small-group teacher-directed instructional activities for each major content area covered throughout the year. These activities were generated so that each type of task (i.e., independent fluency tasks, group generalization tasks, small-group activities) was created for low-, medium-, and high-performing students. This way, every day during core instruction all students would have opportunities for guided practice with current content, fluency practice at each student's instructional level, generalization activities organized by skill proficiency levels, and teacher-directed small-group instruction that provided either repetition of prerequisite skills, current content, or enrichment.

In summary, these data suggest that while time is allocated for providing students with instruction on skills and concepts associated with basic number operations, there are few opportunities within core instruction or textbook activities for students to build fluency and generalization. For word-problem solving the situation is more concerning because evidence suggests little instruction is provided on acquisition, fluency building, or generalization in this content area. Therefore, classwide interventions targeting computation and word-problem solving are appropriate targets for whole classes of students who are displaying math weaknesses in these areas.

CLASSWIDE INTERVENTIONS

Below we describe five classwide math interventions found in the peer-reviewed literature that can be used to address specific areas of math difficulties experienced by all students in the classroom (see Table 4.2 for more details). Classroom Hot Math (Fuchs, Seethaler, et al., 2008) is the only intervention described below that targets word-problem solving and is commercially available. The remaining interventions have been shown to increase computation skills when applied classwide and include CCC, detect–practice–repair (DPR), taped problems, and explicit timing. Time allotted to these instructional activities are usually short in duration (approximately 5–10 minutes) and materials needed to implement these interventions can be created using materials already existing in classrooms or by visiting websites for free resources. These interventions target key foundational skills and are used to supplement the core curriculum. Proficiency (i.e., meeting mastery criteria for fluent

TABLE 4.2. Classwide Interventions That Improve Computation and Word-Problem-Solving Performance

	Classroom Hot Math	Detect–Practice–Repair	Taped Problems	Cover–Copy–Compare
Treatment components	• Explicit instruction • Strategy instruction • Sequenced instruction • Progress monitoring and feedback • Drill, practice, review • Visual representations	• Sequenced instruction • Progress monitoring and feedback • Drill, practice, review	• Progress monitoring and feedback • Drill, practice, review • Reinforcement	• Explicit instruction • Progress monitoring and feedback • Drill, practice, review • Reinforcement
Level of skill proficiency	• Acquisition • Fluency • Generalization	• Fluency	• Fluency	• Acquisition • Fluency
References	• 5–10 studies	• 5–10 studies	• 5–10 studies	• 5–10 studies
	• Conducted by program authors	• Conducted by program authors	• Conducted by program authors	• Conducted by program authors and other research groups
Grades	3	1–5; middle school grades	1–3	1–4
Target skills	• Basic arithmetic operations • Multidigit arithmetic operations	• Basic arithmetic operations • Multidigit arithmetic operations	• Basic arithmetic operations	• Basic arithmetic operations • Multidigit arithmetic operations
Interventionist	• General ed teacher	• General ed teacher • Student (monitored by adult)	• General ed teacher	• Student (monitored by adult)
Effect size	• Large	• Large	• Small • Large	• Small • Large

responding) in these skills is essential for students to maximize the benefits of instruction targeting conceptual understanding associated with problem solving, critical thinking, and math reasoning skills.

One of the challenges for educators is to locate and access materials to support the delivery of empirically validated interventions. To assist in this effort a variety of teacher-friendly resources to support the implementation of several of the interventions described in this chapter have been developed. These can be accessed at no cost from the OTISS website (*www.otiss.net/assessment-intervention/intervention*) or *www.factsonfire.com*. Specifically, materials are available for CCC, DPR, taped problems, and explicit timing, and include an intervention overview, administration guidelines, student training protocol, treatment integrity protocol, and intervention worksheets across each of the computation skills (*www.otiss.net/assessment-intervention/intervention*). Examples of these resources are included throughout the book.

Cover–Copy–Compare

CCC (Skinner, McLaughlin, & Logan, 1997) has been examined as a classwide intervention to address computation deficits in seven studies (Ardoin et al., 2005; Codding, Chan-Iannetta, et al., 2009; Codding et al., 2007; Grafman & Cates, 2010; Poncy, McCallum, & Schmitt, 2010; Poncy & Skinner, 2011; Poncy, Skinner, & McCallum, 2012). Evidence for using CCC as a classwide intervention has resulted in improved performance with effect sizes ranging from small to large. With CCC, student gains in computation skills were maintained anywhere from 1 day to 2 months after the intervention ended (Codding, Chan-Iannetta, et al., 2009; Poncy et al., 2010; Poncy & Skinner, 2011). In one study, improvement in basic subtraction skills even generalized to performance with 2×1-digit subtraction with regrouping when compared with students who did not receive the intervention (Codding, Chan-Iannetta, et al., 2009). Student acceptability for CCC was assessed ranges from modestly to highly acceptable (Grafman & Cates, 2010; Codding, Chan-Iannetta, et al., 2009; Codding et al., 2007). Teacher acceptability for CCC showed a preference for a modified variation of CCC, which requires students to copy the problem with the answer, as opposed to traditional CCC for which the problem and answer are provided to the student (Grafman & Cates, 2010).

Intervention Description

When reported by empirical studies, implementation of CCC procedures consumes approximately 3–10 minutes of class time and the number of sessions has varied from twice weekly to daily across a total of 2–6 weeks. CCC is a self-instruction procedure that consists of the following five steps (Skinner, McLaughlin, et al., 1997): (1) look at the math problem and answer provided on the left side of the worksheet, (2) cover the problem and answer with an index card or by folding the page in half, (3) write the problem and answer (or just the answer) on the right side of the page, and (4) uncover the problem with the answer, and (5) compare the written response with the model.

CCC worksheets can be constructed by teachers or generated online by using the Math Worksheet Generator available from Intervention Central (*www.interventioncentral. org/teacher-resources/math-work-sheet-generator*), the OTISS website (*www.otiss.net/ assessment-intervention/intervention/math-accuracy*), and *www.factsonfire.com*. For effective use of CCC, identifying specific skill weaknesses via grade-level computation scope and sequence charts and administering CBA, CAT, or other unit tests that can isolate specific skills can be helpful. Using average class performance to determine the lowest prerequisite skill in the scope and sequence chart that students need additional support with is one way to select the skill the intervention will target (Codding, Chan-Iannetta, et al., 2009; Codding et al., 2007).

Four variations of CCC have been applied that either change the method or type of practice provided or add motivation and self-regulation components. First, rather than provide the problem with the answer on individual worksheets, teachers can provide problems with answers simultaneously to the whole class using Microsoft PowerPoint and a projector or with a standard whiteboard or Smart Board and ask that students copy the problem with the answer on their own papers as the first step (Grafman & Cates, 2010). Subsequent steps would be followed according to the standard version of CCC. Second, rather than selecting single facts for practice; teachers could use worksheets that contain fact-family triangle models that prompt the student to write facts that can be derived from the fact family (Poncy, McCallum, et al., 2010). A student training protocol, sample worksheet, and treatment integrity checklist for the fact-family adaptation of CCC can be found in Form 4.1. Third, using group contingencies (see Chapter 2 for an example) has led to positive impacts on classwide computation skills to motivate students to actively participate in the intervention (Ardoin et al., 2005; Poncy & Skinner, 2011). Students can be rewarded for number of problems completed, effort, engagement in the task, or improved scores. Finally, providing written performance feedback (i.e., number of problems completed correctly) and graphs individualized for each student has produced greater and faster student computation gains than CCC alone (Codding, Chan-Iannetta, et al., 2009).

Pros and Cons of Classwide CCC

An important feature of CCC is the inclusion of a model that prompts the student to accurately respond when answering problems. If the student incorrectly answers the problem, immediate corrective feedback is provided as the student checks the problem and answer against the model. Another useful aspect of CCC is content differentiation. Since the model is the impetus for student responding, the teacher can provide a worksheet that is matched to the needs of each student (e.g., student A works on addition while student B works on multiplication). Students in the classroom will be using the same procedures but will be working on different skills. CCC practice can also be differentiated by providing some students with extra practice opportunities on a smaller set of problems while other students practice a larger set of problems with fewer repetitions of each problem. For example, students working on larger sets of math facts may only practice writing and answering each problem once, whereas students working on a smaller set of problems might repeat the CCC procedure for each problem four times. Drawbacks to CCC center on decreased student response rates that result from the procedures of looking at, covering, writing the problem and/or answer, and checking response accuracy. This decrease in problems completed per minute may necessitate that smaller item sets (e.g., 12–24 problems) be used so that students can practice items multiple times in an intervention session. Although CCC is empirically validated, it is important that educators understand when and when not to use CCC to ensure maximum effect. For example, Codding et al. (2007) compared CCC and explicit timing and found that CCC was the more effective intervention for students who lack computation fluency, while explicit timing was more effective for students who were more fluent. Although additional research is needed to elucidate the specific scores that differentiate intervention effectiveness, these data suggest that it may be important for educators to incorporate initial fluency rates to properly match student intervention selection to patterns in student responding.

Intervention Training

Intervention training is simple and takes as little as 10 minutes of classroom time (Grafman & Cates, 2010). Training is provided by the teachers and is directed to the students, given that CCC is a self-instruction procedure. The teacher explains and demonstrates each of the five CCC steps and guides students through practice examples. Additional teacher training could be provided to assist teachers with administering and scoring a CBA or using CAT to identify which skills to target for intervention first within the instructional scope and sequence chart.

Teacher Responsibilities

Teacher responsibilities for this intervention include (1) determining the target skill for CCC; (2) making CCC worksheets and goal charts (if using); (3) training students on CCC procedures; (4) circulating around the room to oversee accurate implementation of CCC by students; and (5) providing rewards, if using a group contingency.

Detect–Practice–Repair

The DPR intervention has been examined in six studies to date (Axtell, McCallum, Bell, & Poncy, 2009; Parkhurst et al., 2010; Poncy, Skinner, & Axtell, 2010; Poncy, Fontenelle, & Skinner, 2013; Poncy & Skinner, 2011). Across the studies, average student improvement on CBMs from pre- to postintervention increased from five to 25 DCPM, and one study yielded a large effect size (Axtell et al., 2009). DPR may work better for students who demonstrate higher fluency levels in the target skill rather than students who are dysfluent, as DPR procedures isolate facts that are problematic for students (Poncy et al., 2013). If a student struggles across a majority of the problems, DPR likely loses some of the effect, but if the student needs repeated practice to shore up a handful of problems, DPR is very effective.

Intervention Description

DPR was implemented anywhere from 1 to about 4 total weeks on a daily basis for typically 10–12 minutes each day. This intervention consists of three phases: (1) detect, (2) practice, and (3) repair. The purpose of the detect phase is to identify math computation problems that students know automatically. The practice phase permits students to practice unknown math problems using CCC (Skinner, McLaughlin, et al., 1997), described above. Finally, the repair phase includes a math sprint designed to assess students' computation fluency and learning that has occurred during the practice phase. In addition, students use a progress chart to graph and monitor their own performance over time.

During the detect phase, folders are distributed by classroom teachers that contain all of the intervention materials. Students are instructed to select the tap-a-problem sheet containing 48 problems. The teacher then starts a metronome (set to 40 beats per minute; this translates into 1.5 seconds per problem), which is placed at the front of the room. Students are instructed to write the answer to the problem before the click of the metronome. An alternative to using the metronome is to create a slide show using Microsoft PowerPoint that is then projected to the class. The slide show should be paced so that one problem is presented automatically every 3 seconds (Parkhurst et al., 2010). After about 1 minute, students examine their "detect" sheets to locate the first five problems they were unable to complete on time by referencing an answer board placed in the front of the classroom or viewing the Microsoft PowerPoint slide that displays the problems and the correct answers in the order they were presented.

During the practice phase, students write the first given problems that were not completed within the detect phase on a CCC matrix under the corresponding problem and answer boxes. If students were unsure of the answers, they could reference an answer board (this board was made visible after the detect phase to prevent students from practicing errors). After the problems and answers are written, students read each printed problem and answer to themselves, cover each problem and answer, write each problem with the answer, and then check the accuracy of their own response by comparing it with the written model. When errors are made, students put a line through the incorrect response and copy the correct problem and answer. Students continue working until all five target problems are correctly written and answered five times each. This phase takes approximately 5 minutes to complete.

During the third and final phase, repair, the teacher removes the answer board and students take out the sprint worksheet from their own folders and complete as many problems as possible in 1 minute. After 1 minute, students stop working, score their papers, count the number of problems completed correctly, and record this number on a graph stapled inside their folder. Form 4.2 provides the treatment protocol for DPR along with a sample CCC worksheet and DCPM graph template.

Pros and Cons of DPR

This intervention was developed in an effort to differentiate target problems for each student in a classwide setting (Poncy, Skinner, & O'Mara, 2006). Similar to CCC, content can be differentiated with students working on different skill areas across the classroom (e.g., some students work on addition, others subtraction). However, DPR takes differentiation a step further with the paced pretest designed to identify problems specific to each student's skill set instead of having all students in the target area practice the same problems. DPR is unique in that it has been used to individualize math practice across a classwide setting; however, when compared with other computation interventions such as CCC, taped problems, and explicit timing it may be relatively difficult to implement and manage. Specifically, students may have trouble adhering to the cues that pace the pretest and invalidate the identification of the dysfluent problems. Teachers may be resistant to making daily packets and find it cumbersome to navigate through the four steps each day. Lastly, research has been conducted to validate the effectiveness of DPR but comparative intervention studies controlling for cumulative instructional time and session length need to be done to gauge the relative effectiveness of DPR to simpler computation approaches such as CCC, taped problems, and explicit timing.

Intervention Training

Teacher training on DPR was not widely reported across studies, so the procedures described represent one strategy employed within one study (Axtell et al., 2009). Three training sessions were conducted by graduate students in the research lab of the DPR developer. These training sessions consisted of one session describing general procedures for scoring CBMs and two sessions teaching the DPR procedures. A written protocol was provided to teachers. On-site support was provided daily by researchers who oversaw CBM administration and intervention implementation. Student training on the DPR procedures was conducted during one session by the researcher and consisted of implementing the complete intervention using simple skills (i.e., single-digit addition facts) that students had already mastered.

Teacher Responsibilities

Teachers are responsible for filling, distributing, and collecting intervention folders. Teachers manage the intervention procedures by directing students through each of the three DPR phases, managing all timed elements, and circulating around the room to ensure correct student implementation as well as answer any student questions.

Taped Problems

The taped problems intervention has been evaluated as a classwide intervention that addresses computation skills in six studies (Aspiranti, Skinner, McCleary, & Cihak, 2011; McCallum, Skinner, Turner, & Saecker, 2006; McCleary et al., 2011; Miller, Skinner, Gibby,

Galyon, & Meadows-Allen, 2011; Poncy et al., 2012; Windingstad, Skinner, Rowland, Cardin, & Fearrington, 2009). Effect sizes ranged from small to large with improvements in CBMs found for all students in the classroom (Kleinert, Codding, Sheppard, Silva, & Gould, 2015). However, students who displayed lower performance in computation skills at the start of the classwide intervention made fewer gains (e.g., Aspiranti et al., 2011; McCallum et al., 2006) and group contingencies were necessary to improve student engagement partway through another study when more challenging material was targeted (McCleary et al., 2011). Average classroom performance increases were maintained in all studies that assessed for retention and in one study performance generalized to problems representing the inverse of the targeted facts (e.g., Miller et al., 2011).

Intervention Description

Taped problems was implemented typically 3–8 total weeks with three to five sessions weekly. Each session lasted 8–15 minutes. The taped problems intervention requires that the teacher records the sessions, using an audiocassette recorder or computer technology, arithmetic problems, and their answers. Teachers vary the intervals between stating the problem and the answer so that the problems and answers are read with no delay, 1-second delays, and 2-second delays. Students listen to math fact problems and answers presented from the recording. Students are given a printed copy of the problems without the answers and are instructed to try to "beat the tape" by writing the correct answer to each problem before the answer is provided on the tape recording. Teachers circulate around the room ensuring that students do not work ahead of the tape and prompt students to correct errors. The worksheet includes three columns, one for each time interval. Individual and group contingencies can be provided (e.g., Aspiranti et al., 2011). For example, each student can be provided with performance feedback using graphs that display their performance from the previous intervention session and then be provided with educationally relevant rewards (e.g., stickers, computer time, line leader, erasers) when they improve their scores. Group contingencies can be provided to encourage participation from the whole class.

Pros and Cons of Taped Problems

The primary strength of the taped problems intervention is the incorporation of immediate corrective feedback and rapid pacing, a combination that results in high rates of active, accurate responding. Also, whereas CCC provides students with a model including the answer, taped problems prompts students to generate the answer themselves, which may shape students toward independent and automatic responding. This intervention is also low effort, as the teacher has to simply distribute the worksheets and begin the audio recording. A notable limitation of the taped problems intervention is the inability for content differentiation. Since the class is listening to the same audio recording all students must work on the same operation and problems. Another potential downfall is that students could just write in answers when they are read by the tape and not actively try to beat the tape.

Intervention Training

Training requirements for this intervention were not explicitly reported by these studies. The primary preparation for the intervention involves the creation of the taped voice recording of the problems and answers, as well as the creation of worksheets that match the voice recordings. Explanation of the intervention to students in the classroom is relatively simple. Teacher training may be necessary on how to implement a group contingency program if teachers are interested in adding this treatment element.

Teacher Responsibilities

Teachers are responsible for selecting the number combinations that will be addressed with the intervention, as well as creating the voice recordings and corresponding worksheets. Teachers manage the intervention procedures by providing the intervention instructions to the students prior to beginning the intervention and circulating around the room to ensure correct student implementation, as well as answer any student questions.

Explicit Timing

Explicit timing is an antecedent timing procedure used in conjunction with practice activities (e.g., computation worksheets, oral counting, number writing) and should be used only when students have evidenced accurate responding across the target problem set. Van Houten and Thompson (1976) showed that overtly timing students increases both rates of responding and learning outcomes. Subsequently, explicit timing has been shown to be an effective intervention component for increasing DCPM scores across numerous skills, populations, and settings (see Duhon, House, Hastings, Poncy, & Solomon, 2015; Duhon, House, & Stinnett, 2012; Poncy, Duhon, Lee, & Key, 2010; Rhymer & Morgan, 2005; Rhymer, Skinner, Henington, D'Reaux, & Sims, 1998; Rhymer et al., 2002; Schutte et al., 2015). In addition, the effectiveness of explicit timing has been supported by multiple meta-analyses (Burns et al., 2010; Codding, Burns, et al., 2011; Codding, Hilt-Panahon, Panahon, & Benson, 2009; Methe, Kilgus, Neiman, & Riley-Tillman, 2012; Poncy, Solomon, Duhon, Skinner, Moore, et al., 2015).

Intervention Description

The explicit timing intervention is very simple, as it requires two things. First, students need to be able to accurately and independently complete the assigned practice activities (e.g., a math fact worksheet). This provides students with a relatively easy task where they can focus on working as quickly as possible without making errors. Second, the teacher informs students that they will be given a finite amount of time to complete as many problems as possible. Across the literature, researchers have used differing amounts of total time and have separated these times into various blocks (e.g., 1 minute, 2 minutes, 4 minutes). Regardless, the literature agrees that overtly employing explicit timing procedures is effective in increasing rates of responding and learning outcomes (Schutte et al., 2015). Last, other components are often incorporated along with explicit timing to increase the effectiveness of practice activities including goal setting, performance feedback, self-graphing, and reward (Skinner, 1998).

Pros and Cons of Explicit Timing

The biggest advantage of explicit timing is the ease with which it can be incorporated into practice activities. It is low effort and inexpensive, and when students are matched with appropriate materials it allows them to successfully build fluent responding and provides a context for the teacher to link effort and practice with learning. Similar to CCC and DPR, content can be differentiated when explicit timing is used, ensuring that all students in the class practice items that are appropriate to their skill levels. The most difficult component of successfully implementing the explicit timing procedure is matching the student to the correct skill and moving the student to the next skill at the correct time. In order to do these things, teachers need to identify an appropriate skill sequence, access appropriate practice worksheets, be proficient with CBM procedures, assess and identify the starting skill for the student(s), and be knowledgeable of scores that demonstrate mastery. The combination of these skills will aid the teacher in appropriately placing the student with the correct practice materials and will alert the teacher when to move the student to the next skill.

Intervention Training

Training the teacher how to implement explicit timing is very simple. Teachers are given a script to read or are instructed to inform students that they will be given a set amount of time to complete as many problems as possible. Students are taught to follow teacher directions for when to start and stop completing the task and told to draw a line to show where they were at the conclusion of the timed practice session. Teachers will also need to know the total time the students will practice and how the time will be divided (e.g., 10 total minutes split into five 2-minute sessions).

Training Responsibilities

To successfully employ explicit timing classwide, the teacher must organize and distribute worksheets. We have found it useful for the teacher to make weekly packets, place them in folders, and have students keep these in their desks. The teacher must also score probes to inform decision making about whether to move back a skill (student is inaccurate), continue with the current skill (student is accurate), or to move to the next skill (student has eclipsed mastery criteria). We recommend that the teacher collect the folders once a week and extract a DCPM score from 2 days of the practice materials. If the teacher thinks that the sample data are invalid, they will need to pull the student and assess using CBM procedures. Similar to all the interventions reviewed it is imperative that the teacher circulates around the room to provide behavior-specific praise to students in regard to procedural integrity and effort.

Classroom Hot Math

Classroom Hot Math (Fuchs, Seethaler, et al., 2008) is a companion to a small/individual group tutoring program called Hot Math Tutoring, both of which use schema-broadening instruction. Schema-broadening instruction consists of four components that explicitly teach students to (1) understand the underlying mathematical structure of the problem type, (2) recognize the basic problem-type category, (3) solve the problem type, and (4) transfer problem-solving skills. Classroom Hot Math is designed for whole-class supplemental instruction that is provided to third-grade students (Fuchs, Seethaler, et al., 2008). There are five empirical studies examining Classroom Hot Math (Fuchs et al., 2003a, 2003b; Fuchs, Fuchs, Finelli, Courey, & Hamlett, 2004; Fuchs, Fuchs, Prentice, et al., 2004; Fuchs, Seethaler, et al., 2008); these studies demonstrated the benefits of delivering these problem-solving lessons classwide for high-, average-, and low-performing students (Fuchs, Fuchs, & Hollenbeck, 2007). Across problem-solving outcomes a large effect size was found supporting Classroom Hot Math over conventional instruction (Fuchs, Seethaler, et al., 2008); the program is available for purchase through the following website: *http://kc.vanderbilt.edu/pals/pdfs/hot_math.pdf.*

Intervention Description

Classroom Hot Math is designed to be implemented for 12 weeks with lessons occurring twice weekly. The program consists of four 3-week units (plus an introductory unit) and each unit contains six sessions (Fuchs, Fuchs, & Hollenbeck, 2007). The first four sessions within each unit emphasize skill acquisition with cumulative review. During the remaining two lessons, given in the third week of each unit, specific emphasis is on the transfer of problem-solving skills so that students can identify which problem type applies to new problems and find the solution. Within each of the four units, two lessons are designed to last 40 minutes and each remaining lesson is 30-minutes long. An introductory unit teaches students basic problem-solving information such as checking answers to be sure they make sense, lining up numbers from the text to perform math operations correctly, and label their work with words and numerical symbols. The remaining four units focus on one problem type each including "buying bags" problems (solve problems for buying items in groups), "shopping list" problems (solve multistep problems with multiple prices), "half" problems (strategies for finding half of a group), and "pictograph" problems (using pictographs to solve problems). The same structure is applied to each session across problem types (see Figure 4.1). Self-regulated learning strategies are incorporated by asking students to score their independent work using an answer key, graph scores on a thermometer chart, and compare scores to see whether they improved on their highest score.

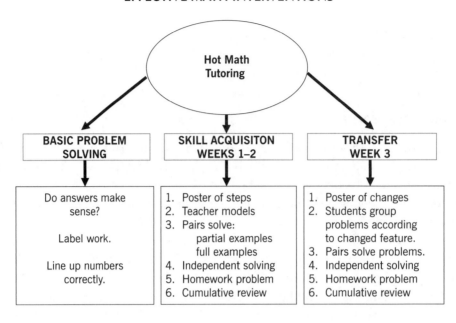

FIGURE 4.1. Hot math tutoring structure. For more details, see Fuchs, Fuchs, and Hollenbeck (2007).

Intervention Training

According to the National Center on Intensive Intervention (*www.intensiveintervention. org*), the tutoring variation of Hot Math requires that training be provided by developers. Once scheduled, training consumes 1 full day. A teacher/tutor manual is also provided that contains scripted lessons and masters of all required materials. The National Center on Intensive Intervention website suggests that school professionals within the local school or district provide follow-up support to teachers to assist with implementation.

Teacher Responsibilities

All sessions are scripted. Teachers are responsible for providing explicit instruction on basic problem-solving skills, problem-solving types using schemas, the concept of transfer, and problem features that change using the provided poster displays. Teachers then demonstrate how to use the steps to solve several problems, circulate around the room during peer-pair practice to ensure that students are engaged, correct student errors as needed, and distribute and correct homework.

DIFFERENTIATING INSTRUCTION AT THE CLASSWIDE LEVEL

We have already described how many students struggle with computation skills and as a result students' ability to solve more complex math problems is affected. This makes sense as nearly all application and/or word problems contain numbers and operations in some form. Therefore, computational proficiency is essential, as it provides a foundation for students to benefit from instruction targeting skills such as problem solving and math reasoning. One way to prevent and remedy deficits in computation skills is the use of classwide interventions; however, to maximize outcomes practitioners must differentiate instruction across students. This vignette describes a case where DPR was used with a class of students to remediate deficits in basic fact fluency.

> Mrs. Melrose requested consultative assistance with her fourth-grade class of 22 students to increase basic fact fluency. Specifically, she reported that help was needed for her to address a wide array of skill needs in the class. To address this issue we first tested all students in her class across basic computation skills. We used CBM procedures across single-skill addition, subtraction, multiplication, and division probes and compared student performance with a performance criterion of 20 DCPM. The target skill was identified as the skill for which students first obtained a score below 20 DCPM. Assessment data determined that three students needed practice in addition, five in subtraction, eight in multiplication, and four in division (the other two students met the criteria across operations and practiced multidigit multiplication worksheets during this time).
>
> Once each student was appropriately placed with a target skill, Mrs. Melrose was given a choice of classwide interventions and decided to use DPR. She chose the DPR intervention because it incorporated a test–teach–test format to individualize each student's target items in a group setting across skills. Each day students were provided with a packet comprising materials using the identified target skill. A paced pretest was administered that incorporated an audio cue prompting students to attempt a problem every 2 seconds on a single-skill probe in his or her target area. Once the pretest was finished, students identified the first five problems that they failed to complete (or completed incorrectly) and wrote the correct problem and answer on a CCC worksheet. Then the class was given 5 minutes to practice those five problems. The session finished with a 1-minute explicit timing practice after which students totaled the number of digits they computed correctly and graphed their performance. The entire DPR intervention took approximately 15 minutes a day and was run for 3 weeks. The mean DCPM increase for the class was around 10 (an approximate increase of 0.7 digits correct per session and 3.3 digits correct per week).

This case highlights two important facets of implementing classwide interventions: (1) use assessment and performance criteria to instructionally group students, and (2) choose intervention procedures that are standardized across skills. Traditional math instruction often consists of all students in the general education setting working on the same task regardless of prior skill knowledge. For younger students who display more homogeneous skill weaknesses, this is less of a concern. For example, in a second-grade classroom, you would likely be able to use a taped problems intervention targeting addition facts, single-digit addends sums to 18. However, the more heterogeneous the skill set of the class, the more important differentiation of both what is taught (i.e., curriculum) and how it is taught (i.e., instruction) becomes. In the current example, DPR was chosen and worked well. This was due, in part, to the successful differentiation of the curriculum based on the preassessment data—that is, the preassessment data were used to properly assign a target skill to each student and then the paced pretest was used to differentiate specific items for each student to practice. The success of the DPR intervention is also due, in part, to the standardized multicomponent composition of the procedures. The DPR intervention combines acquisition (CCC; errorless learning with model), fluency (explicit timing; timed drill and practice), and motivation (self-graphing; performance feedback) strategies across skills. This uniform structure allowed students working on different skills to practice target items appropriate to their skill development while in a classroom setting.

In this case example, DPR produced improved student outcomes but some may find that implementing this intervention is costly in terms of instructional time (15 minutes/day), preparation time (daily construction of a four-sheet packet for 20 students), and teacher effort (e.g., the multistep procedures may be more difficult to implement accurately and consistently). Fortunately, there are other intervention options! Just as with DPR, you would still assess to identify each student's appropriate target skill. However, you could choose to use intervention procedures such as CCC and explicit timing in isolation. This would provide a less costly alternative as skill-specific instructional packets for each student could be made weekly, implementation would be more straightforward, and instructional time could be negotiated (e.g., the teacher uses explicit timing for 1-minute timings). The caveat is that you would want to determine students' skill weaknesses and match them to the appropriate intervention; either the acquisition-based intervention (CCC) or the fluency-based intervention (explicit timing), depending on CBM scores.

CONCLUSION

Students in the United States continue to perform poorly in math on various national and international assessments. Given these deficits in math achievement it is imperative that efficient and effective Tier 1 interventions be implemented to prevent and remedy these problems. In this chapter, we described five empirically validated classwide interventions that have been shown to improve computational fluency or word-problem solving. These interventions are meant to supplement and enhance the core curriculum by increasing proficiency in keystone skills essential to student learning. We reviewed the pros and cons that contribute to unique characteristics that need to be taken into account when selecting an intervention to best meet the needs of your school or classroom. To maximize student learning it is essential that valid assessment data are used to link student response patterns (e.g., the student is accurate but slow) to intervention selection and monitor progress to inform educational decision making. Classwide applications of these interventions will not work for all students; however, each of these interventions can be adapted and intensified (e.g., increase time, decrease the targeted item set) for use with small groups and/or individuals. The individual adaption of each of these interventions will be discussed in subsequent chapters.

Cover–Copy–Compare: Fact Families

CCC: Fact Families—Student Training Protocol

This training script was written for a classwide application; however, it should be fairly easy to adapt to either a small group or individual student. The steps are as follows:

1. Pass out the CCC sheets to students and instruct them to write their names at the top of the paper.

2. Read the following directions: "Today we are going to do something new. We are going to do math problems using cover–copy–compare. (*pause*) Look at your worksheets. On the worksheet you will see columns of math fact families with two empty spaces next to each fact family. You will use cover–copy–compare to complete these."

3. Continue reading: "Doing cover–copy–compare is easy. Look at the first fact family. It is [read fact family]. When doing cover–copy–compare, you begin by looking at the fact family, making a problem from the family, and saying it to yourself. With this fact family a possible problem is [read problem and answer]. Next, you cover the fact family with your hand, and you write the problem and answer in the space directly next to it. Now, everybody write the problem and answer. After you have written the problem and answer, uncover it and check to see if what you wrote is correct. (*pause*) Now, in the space next to the problem you just wrote, I want you to write the reciprocal fact. [Teacher will need to preteach what this is; terminology can be changed.] Did everyone write the two correct problems from the fact family? If you have written a wrong problem and answer, then cross it out and write in the correct problem or answer. Does anyone have any questions? (*pause*)"

4. Continue reading: "Now let's try the next family. It is [read fact family]. Remember to look at the family, make a problem from the family, say it to yourself, and then cover it. Next, write the problem and answer (*pause for students to complete the step*). Last, uncover the problem to see if you did it correctly. When you have written the problem and answered it correctly, then write the reciprocal problem. Go to the next family and complete these until you have finished the sheet."

5. If anyone has any questions, or is unsure of how to do cover–copy–compare, then raise your hand and I will come to your desk and show you how to do this."

6. Repeat as necessary.

As you are reading the directions, circulate through the room to check for adherence to protocol. In addition, point out students who are doing the steps correctly and provide behavior-specific praise for correctly implementing the CCC steps.

(continued)

CCC: Fact Families Worksheet

Name: _____   Date: _____

72 / 8 — 9		42 / 6 — 7	
15 / 5 — 3		54 / 9 — 6	
49 / 7 — 7		16 / 2 — 8	
10 / 2 — 5		24 / 8 — 3	
30 / 6 — 5		36 / 9 — 4	
9 / 3 — 3		16 / 4 — 4	

(continued)

CCC: Fact Families—Treatment Integrity Protocol

This is to be used by teachers when they are prompting students to use the CCC: Fact Families procedure. It is meant to ensure adherence to treatment and should be used the first few times when you are administering the CCC: Standard Worksheet or when you feel you may need a refresher on the procedures.

Student(s): _____ Date: _____ Start/End Time: _____

Materials

Required: ☐ CCC: Fact Families Worksheet   ☐ Implementation Checklist   ☐ Pencil

Optional: ☐ Timer   ☐ Graph (for self-graphing)   ☐ Rewards

Intervention Procedures

1. Document date, start time, and end time: This is useful when investigating student response to intervention. You can answer how often and consistently CCC: Fact Families was done and how many instructional minutes were spent with the student engaged in the procedure.

2. Pass out the CCC: Fact Families Worksheets to students and have them put their name at the top of the paper. If using performance feedback and/or reward, instruct them to see if they can beat their score from the previous day and what reward they may be able to obtain.

3. Read the following directions if giving the student *unlimited time* to complete the CCC: Fact Families Worksheet: "Here is/are your CCC: Fact Families Worksheet(s). I want you to complete all of the problems. When you have finished all of the problems, raise your hand and I will collect your worksheet(s). Ready? Begin."

If you are timing the student, read the following directions: "Here is your worksheet. You will have [amount] minutes to do as many problems as you can using the cover–copy–compare worksheet. If you finish all of the problems, raise your hand and I will bring you another worksheet. When I say 'Stop,' put down your pencil and I will collect your paper. Ready? Begin."

4. If timing, stop them after _____ minutes and have them hand in their worksheet.

Remember to constantly circulate around the room to prompt and/or help students who are not working. Look for any mistakes and give students feedback so they can correct any incorrect response(s).

Note. Reprinted with permission from Brian C. Poncy and Gary Duhon. Copyright © 2015.

Detect–Practice–Repair
DPR Treatment Protocol

Target Behavior

DPR was designed to be used with groups of students who need to increase fluency when completing basic math facts (i.e., addition, subtraction, multiplication, division). This intervention is appropriate for students who complete math facts accurately but slowly (e.g., 20 DCPM) and who use counting strategies to arrive at accurate answers. While DPR will primarily be used in elementary grades, older students with fluency deficiencies in basic fact skills could benefit as well.

Materials

Metronome, tape recorder (play beat tape), stopwatch, alternate forms of basic fact probes (+, −, ×, ÷), CCC Standard Worksheet, student graph, student folders

Procedures

1. *Preparation: Get the materials ready for the efficient delivery of DPR.*
   - Make a packet for each student folder containing the following: (1) Basic Fact Probe, (2) CCC Standard Worksheet, (3) a student graph.
   - Pass out student folders and have the students take out the DPR packet and place it face down.

2. *The Tap a Problem: Identify items needed for each student to practice.*
   - Introduce and start DPR: "Today we will be working on increasing how quickly and accurately we can do basic fact problems. Remember, it is very important to get the problems right. If you use your fingers or count in your head, you will not have enough time to complete the problems. Begin after the tap [set metronome at 30–40 beats per minute]—go."
   - Continue with the tap-a-problem pretest for 2 minutes or until each of the problems on the worksheet can be completed.
     - Monitor student performance: The tap a problem may be difficult for some, especially when learning to use the intervention. The teacher will need to prompt students to complete problems with the "tap" of the metronome to ensure that the correct items are identified.
   - Have each student identify and circle the first five problems that have been left blank to make up the item pool that will be practiced. If five problems are not left blank, help the student in selecting problems.
   - Instruct the students to turn to the second page of their packet, the CCC Standard Worksheet.

3. *Cover–Copy–Compare (CCC): Using accurate models to prompt repeated practice.*
   1. The student writes down the five circled problems in the column on the CCC Standard Worksheet labeled "Problem and Answer" (one problem per box).
   2. The student looks at the first problem and rehearses it, covers it with his or her hand, writes down the problem and answer, uncovers the model to check for accuracy, and recites the problem and answer five times.
      - Have students mouth/whisper the verbal rehearsal of the problems to allow the teacher to monitor whether students are completing this step.

(continued)

Note. Reprinted with permission from Brian C. Poncy and Gary Duhon. Copyright © 2015.

3. These steps are repeated for the remaining four boxes going *across* the CCC Standard Worksheet, with the student writing the problem and answer once and saying it five times for each box, resulting in 30 repetitions for each identified problem.
4. The student repeats this process for the remaining four problems.
   - During CCC, teachers should circulate around the room to praise students for accurately doing problems and for correctly using the procedures.

4. *Mad Minutes with Self-Graphing: Apply skills and present performance feedback.*
   - Have students turn to the next page in their packet labeled "Student Graph: DCMP"; instruct them to accurately complete as many problems they can in 2 minutes and have them begin.
   - When the 2-minute sprint is finished, have each student count the number of digits written and chart the amount on their graph.
     o The teacher needs to circulate around the room to make sure that student answers and charting practices are accurate.
   - Teachers should, if at all possible, have students tell them when they have beaten a previous score and/or an established standard (e.g., 60 written digits) so that they can receive praise.

(continued)

DPR: Basic Fact Probe

Name: _____   Date: _____

8 ×9	3 ×3	7 ×7
3 ×5	7 ×6	9 ×4
7 ×7	6 ×9	4 ×4
2 ×5	4 ×4	6 ×9
8 ×2	8 ×3	7 ×6
9 ×4	5 ×6	8 ×9

(continued)

CCC: Standard Worksheet

Name: _____   Date: _____

$\begin{array}{r} 8 \\ \times\,9 \\ \hline 72 \end{array}$		$\begin{array}{r} 3 \\ \times\,3 \\ \hline 9 \end{array}$		$\begin{array}{r} 7 \\ \times\,7 \\ \hline 49 \end{array}$	
$\begin{array}{r} 3 \\ \times\,5 \\ \hline 15 \end{array}$		$\begin{array}{r} 7 \\ \times\,6 \\ \hline 42 \end{array}$		$\begin{array}{r} 9 \\ \times\,4 \\ \hline 36 \end{array}$	
$\begin{array}{r} 7 \\ \times\,7 \\ \hline 49 \end{array}$		$\begin{array}{r} 6 \\ \times\,9 \\ \hline 54 \end{array}$		$\begin{array}{r} 4 \\ \times\,4 \\ \hline 16 \end{array}$	
$\begin{array}{r} 2 \\ \times\,5 \\ \hline 10 \end{array}$		$\begin{array}{r} 4 \\ \times\,4 \\ \hline 16 \end{array}$		$\begin{array}{r} 6 \\ \times\,9 \\ \hline 54 \end{array}$	
$\begin{array}{r} 8 \\ \times\,2 \\ \hline 16 \end{array}$		$\begin{array}{r} 8 \\ \times\,3 \\ \hline 24 \end{array}$		$\begin{array}{r} 7 \\ \times\,6 \\ \hline 42 \end{array}$	
$\begin{array}{r} 9 \\ \times\,4 \\ \hline 36 \end{array}$		$\begin{array}{r} 5 \\ \times\,6 \\ \hline 30 \end{array}$		$\begin{array}{r} 8 \\ \times\,9 \\ \hline 72 \end{array}$	

(continued)

Note. Reprinted with permission from Brian C. Poncy and Gary Duhon. Copyright © 2015.

Problem and Answer	Practice #1	Practice #2	Practice #3	Practice #4	Practice #5

(continued)

Student Graph: DCPM

Name: _____ Date: _____

Did You Score More Digits Correct?

40						
35						
30						
25						
20						
15						
10						
5						

Digits Correct per Minute

Date

CHAPTER 5

Computer-Assisted Math Instruction in Schools

with Genevieve Krebs

COMPUTERS IN SCHOOLS

Interest in computers as vehicles for instruction developed swiftly from the earliest days of electronic computing. Only 25 years after the launch of the Electronic Numerical Integrator And Calculator (ENIAC) in 1946—widely considered the first general-purpose programmable electronic computer—Lekan (1971; as cited in Suppes, 1979) reported 1,264 CAI programs had been created. In 1982, 80% of 13-year-olds said they had used a computer to play a game and 23% reported using computer instruction to study math (Carpenter, Lindquist, Matthews, & Silver, 1983). As early as the 1980s programs had become available for a variety of academic subjects including math, reading, and physics. One relevant example is the PLATO system. One of the many components of this system was the Speedway lesson, which was used to teach elementary school students (e.g., grades 4–6) a variety of skills including math combinations (i.e., addition, subtraction, multiplication, and division), fractions, and graphing. It included a game-like component in which students' speed and accuracy in solving problems propelled a race car on a virtual racetrack (Slattow, 1977).

In response to this technological expansion and diversity, Taylor (2003) designated three functional categories—tutor, tool, and tutee—to classify computer use and applications in education. The tutor category referred to the use of computers to deliver instruction or for practice (e.g., modeling problem solutions, providing practice problems, providing immediate performance feedback). The tool category referred to instances where computers simpli-

Genevieve Krebs, MS, CAGS School Psychology, is a licensed school psychologist in Massachusetts. She is currently a School Psychology doctoral student at Northeastern University. Her research interests include intervention and prevention.

fied other work (e.g., calculators, spreadsheet programs). The last category, tutee, referred to the student teaching the computer by programming code (Taylor, 2003). Although computers and their use have evolved since the time these categories were delineated, they still apply to computer use in schools today. The tutor application of computers (e.g., for drill and practice and tutorials) is now more commonly called *computer-assisted instruction* (CAI) and is the focus of this chapter.

COMPUTER-ASSISTED INSTRUCTION

In a recent survey, 56% of elementary school teachers reported "sometimes" or "often" using CAI (Gray, Thomas, & Lewis, 2010). With more than half of elementary school teachers reporting that students are using computers for learning at school, it is imperative to understand how computers are best used for learning and what programs benefit students. The purported benefits of CAI include increasing motivation, improving academic functioning, facilitating independent learning, and differentiating instruction (de Koster, Kuiper, & Volman, 2012). Indeed, the use of incentives (e.g., points for accurate responses) and the judicious use of animations in many game-format CAI programs have been found to have positive effects on academic engagement (Ford, Poe, & Cox, 1993; Ota & DuPaul, 2002). Similarly, CAI allows for differentiated instruction (i.e., modifying instruction to meet the needs of individual students), which increases rates of success and is thought to increase student motivation (Chang, Sung, Chen, & Huang, 2008; Kebritchi, Hirumi, & Bai, 2010; Mautone, DuPaul, & Jitendra, 2005; Schoppek & Tulis, 2010). Some other appealing aspects of CAI are that it requires less educator involvement, provides frequent performance feedback to students, and can collect and store student progress data.

Despite the widespread use of CAI in schools in the United States, the evidence base for its use in math instruction is relatively sparse. The efficacy of the majority of CAI programs for math has not been systematically evaluated and, of those with empirical support, many are no longer available (Slavin & Lake, 2008). Further, attempts to synthesize the literature on CAI for math have been thwarted by a scarcity of high-quality studies to analyze (Seo & Bryant, 2009; Slavin & Lake, 2008). In summary, despite widespread use of CAI for math, little information exists to guide educators in their adoption of specific programs. In this chapter, we review the available research concerning CAI in math to examine the evidence for its efficacy and consider what features are most likely to benefit students. Also, we offer some guidelines for the evaluation of software programs and systems being considered for adoption.

CAI AND THE INSTRUCTIONAL HIERARCHY

CAI programs can have multiple components including instruction, drill and practice, and gaming, each of which is beneficial to students (see Table 5.1 for a summary of these components and their corresponding uses). These diverse components allow for educators to

TABLE 5.1. Instructional Hierarchy and Program Components

Component	Corresponding instructional levels	Corresponding student needs	Best use
Instructional	Acquisition	Review of concepts	Provide additional teaching; modeling and demonstration
Drill and practice	Fluency	Reinforce skills in learned concepts	Extra practice in specific skills
	Maintenance	Review known material	Preserve learned skills
Gaming	Generalization	Applying skills in new settings or situations	Facilitate generalization
	All levels	Motivation	Improve attitude toward math; increase motivation to practice

match students to programs that best meet their current needs. In particular, each student's current stage in the instructional hierarchy for the target skill should be considered (see Chapter 1 for a full discussion of the instructional hierarchy). When students are first introduced to a topic, components intended for instruction are most suitable. Instructional components can independently teach new skills or supplement classroom instruction by providing a review of skills the student did not master. Typically, this element includes a brief tutorial followed by practice and immediate performance feedback. For example, Shiah (1994) created a program that taught students with learning disabilities a seven-step cognitive strategy for solving word problems. This was done by providing a demonstration with animations or static pictures to model each step of the strategy. Then, the program guided the student through the steps, requiring the student to use each step and providing an explanation of the step as it was practiced.

Next, when students have acquired the skills, drill-and-practice elements are most appropriate as they reinforce these skills and build automaticity. Typically, this consists of repeated practice on a fixed set of skills. For example, in the Math Masters program, students are presented with a calculation problem and required to select the correct answer for as many problems as possible in 2 minutes. Correct answers are rewarded with a smiley face icon displayed on the screen (Seo & Bryant, 2009).

Finally, when students are at the maintenance and generalization stages, gaming elements can be motivating ways to practice skills and may improve attitudes toward math. Many programs incorporate educational concepts into game-like scenarios. For example, in Math Smash: Animal Rescue (*www.mathgames.com*), students help rescue trapped creatures by correctly answering problems that are presented on the screen. Students also earn coins and power-ups by answering quickly. In addition to games, real-world, project-based, and collaborative formats are also beneficial for increasing generalization (Brophy & Good, 1986; International Society for Technology in Education [ISTE], 2008). These approaches provide opportunities to use skills and knowledge in diverse ways, thereby building procedural fluency and generalization.

Ideally, programs will include a few or all of these elements in order to adapt to student needs as they move through the levels of instructional hierarchy across skills. Gaming elements are particularly beneficial at all stages and are often incorporated across learning as they increase student motivation and interest in the program. In particular, students with attention-deficit/hyperactivity disorder (ADHD) have demonstrated lower levels of off-task behaviors and higher levels of academic engagement during CAI than during typical classroom instruction (Mautone et al., 2005; Ota & DuPaul, 2002).

The Effectiveness of CAI

Several meta-analytic studies have provided evidence for the effectiveness of CAI—however, what the term *CAI* specifically refers to differs across studies. In particular, many studies have not differentiated CAI from other forms of technology (e.g., audio and video programs, calculators, and computers for data management) and have instead looked at the impact of all of these elements together. Thus, for consistency, within this chapter the term *technology* is used when CAI is not differentiated from other technologies. In contrast, the term *CAI* is used to indicate computer use in the "tutor" sense (i.e., for teaching through tutorials, drill and practice, and games).

Multiple meta-analyses have been conducted in order to determine the effectiveness of technology and CAI. They have examined the impact of technology and CAI across ages, education levels, and multiple academic areas, as well as comparing effects on different groupings. Results of these investigations have varied widely, yet overall they have been shown to be effective in an array of contexts. Most generally, empirical evidence suggests that CAI is moderately effective across academic subjects and grade levels (see Table 5.2 for a summary of effect sizes; Fletcher-Flinn & Gravatt, 1995; Kulik & Kulik, 1991). CAI seems to be particularly effective for students in the primary grades (Kulik, Kulik, & Bangert-Drowns, 1985) as demonstrated in meta-analyses that have compared grade and age levels—in fact, CAI is more effective for younger as compared with older students (Fletcher-Flinn & Gravatt, 1995; Li & Ma, 2010; Tamim, Bernard, Borokhovski, Abrami, & Schmid, 2011). One hypothesis to explain this finding is that the appeal of technology wears off as it becomes less novel, and that younger students benefit more from the interactive learning style used in CAI than older students (Fletcher-Flinn & Gravatt, 1995; Li & Ma, 2010). CAI is most beneficial when added to supplement traditional classroom instruction, as it increases student academic achievement (Christmann & Badgett, 2003; Tamim et al., 2011). Although CAI can be beneficial for all students, it should not replace instruction from qualified educators (Kroesbergen & Van Luit, 2003).

Of interest, interventions provided over shorter durations are associated with larger effects (Kroesbergen & Van Luit, 2003; Kulik & Kulik, 1991; Li & Ma, 2010). This is counterintuitive; if programs are effective, then more time using the program should be associated with greater improvements in performance. However, programs with a narrow focus (i.e., finite instructional targets) should take less time and are likely to be associated with

TABLE 5.2. Meta-Analysis Effect Sizes for Technology and CAI across Academic Areas

	MES	Grade levels	Academic areas included
General effects			
Fletcher–Flinn & Gravatt (1995)	0.26	1–6	Math, reading/writing, science/medicine, arts, not categorized
Kulik, Kulik, & Bangert-Drowns (1985)	0.47	1–6	Math, language/reading, combined
Kulik & Kulik (1991)	0.36	All	Math, science, social science, reading and language, combined, vocational training, other
Supplemental instruction			
Christmann & Badgett (2003)	0.34	Elementary	Not reported
Tamim, Bernard, Borokhovski, Abrami, & Schmid (2011)	0.42	All	Math, science and health, engineering, language, information literacy, combination

Note. MES, mean effect size; see meta-analysis for description of effect size calculation.

rapid instructional gains (Kroesbergen & Van Luit, 2003). An alternative explanation is that programs used over shorter durations may be used more consistently.

The Effectiveness of CAI for Math

CAI (i.e., computer use for teaching through tutorials, drill and practice, and games) for math has also resulted in small to moderate gains in academic achievement (see Table 5.3 for a summary of effect sizes; Cheung & Slavin, 2013; Fletcher-Flinn & Gravatt, 1995; Kulik & Kulik, 1991; Kulik et al., 1985; Li & Ma, 2010; Slavin & Lake, 2008). In fact, the effects of math CAI were greater than for CAI in other academic areas (Fletcher-Flinn & Gravatt, 1995; Kulik et al., 1985). Promisingly, students with learning disabilities and intellectual disabilities particularly benefit from CAI and technology use (Kroesbergen & Van Luit, 2003; Li & Ma, 2010). Thus, there is considerable evidence that using technology—particularly CAI—benefits students of all ages and ability levels and improves performance in all academic areas including math. Of the available CAI programs, most address one of two areas: word-problem solving or computational fluency.

CAI FOR WORD-PROBLEM SOLVING

Within the broad scope of conceptual knowledge in math, CAI research has focused on word problems. Large effects of CAI and assistive technology (e.g., video based, calculators, cassettes) on students' word-problem-solving performance have been demonstrated by meta-analytic studies (Xin & Jitendra, 1999; Zhang & Xin, 2012).

TABLE 5.3. Meta-Analysis Effect Sizes for Technology and CAI for Math

	MES
General effects	
Cheung & Slavin (2013)	0.16
Fletcher-Flinn & Gravatt (1995)	0.32
Kulik, Kulik, & Bangert-Drowns (1985)	0.54
Kulik & Kulik (1991)	0.37
Li & Ma (2010)	0.28
Slavin & Lake (2008)	0.19
Effects for students with disabilities	
Kroesbergen & Van Luit (2003)	1.65
Li & Ma (2010)	1.51

Note. MES, mean effect size; see meta-analysis for description of effect size calculation.

Primarily CAI targeting word-problem solving has provided cognitive strategy instruction or schema instruction and representation techniques through a computer program (i.e., tutorial format; Xin & Jitendra, 1999; Zhang & Xin, 2012). This often includes virtual pictorial representations or schematics with interactive features and animation embedded. Reinforcement is provided through praise, flashing colors, and opportunities to earn and collect virtual prizes. Unfortunately, there are few available CAI programs that target math word-problem solving (Seo & Bryant, 2009). We describe two programs below.

Math Explorer. Math Explorer (Seo & Bryant, 2012) was designed to provide instruction to second and third graders on one-step addition and subtraction word problems using a four-step cognitive strategy and a three-step metacognitive strategy. The program incorporates the following cognitive strategy: reading, finding, drawing, and computing. The metacognitive strategy applied to each cognitive strategy step is do activity, ask activity, and check activity. Math Explorer includes instructional goals, step-by-step modeling, opportunities for guided and independent practice, review of vocabulary and prerequisite skills, visual representations, feedback, and text-to-speech functionality. The program uses a Windows interface that can be installed on standard desktop or laptop computers. Math Explorer was designed to be implemented 20–30 minutes per day for a maximum of 5 days per week. We could not locate whether this program is available for free trial or purchase; we encourage readers to contact the authors.

GO Solve Word Problems. GO Solve Word Problems is commercially available from Scholastic as part of the FASTT math program (*http://teacher.scholastic.com/products/ product_info/edtech3.htm*). The program uses schema-based instruction, guided practice, and adaptive practice to teach students in grades 3–6 word problems that address all four math operations. A text-to-speech feature is available, animation is embedded, and word problems can be customized. Error corrections, hints, and prompts along with progress reports are provided to the student (Leh & Jitendra, 2012). Program developers also included graphic organizer sheets that mimic the strategy provided through the computer program so that students can transfer the strategies to actual classroom applications. No specific information on cost is provided on the website; to find this information one must contact the company directly.

CAI FOR COMPUTATIONAL FLUENCY

Although computational fluency is a common focus in CAI programs, our review of the literature found no meta-analyses that examined CAI programs targeting computational fluency alone. A few analyses have considered drill-and-practice programs separately from other approaches (Fletcher-Flinn & Gravatt, 1995; Kulik et al., 1985; Niemiec & Walberg, 1985), but none specifically examined CAI addressing computational fluency.

Method. To examine the impact of CAI programs targeting computational fluency, we searched abstracts of psychology and education journals and dissertations published between 2002 and 2014. Our search identified 1,804 studies for potential inclusion. To be included in our review, studies must have evaluated the efficacy of a CAI program targeting whole-number mathematical computation for students (i.e., grades 1–6) using a group design where sufficient data (i.e., group sizes, pre- and posttest scores for each group, and standard deviations of posttest scores for each group) were available to calculate effect sizes. We limited our review to dissertations or studies in press or published in peer-reviewed journals and available in English.

Results. Ten studies satisfied the inclusion criteria yielding 11 effect sizes (see Table 5.4 for a summary of included studies and their effect sizes). Standard mean difference scores (d) were calculated using posttest means and pooled standard deviations. The range of effect sizes was −0.57–1.1. This variability in effects was generally attributable to differences in outcome measures (e.g., general achievement tests vs. progress monitoring measures of target skill) and comparison groups (e.g., students receiving an alternate math intervention vs. students receiving traditional instruction). Despite this variability, we found an overall modest positive effect (mean $d = 0.36$) consistent with previous similar investigations. Therefore, on average, these programs are useful in helping students improve their knowledge of math facts.

In addition to variability in outcomes, the studies themselves were quite diverse including students in grades 1–6 and students considered to be at risk, as well as in general and special education. Program construction was also very diverse; some programs presented problems in a flash-card format, whereas others utilized a game format. Further, response style differed across programs; some were open-ended and others were multiple choice. Sessions ranged from one to five per week and lasted as long as 2–70 minutes each time. Total time spent on the programs was the most variable ranging from 40 to 800 minutes.

The programs included in the reviewed studies included Fluency and Automaticity through Systematic Teaching and Technology (FASTT), Exuberant Eye!, multiplication.com, Math Facts in a Flash, Math Flash, Practice Mill, the Cognitive Aptitude Assessment System, and programs created by the researchers. Many of the reviewed programs are no longer available, and of those that are available, most require a paid subscription (see Table 5.5 for a list of reviewed programs currently available). However, there are several other programs available online for free, two of which are described below.

TABLE 5.4. Studies Included in Meta-Analysis of Computational Fluency

Study	Effect Size[a] (95% CI)	Program	Population
Bochniak (2014)	1.1 (0.42, 1.74)	FASTT Math	General education[b]
Buchik (2009)	0.14 (−0.31, 0.60)	Exuberant Eye!; Multiplication.com	General education
Burns, Kanive, & DeGrande (2012)	0.36 (0.12, 0.59)	MFF	At risk
Burns, Kanive, & DeGrande (2012)	0.49 (0.17, 0.80)	MFF	At risk
Chang, Sung, Chen, & Huang (2008)	0.77 (0.13, 1.39)	Experimenter created	General education
Duhon, House, & Stinnett (2012)	−0.57 (−1.27, 0.16)	Experimenter created	General education
Fuchs, Fuchs, Hamlett, et al. (2006)	0.48 (−0.23, 1.16)	Math Flash	At risk
Nelson, Burns, Kanive, & Ysseldyke (2013)	0.57 (0.01, 1.11)	MFF	At risk
Reynolds (2010)	0.04 (−0.29, 0.36)	Practice Mill	General education
Smith (2010)	0.34 (−0.11, 0.85)	FASTT Math	At risk
Walles (2008)	0.07 (0.05, 1.27)	CAAS	General education

Note. CAAS, Cognitive Aptitude Assessment System; CI, confidence interval; FASTT Math, Fluency and Automaticity through Systematic Teaching and Technology; MFF, Math Facts in a Flash.
[a]Standard mean difference at posttest.
[b]No special education students included.

TABLE 5.5. Computational Fluency Programs Reviewed and Available

Program	Mean effect size (as reviewed)	Available at . . .
CAAS: Cognitive Aptitude Assessment System	0.67	*https://simerr.une.edu.au/quicksmart/ pages/index.php* (potentially available as part of research program)
Exuberant Eye!; Multiplication.com	0.14	*www.fun4thebrain.com*; *www. multiplication.com*
Accelerated Math Fluency (formerly called MFF: Math Facts in a Flash)	0.42	*www.renaissance.com/resources/ datasheets/mathfacts-in-a-flash/*
FASTT: Fluency and Automaticity through Systematic Teaching and Technology	0.63	*www.scholastic.com/fastt-math*

XtraMath. XtraMath (*https://xtramath.org*) is a web-based drill-and-practice program for basic computational skills. It is intended as supplemental practice for students to gain fluency with computation skills. Educators can create profiles for individual students and select the skill (i.e., addition, subtraction, multiplication, and division) they should practice. Initially, students take a practice quiz to determine which facts they need to work on within the skill, and each time they begin the program another short quiz is given to monitor progress. The program then selects items that have not been mastered and has the student practice them. Each item is to be answered within 3 seconds. If it is incorrect or not answered, the answer is supplied, and the student is required to replicate that answer to move on. The program can be used through the website on computers and tablets. It is recommended that students use the program daily.

Math Games. Math Games (*www.mathgames.com*) is a web-based gaming program to improve math skills. It includes five games: King of Math, Math Smash: Animal Rescue, Math Buzz, Math Leaper, and Math Missile. Each game can be used to practice a variety of skills. In the Math Buzz game, correctly answering target problems propels a bee through the sky. As the student keeps the bee flying, he or she progresses through the levels, and items increase in difficulty across the target skill. This program is available through the website and students and educators can register to track progress. Additionally, targets at each grade level are designed to align with the Common Core (NGA & CCSSO, 2010).

IMPLEMENTATION CONSIDERATIONS

In general, it is well established that CAI can be used to improve academic achievement. Yet, as previously noted, the available literature is quite difficult to apply because of the rapid changes that characterize technology and the resultant frequent turnover in programs. Many previously reviewed programs are no longer available and a plethora of new programs, including applications and websites, have emerged. Consequently, rather than recommending particular programs, we provide an evaluation framework that can be applied to programs being considered for adoption. The components that make up this framework are derived from research in CAI and best practices for instructional design (Baker et al., 2002; Brophy & Good, 1986; Cheung & Slavin, 2013; Deubel, 2002; Fitzgerald, Koury, & Mitchem, 2008; Fletcher-Flinn & Gravatt, 1995; Ford et al., 1993; Kroesbergen & Van Luit, 2003; Li & Ma, 2010; Rivera & Bryant, 1992; Seo & Bryant, 2009; Simonsen, Fairbanks, Briesch, Myers, & Sugai, 2008; Slavin & Lake, 2008; Weinert, Schrader, & Helmke, 1989).

In order to choose and implement a program with fidelity, several considerations must be made. First, one must determine readiness by evaluating what resources are available and if the implementing educators have the necessary preparation to use the selected program. Second, what system level the program will be used for must be decided. Third, individual student variables should be considered, including what skill will be targeted and what accommodations the student might need. Finally, the logistics should be decided such as where and how often the program will be used. The following sections review each of these considerations in more detail (see Form 5.1 for a template for summarizing these factors).

Evaluating Readiness

Before beginning any intervention, a review of available resources is encouraged (see Box 5.1). Key resources to consider are (1) access to technology (e.g., well-functioning computers or tablets), (2) support personnel (e.g., general and special educators, aides), (3) funding (e.g., for software, personnel, and technology), and (4) time to allot to program use. These basic resources and their availability are critical factors in determining what programs have the most potential to be successfully implemented and used as intended.

In addition to reviewing available resources, it is important to determine whether the educators themselves are prepared and able to implement the program with fidelity. Specifically, one should evaluate the implementing educators' knowledge of CAI programs, interest in their use, and commitment to implementation fidelity (i.e., using programs as intended). Educators need to understand basic computer operation and be willing to obtain training in the selected program (Archer et al., 2014; ISTE, 2008; Jitendra & Xin, 1997). Further, and perhaps most importantly, educators must evaluate their ability and commitment to deliver the program with fidelity. Lack of implementation fidelity decreases intervention effective-

---

BOX 5.1. Practical Considerations

- What technology do you have access to?
- Who will help implement the program?
- What funding do you have or need?
- What time do you have for the student to use the program?

ness (Archer et al., 2014; Heinecke, Milman, Washington, & Blasi, 2001; Ysseldyke, Thill, Pohl, & Bolt, 2005). When using CAI it is important to remember that teachers or other professional staff are required to monitor student engagement with the computer program, ensure students are using the program accurately, and provide technological assistance such as using and manipulating the computer mouse, keyboarding skills, and access to the software program (Leh & Jitendra, 2012; Seo & Bryant, 2012).

System-Level Considerations

CAI is beneficial at all system levels, but it is important to determine how CAI will be used before selecting a program. CAI can be used with one classroom, a group of students, or individually and to address computation or word-problem-solving skills. Because opportunities to practice word-problem solving and computation skills are needed and often not sufficiently provided within core instructional practices (NMAP, 2008), CAI is a good option to supplement classroom instruction. Used in this way, CAI can reinforce classroom learning and provide novel, engaging opportunities to practice fundamentals that facilitate fluency and generalization. At this level, CAI is especially beneficial as it helps differentiate across a variety of instructional and skill levels. For example, one implementation study used computer programs to differentiate practice across nine third-grade classes (Schoppek & Tulis, 2010). These students used the program once a week for an hour. Another study examining the use of Math Facts in a Flash across classrooms required teachers to have students use the program daily for 5–15 minutes (Ysseldyke et al., 2005).

In addition to use for all students, CAI can be beneficial to individual students who need extra support and practice. Because of their history with math, these students may be resistant to engage in the drill and practice necessary to build fluency. Because CAI can increase motivation to do math as well as the appeal of math activities, as student skills improve, so may their attitudes toward math (Ysseldyke et al., 2005).

Student Considerations

In addition to system-level considerations, educators must evaluate several student variables—including *who* are the student(s) of interest? and *what* are these students' areas of need?—to determine whether CAI is an appropriate tool for a given student (see Box 5.2). These needs can be threefold, including stage of the instructional hierarchy, level of instructional support required, and accommodations necessary. Academically, it is important to review the student's previous performance and decide what aspects of the instruc-

---

BOX 5.2. Student Characteristics to Consider

- Who will the intervention target?
- What are the students' areas of need?
- When, where, and for how long will the program be used?
- What are the intervention goals?

tional hierarchy to target: acquisition (i.e., direct or schema-based instruction), fluency (i.e., opportunities for practice), or generalization (i.e., gaming). School professionals should also consider the level of initial and continued instructional support a student requires to use the software correctly, as well as how interactive the program needs to be to increase motivation and sustain engagement. Finally, it is important to determine whether any accommodations are necessary for the student to successfully access the software. For example, students' reading ability is important to take into account when selecting a program so that reading difficulties do not impede math learning (Deubel, 2002). Similarly, for a student with a vision impairment, school professionals should evaluate the size of print and clarity of graphics. Furthermore, the students' keyboarding and computer skills should be tested, as these will have important implications for their access to the program (e.g., lack of keyboarding fluency may impact student response times and interfere with learning).

Intensity and Implementation Considerations

The final aspects of implementation that should be considered are *when, where,* and *for how long* will the program be used? CAI can be implemented across the school day including before or after school, during a math period, or during free time. In addition, the educator must decide how often and for how long (e.g., minutes or hours) the student will use the program, which may be constrained by the available classroom time. Locations could include home, school (e.g., in a classroom, computer room, or library), or both. Programs intended to be used both at home and school should keep track of progress across locations. Additionally, school professionals should determine the total duration of time the intervention will be applied (e.g., weeks or months). Programs should be planned only for as long as the educator can be confident CAI will be implemented well, as fidelity (i.e., implementation integrity) has been found to be a crucial element of intervention effectiveness (Ysseldyke et al., 2005).

In the next section, we discuss program characteristics that are useful for evaluating specific programs (see Tables 5.6 and 5.7, respectively, for a list of some currently available programs and websites that review programs).

PROGRAM EVALUATION

Ideally, CAI programs should have independent research that supports their effectiveness. If this is available, educators are encouraged to use it to choose programs—however, as previously discussed, minimal independent research about individual programs is available. Thus, in lieu of this, one can review related research such as evidence-based instructional methods and CAI characteristics to identify efficacious program elements (see Box 5.3). Review of these related research areas indicates that CAI should include five key aspects: evidence-based teaching practices, correspondence to classroom teaching, use of data for individualization, feedback to students, and engaging programming (see Form 5.2 for a Program Evaluation Checklist).

TABLE 5.6. Additional Programs Available

Program	Available at . . .
DreamBox	*www.dreambox.com*
IXL Math	*www.ixl.com/math*
Compass Odyssey	*https://compasslearning.com*
Reflex	*www.reflexmath.com/home*
TenMarks	*www.tenmarks.com*
XtraMath	*https://xtramath.org*
Math Games	*www.mathgames.com*
Splash Math	*www.splashmath.com*
FunBrain—Math	*www.funbrain.com/brain/MathBrain/MathBrain.html*

TABLE 5.7. Websites That Review and/or List Programs

LearningWorks for Kids
http://learningworksforkids.com

TechMatrix
http://techmatrix.org

Common Sense Education
www.commonsense.org/education

What Works Clearinghouse: Education technology
http://ies.ed.gov/ncee/wwc/Topic.aspx?sid=5

Educational Technology Clearinghouse at the University of South Florida
http://etc.usf.edu/math

The Math Forum at Drexel University
http://mathforum.org/library/resource_types/software

> ## BOX 5.3. Key Program Characteristics
> - Evidence-based teaching
> - Corresponds to classroom teaching
> - Uses data for individualization
> - Feedback to students
> - Engaging programming

Evidence-Based Teaching Practices

Common sense and research dictate that programs should use evidence-based teaching practices (Bishop & Santoro, 2006; Hall, Hughes, & Filbert, 2000). Explicit teaching or direct instruction both have a strong evidence base, particularly for children with learning disabilities (Burns & Ysseldyke, 2009; Gersten et al., 2009). Heuristics and mnemonics are also evidence-supported approaches for children with learning disabilities (Burns & Ysseldyke, 2009; Gersten, Chard, et al., 2009). Since these approaches benefit students with learning disabilities, the benefits would likely extend to all students.

Beyond the instructional approach, the program must use a sequential, systematic framework to approach instruction (Bishop & Santoro, 2006; Brophy & Good, 1986; Deubel, 2002; Hall et al., 2000; Hasselbring, Lott, & Zydney, 2005; Weinert et al., 1989). In teaching, organization ($r = .40$) and clarity of instruction ($r = .39$) have demonstrated strong effects on student outcomes (Weinert et al., 1989); therefore, organization in CAI should include a logical progression of skill development (Bishop & Santoro, 2006; Weinert et al., 1989). Further, tasks should be broken down (DuPaul & Eckert, 1998), concepts taught should be scaffolded (Fitzgerald et al., 2008), and material should be covered in-depth (Simonsen et al., 2008).

In addition to the general instructional approach, it is important to consider the amount of information the child is able to learn. This is often described as the student's acquisition rate or "the relative ease with which a student learns new information" (Kovaleski, Tucker, & Duffy, 1995, p. 4). It is particularly important to pay attention to the acquisition rate in drill-and-practice and instructional approaches as the amount of information the student is expected to learn or practice can affect behavior (Simonsen et al., 2008) and recall (Haegele & Burns, 2015). Thus, programs should introduce only manageable amounts of new material in each session, and students should focus practice on a small discrete set of skills. For example, a student who is learning multiplication facts for sevens should learn and practice a few (e.g., three to five) facts in each session, rather than the entire set of sevens' facts. When students are taught an appropriate amount of information, recall improves and intervention time is used more efficiently (Haegele & Burns, 2015).

Correspondence to Curriculum

To facilitate learning, skills targeted via CAI should correspond to classroom teaching (Bishop & Santoro, 2006; ISTE, 2008; Rivera & Bryant, 1992). Skills and concepts taught in each component of the program should be available to educators as clear objectives and learning goals (Deubel, 2002; DuPaul & Eckert, 1998), and educators should use these to evaluate the program's correspondence to the goals of CAI use. Specifically, educators should be able to choose learning objectives that align with current classroom curriculum. For example, IXL Math (*www.ixl.com/math*) has students or educators select skills, divided by grade level, that can be coordinated to classroom learning (e.g., directing students to practice "third-grade: estimate sums," concurrent with a unit on estimation). Drill-and-practice goals should be roughly compatible with classroom learning (e.g., practicing multiplication tables after introducing them in the classroom) and aligned with student needs as indicated by data from student performance on progress monitoring measures. Websites such as XtraMath (*https://xtramath.org*) allow the educator to choose the target skill (e.g., multiplication or addition) and then use initial assessment and progress monitoring data to dictate what to focus on within the selected skill. Finally, for students practicing for maintenance and generalization, programs should not include new skills; instead, they should integrate previously learned concepts.

Data-Driven Individualization

It is well documented that individualized instruction increases engagement (Simonsen et al., 2008) and improves academic outcomes (Bishop & Santoro, 2006; Brophy & Good, 1986; Deubel, 2002; DuPaul & Eckert, 1998; Fitzgerald et al., 2008; Hasselbring et al., 2005; ISTE, 2008; Rivera & Bryant, 1992; Schoppek & Tulis, 2010; Seidel & Shavelson, 2007; Weinert et al., 1989). Therefore, an important element of CAI is the use of initial assessment and progress monitoring data to individualize programming. Further, this information should be readily available to educators. Given that data direct individualization, particularly with well-integrated programs, these principles are reviewed together.

Initially, the program must include an assessment to place the student at the appropriate instructional level within the program's objectives (Deubel, 2002; Rivera & Bryant, 1992; Simonsen et al., 2008). This decreases behavior problems, as students working at their instructional level are more successful and less frustrated (Simonsen et al., 2008). After initial placement within the program, data should be collected across the program to monitor student progress, and also, to adjust instruction accordingly (Bishop & Santoro, 2006; Brophy & Good, 1986; Burns & Ysseldyke, 2009; Deubel, 2002; Rivera & Bryant, 1992; Seidel & Shavelson, 2007; Simonsen et al., 2008). Many CAI programs automatically adjust instruction to students' level of accuracy and fluency, provide cumulative review when necessary, and provide advanced problems when prerequisite skills are mastered.

Further, data should be readily accessible to educators in a format that allows for monitoring student progress and evaluating response to the intervention and rate of improvement (Baker et al., 2002; Bishop & Santoro, 2006; Gersten, Beckmann, et al., 2009). By having these data available, the educator can continually monitor a student's needs and see whether the student is on track to meet his or her goals. Additionally, the program should allow the educator to see how much time is spent on program activities as well as the student's level of accuracy or fluency. This information can assist in determining whether the program is being used as intended and provides valuable information about the program's efficiency. Also, educators can use these data in instructional decision making for classroom teaching. As an example, the XtraMath website provides multiple forms of feedback including (1) a calendar of days that the student practiced and his or her performance, (2) a graph of student progress over time, and (3) a matrix of problems and the student's level of mastery with each problem.

Feedback to Students

Another essential element is feedback to students (Gersten, Chard, et al., 2009; Seidel & Shavelson, 2007; Weinert et al., 1989). In particular, feedback is most effective when it is immediate, embedded, and elaborate. Provision of feedback is highly correlated with overall outcomes; in particular, it has been found to improve accuracy (Gross & Duhon, 2013; Seidel & Shavelson, 2007; Skinner, Fletcher, & Henington, 1996). CAI programs can provide feedback in multiple ways such as requiring students to supply the correct answer to move on to the next item or providing the correct answer and prompting the student to repeat it. These procedures are important as they build knowledge where gaps exist and are less likely to reinforce careless or avoidant behavior. Learning is also improved when feedback is elaborate. Elaborate feedback can include providing help for problem solving when needed (Brophy & Good, 1986) by highlighting errors, providing error corrections (Deubel, 2002; Hall et al., 2000), and requiring additional practice with skills (Hall et al., 2000). Beyond specific feedback and extra practice, students benefit from feedback on their overall progress (Bishop & Santoro, 2006; Ota & DuPaul, 2002), as this improves performance and increases motivation (Mautone et al., 2005; Schoppek & Tulis, 2010). Many programs include this feedback by visual depiction (e.g., graphs) or levels to indicate student progress. As an example, XtraMath provides this feedback each time the student completes a session, using colors (i.e., green for mastered problems) and symbols (i.e., smiley faces).

Engaging Programming

Finally, interactive and fun programming should include frequent opportunities to respond, thereby eliciting a high level of engagement. Just as teaching that includes active participation increases student engagement and decreases problem behavior (Simonsen et al., 2008), CAI programs can increase student engagement by being fun, interesting, and stimulating (Bishop & Santoro, 2006; Ota & DuPaul, 2002). Games generally do this and are especially appealing to students (Gross & Duhon, 2013). However, it should be noted that game programs vary in the number of opportunities students are provided to practice skills and concepts. Although many require continuous responding to maintain progress in the game, others have minimal responding and include long animations and distracting features. Consequently, the latter type of program is unlikely to have a substantial effect on academics (Ford et al., 1993).

In addition to these five key aspects, practical considerations indicate that programs also need to be accessible for both students and teachers to use and customize. First, the program should have an easy-to-use interface with clear directions so students can work independently. Students should also be able to make meaningful progress during the allot-ted time and save their progress throughout sessions (Bishop & Santoro, 2006). This includes being able to create a student or teacher log-in to track student progress—in which case, it is important to evaluate the program's data security. Finally, the program should allow educa-tors to adjust features based on student needs including font size, volume, and distracting features such as music and animation (DuPaul & Eckert, 1998; Jitendra & Xin, 1997).

CONCLUSION

Given the widespread use of computers in education and in math, it is encouraging that 30 years of history indicate that CAI can be effective for improving student outcomes. How-ever, effectiveness has been shown to vary depending on the CAI software utilized, thereby illustrating the importance of both choosing a program that is appropriate for individual students and monitoring student progress during use of CAI. It is also important that CAI be applied with fidelity. Fidelity can be optimized by carefully considering implementa-tion factors including availability of resources, educator readiness and commitment, and student needs and instructional goals. These factors should also be used to assess program fit (i.e., determining the most appropriate program for the target student). Although pro-grams should be chosen to meet individual needs, all programs should also meet basic criteria. CAI may provide the most impact on math performance when (1) incorporating evidence-based teaching practices, (2) corresponding to classroom teaching, (3) using data for individualization, (4) providing consistent feedback, and (5) including elements such as animation and sound to encourage engagement and persistence. Through evaluation of program design, educator readiness and acceptability, and student characteristics school professionals can select and implement CAI programs to benefit their students.

Implementation Considerations

Resources: What is available? What is needed?			
Technology:	Personnel:	Funding:	Time:

What knowledge do you have of technology?	
Are you willing to learn more to use the technology?	
Are you able to implement the program as it is intended?	
Who are the students of interest?	☐ All students, supplemental support ☐ Specific students who need extra/intensive support
What are their areas of need?	Stage of instructional hierarchy in target areas: ☐ Acquisition ☐ Fluency ☐ Generalization Level of instructional support needed: ☐ Low ☐ Medium ☐ High Level of interactivity/motivation needed: ☐ Low ☐ Medium ☐ High Accommodations: _____
When, where, and for how long will the program be used?	When: _____ Where: ☐ Classroom ☐ Home ☐ Other _____ How long: _____
What are the target skills?	☐ Word problems: _____ ☐ Computational: _____

Program Evaluation Checklist

Program name: _____	**Cost:** _____

Format: ☐ Computer   ☐ Tablet   ☐ Other _____

Components included: ☐ Instruction   ☐ Drill and practice   ☐ Gaming

Evidence base	☐ Uses direct instruction ☐ Uses heuristics/mnemonics ☐ Has one or more research studies supporting efficacy
Practicality	☐ Easy to use ☐ Clear directions ☐ Progress can be saved ☐ Data is secure ☐ Features can be adjusted (size, volume, music)
Instruction/ objectives	☐ Correspond to classroom instruction ☐ Educator can choose objectives to work on ☐ Systematic and sequential
Data	☐ Used to select instructional targets within the program ☐ Used for progress monitoring ☐ Used to modify progress through program ☐ Is available for educator to review
Feedback	☐ Immediate ☐ Embedded ☐ Elaborate ☐ Indicates student progress
Programming	☐ Engaging ☐ High level of opportunities to respond/interactive ☐ Fun and interesting

CHAPTER 6

Motivation and Math

Why are you reading the words on this page? You must have some impetus to do so. Otherwise, you would be doing something else—that is, you might find reading some other book, watching a television show, or talking to a friend more to your liking. Are you still here? If the answer is yes, your motivation to read this chapter evidently is sufficient to enable you to resist the urge to do those other things, and instead focuses your attention to this page. Being motivated means "*to be moved* to do something" (Ryan & Deci, 2000, p. 54; emphasis in original). In other words, motivation is a drive to do some particular thing at a given time.

So your motivation to read this chapter helped you initiate the process of reading it and to continue reading these words. Still, there are many different ways one might go about accomplishing the task. You could take a very passive approach to reading these words, without giving the process much thought. You might not be surprised to learn that such a reactive approach is associated with poor learning outcomes. Indeed, sometimes when our attention wanes we can read several lines before we realize that we have not comprehended a passage at all. It most certainly would be more effective to employ a set of metacognitive tools while reading, such as setting specific learning goals and carefully attending to the learning process throughout your reading (e.g., monitoring for attention, taking notes [Brown, 1981]). The degree to which you can maintain your motivation throughout your reading impacts how well you will be able to employ these processes, and how successful you are in attaining your goals influences your motivation in several important ways (Zimmerman, 2002). This process of transforming your mental abilities into academic skills is known as self-regulated learning (e.g., Schunk & Zimmerman, 2008). To complete any challenging task, we must have the will to do it and stick with it (motivation), but we must also have the cognitive skills to see it through. The integration of motivational and cognitive factors in understanding how students succeed in school has received much research attention in the last 30 years. The literature concerning motivation is vast and rich; it is most certainly beyond the scope of this chapter to provide a comprehensive review.

Motivation is often misunderstood. In our work in the schools, we often hear talk of students who are unmotivated and disengaged, as if the students in question were not motivated to do anything at all and this was a stable global trait. This view of student motivation is unfortunate because it implies that motivation is static, one-dimensional, and unchangeable. The rich literature on student motivation indicates that motivation is not global, but situated and specific to different domains, and that it is not stable, but malleable (see Linnenbrink & Pintrich, 2001). There are many potential sources of motivation, including interest in the topic, what one hopes to get out of the experience, and one's expectations as to whether the goal will be achieved (e.g., Dweck, 1999; Schunk & Zimmerman, 2008). Motivation does not derive from any given activity, instead it is generated through self-regulatory practices and the effects they have on our beliefs of ourselves (Zimmerman, 2002). In this chapter, we focus on a few important themes that you should consider in thinking about students' self-regulated learning strategies and some general guidelines and considerations for applying this knowledge to your work with students who are struggling in math.

SELF-REGULATED LEARNING

Self-regulated learning in school-age students is an area that has received much attention in the literature (see Bandura, 1997; Boekaerts, Pintrich, & Zeidner, 2000; Deci & Ryan, 1985; Pintrich & Schunk, 2002; Schunk & Zimmerman, 1998, 2008), and the association between the use of self-regulated learning and academic achievement is well documented (e.g., Murayama, Pekrun, Litchfield, & vom Hofe, 2013; Pintrich & de Groot, 1990; Zimmerman & Martinez-Pons, 1988). These findings have led researchers to study methods to increase student use of these strategies across a range of academic subjects. Before we begin our discussion of supporting appropriate self-regulated learning in our students, we start with a brief discussion of the elements of the process and how they interact to support one's learning.

Much of the work of social learning theorists pertaining to the relationship between learning and motivation can be summarized in a three-phase model of self-regulated learning (Zimmerman & Campillo, 2003), which is illustrated in Figure 6.1. The three phases illustrate what occurs before (forethought phase), during (performance phase), and after (self-reflection phase) learning activities in self-regulated learners.

Forethought Phase

Prior to learning, the thoughts we have about the learning task and its outcomes play an important role in how we regulate our learning. Two types of thoughts that occur in the forethought phase have been found to be particularly important. The first type, task analysis, comprises *goal setting* and *strategic planning*. Goals serve to specify what is required for success and so can increase one's cognitive and affective reactions to outcomes—students

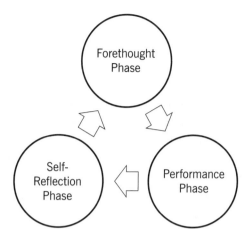

FIGURE 6.1. The three-phase model of self-regulation processes. Based on Zimmerman and Campillo (2003).

can plan strategies to achieve these goals. Goals should indicate a level of performance and a time at which the criterion will be reached. For example, a student might have a goal to earn a good grade on a weekly math quiz or to improve performance on multiplication worksheets that are administered regularly during independent seatwork in math class. A student who is motivated to succeed will develop a plan to achieve these goals (e.g., repeatedly practicing problems, maintaining engagement, asking for additional worksheets). The level of motivation depends on the student's self-motivational beliefs. These include beliefs about one's capability to learn or perform a given task (self-efficacy), the perceived consequences of learning (outcome expectations), interest in the task itself (intrinsic interest), and the specific goal(s) for learning (learning goal orientation). A student who believes that he or she can improve performance, has some interest in the material being learned, and expects that the newly acquired skills will come in handy in the future is more likely to be motivated to do the work to achieve the goal than a student with opposing beliefs, interests, and expectations. We go into more detail concerning goals later in this chapter. It is important to note that self-motivational beliefs are thought to be domain specific—that is, a student may have low self-efficacy for writing, but high self-efficacy for math. Even within the domain of math, for example, a student might have high levels of self-efficacy for algebra but low self-efficacy for trigonometry (e.g., Linnenbrink & Pintrich, 2001).

Performance Phase

The relevant processes that may be employed during learning tasks can be grouped into two classes (self-control and self-observation). During learning tasks learners may employ several processes to focus their attention and get the most out of the task. These include self-instruction, imagery, attention focusing, and task strategies. *Self-instruction* is often readily observable in young children when they are engaged in the performance of a new task, but is more often covert (i.e., unobservable) in older children. Consider a child who is in the early stages of learning to solve addition problems involving regrouping. When solving such problems, the child may whisper to him- or herself the steps in the process ("Add the ones," "Keep the ones in the ones column," "Move the 10 to the tens column," and so on), or say them subvocally. Such a strategy helps the student focus on the appropriate step in the process. Likewise, learners may employ *imagery* to guide themselves through a series of steps. In the previous example, the student may use imagery to remind him- or herself that a 10 must be added to the tens column, or to maintain the important discrimination between the tens and ones columns. Next, *attention focusing* is important to maintain engagement in the task and to avoid distractions. There are so many things competing for a learner's attention that it requires self-control to ignore those distractions and to focus instead on the learning task. Finally, learners can employ *task strategies* to help them focus on the critical parts of a problem.

The other class of processes in the performance phase is self-observation. These processes have been divided into self-recording and self-experimentation. Through these types of self-observation, learners keep track of how well they are performing a task and the conditions surrounding this performance. For example, a student might notice that it takes him or her longer to do homework when the television is on (self-recording) and may conduct a self-experiment wherein he or she compares the amount of time it takes to complete his or her homework with the television on versus with the television off. Such self-observations are considered to be an important source of insight as to how one best approaches a learning or problem-solving task.

Self-Reflection Phase

The self-reflection phase involves the learner's judgments and reactions to his or her performance. The processes in this phase can be divided into self-judgment and self-reaction. Self-regulated learners evaluate their performance against some kind of standard (self-evaluation), which might be the performance of one or more peers, their own prior performance, or some other standard (e.g., getting an "A" or getting all the problems on a worksheet correct). Learners also make judgments as to the cause for their success or failure (e.g., reaching or failing to achieve a specific goal). The attributions learners make as to the cause of their success or failure are critically important, which is an issue we discuss later in this chapter. Also captured in the self-reflection phase are students' reactions to their performance. Whether learners are satisfied (or not) with their performance will also have an impact on their subsequent motivation for that type of task. In addition, a learner's reaction to performance can be adaptive or defensive. For example, an adaptive reaction to poor performance on a math test might be to study more or differently for the next one, while a defensive response might be to protect one's self-image by being absent from school on the date of the next test.

Taken together, the three-phase model illustrates several important aspects to consider in our work with students who are experiencing academic difficulties. First, teaching skills and strategies are necessary, but not sufficient for student success. Student academic motivation is critically important, and failure to consider aspects of student motivation could undermine efforts to support students requiring supplementary instruction. The process by which self-regulated learning strategies are employed and maintained is cyclical. This is an important consideration for students with learning problems who often have a history of failure, which can have a cumulative negative impact at each phase of the self-regulatory process.

STRUGGLING STUDENTS

A useful metaphor in applying this theoretical work to children with learning problems in math is an engine that won't start or runs "rough." Students with a history of learning problems will demonstrate maladaptive cognitions and behaviors related to the academic area(s) in which they struggle (e.g., Bandura, 1997; Licht & Kistner, 1986), and the impacts can be seen at each phase of the three-stage model. For example, in the forethought phase, students with a history of failure in math will likely experience negative self-efficacy beliefs, interest, and expectations for positive outcomes related to their efforts in math activities (e.g., Baird, Scott, Dearing, & Hamill, 2009; Lackaye & Margalit, 2006). It should be noted that many students with ADHD actually overestimate their academic abilities. This is particularly evident in students with elevated hyperactive and impulsive symptoms (see Owens & Hoza, 2003). Whether students have low self-efficacy or overestimate their abilities, these perceptions should have a negative impact on the extent to which these students are able to set ambitious yet attainable goals that would assist them in regulating their learning activities. Conducting assessments designed to optimize the difficulty level of instructional materials is an important consideration, not only to maximize instructional gains but also to enable students to experience improvement and set goals accordingly. Material that is too difficult or too easy will undermine how meaningful goals might be to students and seems to increase off-task behaviors (e.g., Gilbertson, Duhon, Witt, & Dufrene, 2008).

Numerous investigators have established a link between self-motivational beliefs and the adaptive academic behaviors that are exhibited in the performance phase for self-regulated learners. For example, students demonstrating academic underachievement consistently have been shown to avoid challenging academic tasks, and when they do perform such tasks, they tend to demonstrate difficulties in task engagement and task persistence (see Bandura, 1997; Hoza, Pelham, Waschbusch, Kipp, & Owens, 2001). In the self-reflection phase, students with learning problems have been found to demonstrate a negative attribution style (e.g., Tabassam & Grainger, 2002). Compared with typically developing students who are more likely to attribute their success to internal (e.g., effort, ability) and stable factors, students with a history of learning problems are more likely to attribute their success to external and unstable factors (e.g., "I got lucky this time"). This is maladaptive because when students do meet with success they attribute the success to factors outside of their control, which cannot be relied upon in the future. Moreover, students with learning problems tend to view their ability as fixed and do not believe that increased effort will make a difference (see Dweck, 2008). Indeed, they may actually see the need to apply extra effort as indicative of low ability (see Baird et al., 2009).

The discussion of this roughly running engine of motivation is important when considering how best to support students struggling in math. To affect meaningful change in a student's academic development, it is not sufficient to target skills deficits alone. We argue that part of our efforts should focus on getting the engine to turn over and run smoothly. As we have said above, students with a history of failure will tend to avoid the very tasks that could help remediate their skills deficits. A common theme you will see in our discussion of effective interventions to remediate skills deficits in math involves targeting specific skills deficits and increasing opportunities to respond to those specific types of problems. A student's level of motivation for the task serves as a governor that regulates not only the number of such opportunities but also the quality of them—that is, a student with a high level of motivation for the task will stick with it and pay close attention to the assignment. In contrast, a student with little motivation for a task will allocate less attention to each problem and is less likely to sustain engagement throughout the activity (fewer opportunities to respond). Therefore, if we are able to enhance student motivation, we are likely to see benefits in the effectiveness of our intervention efforts.

In sum, students with a history of math problems tend not to engage in key processes that stimulate and maintain motivation for math learning tasks (e.g., self-motivation beliefs, goal setting, self-attributions, interest in the task). To jump start student motivation, these beliefs and behaviors must be considered in our efforts to support the student in math.

TARGETING MOTIVATION

Student motivation is an important consideration in our attempt to increase the rate of achievement in math. We offer some guidance for how to enhance student motivation and self-regulation during math learning tasks below. Supporting student goal setting and self-evaluation is a useful way to structure your efforts to build student motivation for math tasks (e.g., Fuchs et al., 2003a; Schunk, 1985a, 1985b, 1996). The rationale here is that students with a history of failure in a given area may need support in setting appropriate goals, applying self-regulated learning strategies during task performance, and in making adaptive attributions as to their successes and failures. Teaching students the metacognitive skills necessary to regularly make the connection among planning, effort, and positive outcomes is a way to get that "engine" of motivation restarted and running. Student engagement during specific academic tasks is certainly an important goal, but targeting student self-regulated learning strategies is a way to target engagement more broadly and sustainably.

Goals and Goal Setting

Goals have two parts. The first part is the criterion (e.g., 20 DCPM on 1×1 addition problems with sums less than 12). The second part is the time the goal should be reached. The designated time can be almost immediate (e.g., at the end of a brief task) or can be at some later time (end of month, semester, year, or longer). As you may recall, goal setting occurs in the forethought phase of the three-phase model. Goals are important in supporting motivation because they define what is required for success—that is, when a student attains a goal, it is likely that the student's sense of self-efficacy is enhanced because he or she experienced success. Likewise, when a student is making progress toward a goal, it also supports self-efficacy because the student sees his or her skills growing (e.g., Schunk, 1996). This is of central importance to our discussion because when a student sees a goal as attainable, it serves to support the student's use of strategies (if he or she knows the strategies and when to employ them) that might help achieve the goal (performance phase). Reaching goals is highly rewarding, and when we achieve them, we typically then set new ones.

So goals can be very powerful, but their strength on performance depends on several properties. Goals are most effective when they are specific (e.g., "I will get more items correct than I did last time"), short term ("When I am done with this worksheet" as opposed to "3 weeks from now"), and of moderate difficulty (challenging, yet attainable). If goals are too general, too temporally distant, or too easy or too difficult, they are less likely to support positive student learning outcomes (Bandura, 1997), and may lead to decrements in student performance (Morisano & Shore, 2010). Goals also differ in whether they communicate a learning or performance objective. The orientations for learning and performance goals are quite different. Take, for example, a learning goal for this chapter. Your learning goal might be to learn the basics of theories pertaining to motivation because you find the topic fascinating and want to learn as much as you can about this general topic. If that is your goal orientation, you are likely to focus your attention on the concepts being conveyed on this page and monitor your understanding of the text, take notes, and review sections to make sure you are pulling all the pieces together. A performance goal, in contrast, might be to read this chapter before lunchtime, or to read it faster than your classmate or colleague sitting next to you.

Since an ultimate goal for us in targeting student motivation is for students to be able to employ the aforementioned metacognitive skills independently, it would seem that we should have students set goals for themselves instead of having them generated by the teacher or interventionist. Although there is some evidence that self-selected goals may lead to better outcomes than adult-selected goals (e.g., Codding, Lewandowski, & Eckert, 2005; Lee & Tindal, 1994), one study has found that only a minority of middle school students were able to set reasonable reading performance goals that they could meet (see Swain, 2005). It seems clear that many students need support in setting realistic goals. Brief dialogues with students around goal setting may be one way to engender a sense of autonomy, while ensuring that the goals ultimately selected would support student self-efficacy and motivation (see Box 6.1).

Cognitive evaluation theory (CET; Deci & Ryan, 1985) supports the idea of having students set goals. CET is a subtheory of self-determination theory, which postulates that motivation is fueled by three innate psychological needs (competence, autonomy, and relatedness). Perhaps most relevant to the present discussion are the needs for competence (i.e., the need to control outcomes and experience mastery) and autonomy (i.e., the need to have free will). Relatedness pertains to the need to be connected to others (e.g., the need to have positive relationships with teachers and peers). Importantly, CET postulates that enhancing

---

BOX 6.1. Motivation

Teacher: Okay, Matt, I see that you have corrected your worksheet. How many problems did you get correct?

Matt: Mmm, I did 16 problems and got only one wrong, so I got 15.

Teacher: Well, I saw you working really hard at those problems. You were really focused and I see you got two more correct than you did last time.

Matt: Yeah, some of them were really easy.

Teacher: Well, the more you practice, the more problems you come across will seem easy. Let's have you set a goal for next time. What do you think it should be?

Matt: I think I can get 20 problems right!

Teacher: Wow! That sounds pretty ambitious. You seem to be getting one or two more problems right each time you practice these sheets. Ambitious goals are good, but sometimes it takes a little longer to get there. Let's for now talk about how many you will get right next time.

Matt: Okay, I will get 17 right next time.

Teacher: Yes, that sounds real good, Matt. If you keep working as hard as you have been, you might just make it to 20 by the end of the week. That would be pretty cool. Do you want to set that as your goal for the end of the week?

Matt: Yeah, sure.

---

student feelings of competence will support intrinsic motivation only when students also feel autonomous. So according to CET, if we are to support intrinsic motivation for math tasks, we should make sure instructional materials are of moderate difficulty, and assist students in setting goals that result in positive feedback.

Feedback

Feedback to students on their performance can be provided in many different ways, which may have a differential effect on student outcomes (see Gross et al., 2014). In the context of goal setting, at a minimum, the feedback to students should include prior performance, current performance, and whether the goal was met (see Figure 6.2 for an example). Although many students are not able to set effective goals for themselves, numerous studies have demonstrated that students are capable of scoring their own performance with the aid of an answer key and recording their score in writing or graphically (e.g., Codding, Chan-Iannetta, Palmer, & Lukito, 2009; Codding, Chan-Iannetta, et al., 2011; Poncy, Skinner, et al., 2010). Students can graph their progress on a line chart, bar chart, or some other graphic—for example, by filling in performance on a drawing of a thermometer (Fuchs et al., 2003a). The idea here is that the recording of performance should increase the salience of student improvement over time. It seems that for some students, simply recording their performance may be enough to lead to improvements in performance in comparison to no monitoring. Providing a means for students to chart their performance would seem to increase the salience of gains because much information on past and present performance is summarized in an efficient way (i.e., if the student has the ability to interpret the chart).

Compute One MORE Problem Correct

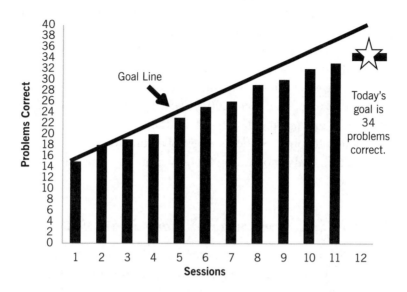

FIGURE 6.2. Sample goal-setting chart with performance feedback.

To take things up one level further, one might add goal lines to the chart (e.g., Figarola et al., 2008; Gross et al., 2014). A goal line (see Figure 6.2) is a line drawn from a starting score to a future goal (end of week or further removed in time). What a goal line does is convey not only whether the student's performance improved over previous efforts but also whether the student is on track to reach the distant goal (e.g., present performance appears on or above the goal line). To increase the saliency of performance even more, one might provide a contingent reward for the attainment of a goal. Such a reward can be provided for short- or long-term goal attainment, or both. This continuum of the saliency of feedback can be thought of as a dial that you can adjust for different situations (see Figure 6.3 for an example).

FIGURE 6.3. Dialing up the salience of performance feedback.

One caveat in regard to providing contingent rewards is that this kind of feedback may not be available to the student for different tasks in other settings. You might have heard that providing rewards for the performance of certain tasks may undermine intrinsic motivation (doing something because it is satisfying/interesting as opposed to doing it for some external outcome) in those tasks (e.g., Deci, Koestner, & Ryan, 1999). Negative effects of reward on intrinsic motivation have been widely studied, but have generated inconsistent results (e.g., Cameron, Banko, & Pierce, 2001; Deci, Koestner, & Ryan, 2001). According to CET, it seems that an important consideration is the extent to which the student feels in control of the situation (autonomy). Students' sense of autonomy will be enhanced when they are responsible for setting goals, monitoring their own progress, and determining when the goal has been achieved.

Promoting Student Self-Monitoring of Math Strategies

Fuchs et al. (2003a) illustrate an excellent model for pulling these themes together in promoting student self-regulated learning while solving math problems. It is beyond the scope of this chapter to go into great detail as to the overall design of the study, but readers are encouraged to read the article in its entirety, as it provides a convincing case for how integrating self-regulated learning strategies into the curriculum can improve math outcomes in addition to student use of important metacognitive strategies that serve to support and maintain student motivation for math, and may generalize to other academic areas. In the Fuchs et al. study, experimental math instruction sessions were conducted two times during the 16-week study. After teacher-led instruction, students in the self-regulated learning condition first worked independently on a unit problem and scored it themselves using an answer key that provided points both for completing the appropriate steps of the problem and obtaining the correct answer. Students then charted their performance by filling in the appropriate area of one of five thermometers presented in an array to represent five consecutive exercises (see Forms 6.1 and 6.2 for sample forms). At the beginning of each session students were instructed to examine their charts, with the short-term goal being to beat their best previous score. Once students charted their performance on the unit problem they would grade their homework using an answer key and then hand it in. A key focus of the Fuchs et al. study was to promote the transfer of unit strategies. During selected sessions students spoke with classmates about ways they applied the unit strategy outside of class. Finally, the teacher recorded on a class chart the number of students who had submitted homework and the number of pairs of students who had noted a transfer of strategy outside of school.

Numerous studies have demonstrated the added value of goal setting (with or without a contingent reward) to academic interventions (e.g., Morgan & Sideridis, 2006), and many others have demonstrated the positive effects for teachers of using self-regulated learning strategies when teaching computational skills (e.g., Schunk, 1985a, 1985b, 1996). The study by Fuchs et al. (2003a) provides a clear example of how teachers can easily incorporate goal setting and self-assessment/monitoring into math strategy instruction.

CONCLUSION

In this chapter, we provided a very brief review of some of the theories and applied work pertaining to student motivation. We presented student motivation as a dynamic and contextualized construct that is most certainly malleable and is influenced by attitudes, behaviors, and skills. We have offered here a conceptual framework for your work with students who are struggling in math that could guide your efforts to help them make the connection between effort and success. When students are able to make this connection and become involved in the process of determining the definition for success in math (goals), they are well on their way to being engaged and motivated learners in math.

FORM 6.1

Student Self-Charting Form

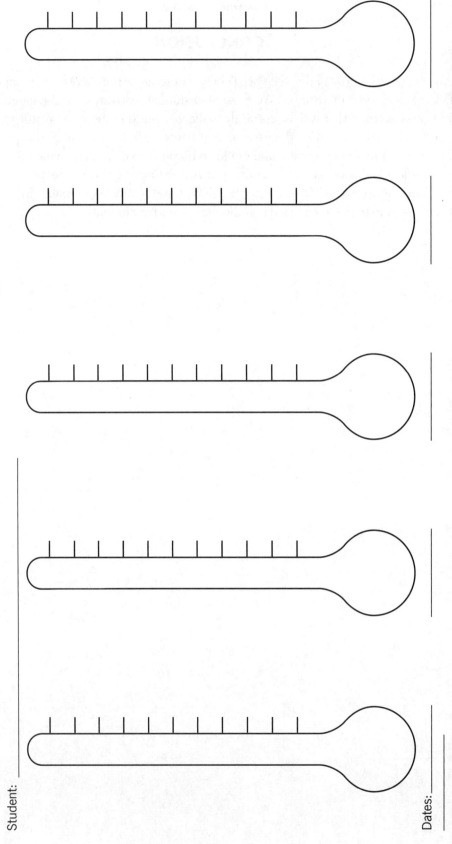

Student: _____

Dates: _____

Goal-Setting Chart

GOAL CHART for _____

Counting	Numbers Named	Missing Numbers	Which Is More?
100	100	30	30
95	95		
90	90	25	25
85	85	20	20
80	80		
75	75	15	15
70	70		
65	65	10	10
60	60		
55	55	5	5

CHAPTER 7

Core Features of Tiers 2 and 3 Math Interventions

Math is a complex content area consisting of many topics that are reflected in the challenges experienced by students. Students may exhibit as many as 32 different types of math difficulties (D. P. Bryant, Bryant, & Hammill, 2000). This chapter begins by discussing common challenges students display with math learning. Next, we describe the rationale for focusing this book on early number skills, computation, and word-problem solving. Finally, we describe key features of intervention components for students who are at risk for or experiencing math learning disabilities.

STUDENTS' DIFFICULTIES WITH MATH

As many as 17% of school-age children will experience substantial math difficulties. About 7% of children or adolescents will be diagnosed as having a learning disability in math, and an additional 5–10% will experience persistent low achievement (Berch & Mazzocco, 2007; Geary, 2007; Shalev, Manor, & Gross-Tsur, 2005). Currently, there is no agreed-upon diagnostic criteria for math learning disabilities and there is no consensus on whether there are different types of math disabilities or what forms they may take (Geary, Hoard, & Baily, 2010; Mazzocco, 2007; Watson & Gable, 2012). That being said, some experts agree that students who consistently (at least 2 consecutive years) score below the 10th percentile on standardized math achievement tests might be categorized as having a math learning disability, whereas students persistently scoring between the 10th and 30th percentile may be described as low achieving (Geary et al., 2010). However, it is important to keep in mind the heterogeneity of math difficulties experienced by students (Murphy, Mazzocco, Hanich, & Early, 2007).

Most research has focused on arithmetic development and has suggested that number sense, semantic memory (leads to challenges with automatic recall and representation of quantities as numerals), working memory (the ability to hold information in mind while using it), and procedural competence represent common deficits associated with math learning disabilities (Baroody, Bajwa, et al., 2009; Geary, 2004; Geary et al., 2010; Watson & Gable, 2012). Children experiencing challenges with math often display difficulty understanding and using the number system and in particular lack mastery over basic skills that serve as the foundation for higher-order math tasks (Jordan, Glutting, & Ramineni, 2010; Lago & DiPerna, 2010). D. P. Bryant and colleagues (2000) solicited a list of 32 math difficulties experienced by students with or at risk for math disabilities (see Table 7.1). This variety suggests that students could exhibit a few or many of these problems with math. Without intervention, difficulties in these core areas remain throughout elementary school (Jordan, Hanich, & Kaplan, 2003b)—math competency in kindergarten is highly predictive of later school achievement (Duncan et al., 2007; Jordan et al., 2009; Morgan et al., 2009).

The five most frequently occurring math problems cited by D. P. Bryant and colleagues (2000) were (1) solving word problems, (2) multistep procedural calculations, (3) math language, (4) checking work and answers, and (5) automatic recall of basic facts.

These first two items, difficulty solving word and multistep computation problems, represent complex tasks that require a number of procedural steps be followed. A task analysis of component skills required to complete these types of problems might be conducted by interventionists, school psychologists, and teachers in order to provide specific student support for these multifaceted math activities (D. P. Bryant et al., 2000; Powell et al., 2013; Stein, Kinder, Silbert, & Carnine, 2006). Word-problem solving can be difficult for a variety

---

TABLE 7.1. 15 Commonly Observed Math Difficulties

1. Has difficulty with word problems.
2. Has difficulty with multistep problems.[a]
3. Has difficulty with the language of math.
4. Fails to verify answers and settles for the first answer.
5. Cannot recall number facts automatically.[a]
6. Takes a long time to complete calculations.
7. Makes borrowing (regrouping) errors.[a]
8. Counts on fingers.
9. Reaches unreasonable answers.[a]
10. Misspells number words.[a]
11. Calculates poorly when the order of the digit is altered.[a]
12. Orders and spaces numbers inaccurately in multiplication and division.[a]
13. Misaligns vertical numbers in columns.
14. Disregards decimals.
15. Jumps impulsively into arithmetic operations.

Note. Adapted from Bryant, Bryant, and Hamill (2000). Copyright © 2000 SAGE Publications. Adapted by permission.
[a]Significantly differentiates students with and without math weaknesses.

of reasons, including reading and interpreting language, understanding the word-problem structure, developing a numerical equation from the narrative, and solving the equation (NMAP, 2008). When solving multistep problems, students experience challenges such as properly aligning numbers when regrouping from one column to the next, subtracting larger numbers from smaller numbers, and borrowing across zeros (Raghubar et al., 2009; Russell & Ginsburg, 1984). These difficulties likely reflect student challenges with conceptual understanding of place value and its application to all number operations, particularly subtraction (Andersson, 2008; D. P. Bryant et al., 2000; Geary et al., 2010).

Challenges with the language of math may reflect the difficulty students have connecting language with quantities of objects as well as numerals and symbols (e.g., <, =, >), often described as the triple-code theory (Dehaene, Piazza, Pinel, & Cohen, 2005). Knowledge of and fluency using number words, numerals and their quantities, and number lines represent critical components that underlie math learning (Geary, 2011b; Geary et al., 2009; Jordan et al., 2009). The language of math is often esoteric to the learning experience or principle instructed (D. P. Bryant et al., 2000). In order to access conceptual understanding of math principles, students need to define the vocabulary words associated with math such as *commutative property, sum,* and *minuend.* Students with math learning disabilities may also display language comprehension deficits that contribute to difficulties understanding math language as well as interfere with problem solving (e.g., Compton, Fuchs, Fuchs, Lambert, & Hamlett, 2012).

Failure to check answers may reflect a number of challenges, including (1) lack of student persistence with problem solving (NGA & CCSSO, 2010; NMAP, 2008); (2) desire to escape from a disliked task (Cates & Rhymer, 2003); (3) skill deficit in knowing how or why checking answers is important (Swanson, 2009); and/or (4) difficulty recognizing the accuracy of an answer or being overconfident in the answers produced, especially on more difficult problems (Rinne & Mazzocco, 2014).

Automatic retrieval of basic facts from memory may represent a signature feature of children with math difficulties (e.g., Geary, Hoard, & Bailey, 2012; Gersten, Jordan, & Flojo, 2005). Students with math learning disabilities also tend to use less sophisticated counting strategies, such as guessing and counting from one when solving simple computation problems, and make more counting errors than their peers (Geary et al., 2004)—that is, these children may not be familiar with the magnitude sequence of numerals, or a mental number line, and therefore can only determine which number comes first (e.g., three or four) by counting from one (Baroody, Bajwa, & Elliand, 2009).

CONTENT AREAS TO TARGET FOR INTERVENTION

Our aim in this book was to target a few key content areas and review the available intervention literature within each: early numeracy, arithmetic computation (also referred to as number combination), and word-problem solving. All three represent areas of difficulty for students struggling with whole-number knowledge (Andersson, 2008; Butterworth, 2010), and each area represents essential aspects of two domains within the CCSS for Mathematics: (1) operations and algebraic thinking, and (2) number and operations in base ten (NGA & CCSSO, 2010).

Early numeracy, or number competence, has been defined as the ability to make judgments about numbers and the order of their magnitudes on a number line, automatically determine the value of small quantities without counting, understand counting principles, and join and separate sets of numbers (Geary, 2011b; Gersten et al., 2005; Jordan et al., 2009; Siegler & Booth, 2004). Early number knowledge includes understanding the counting sequence, developing a mental number line, and developing early reasoning skills about numbers (Sigler & Booth, 2004). Number competencies in kindergarten predict and support more complex math performance in third grade (Jordan et al., 2009). For example, counting knowledge and use of sophisticated counting strategies permits students to solve number combinations fluently, as well as solve novel number combinations (Jordan et al., 2009)—that is, immediate recall of basic facts, a key foundational skill, is difficult to achieve if students do not understand the relationship of numbers to each other on a number line. Number relationships and reasoning assist with the development of strategies that can be applied to more complex word problems (Kilpatrick et al., 2001).

Given the central role of automatic retrieval of basic facts and the frequency with which word-problem-solving difficulties were noted by teachers, we also examined the intervention literature in these two areas (e.g., D. P. Bryant et al., 2000; Gersten et al., 2005; NMAP, 2008). The NMAP (2008) conducted a survey of over 1,000 algebra teachers who suggested that students generally need better preparation of basic skills at the elementary level, and specifically remarked that students were least prepared to solve word problems. Furthermore, arithmetic calculations and word-problem solving have been described as the essential foundations for math competence in elementary school, each representing distinct aspects of knowledge (e.g., Fuchs, Geary, Compton, Fuchs, Hamlett, & Bryant, 2010; Fuchs, Powell, Cirino, Schumacher, Marrin, et al., 2014; Kilpatrick et al., 2001; Swanson, 2006). Intervention studies have shown that providing an arithmetic calculation intervention does not transfer to word-problem solving and vice versa, indicating the necessity to screen for competency in both areas and provide intervention support accordingly (Fuchs, Powell, et al., 2014; Gersten, Beckmann, et al., 2009; Powell & Fuchs, 2014). In other words, if only word-problem solving is problematic, then a specific intervention matched to that skill need should be implemented, whereas if students are exhibiting only computation difficulties, a similarly matched intervention should be given.

These foundational content areas are considered hierarchical and necessary for completing more advanced math tasks (Carr & Alexeev, 2011; Jordan et al., 2009; Sayeski & Paulsen, 2010). Number knowledge skills provide the conceptual understanding necessary to gain fluency with basic facts and, although there is not a transfer of number combination fluency directly to word-problem solving, the ability to solve different number combinations is an essential component of word-problem solving. Likewise, exhibiting fluency with basic facts, understanding place value, and regrouping are necessary to solve multidigit arithmetic problems.

An important consideration that school professionals will need to make as they engage in further assessment of students' skill strengths and weaknesses, is that it is likely that prerequisite skills requiring remediation may not match grade-level content (Gersten, Beckmann, et al., 2009; Swanson, 2009). For example, fourth-grade students with unmastered addition and subtraction facts should receive intervention support that addresses these skills weaknesses prior to focus on multiplication or division facts (Shapiro, 2011). Some experts on math learning disabilities suggest that emphasis on these foundational skills are representative of core math instruction and the Common Core, particularly when students are simultaneously receiving general education instruction with targeted intervention supports (Lembke et al., 2012; Powell et al., 2013). Perhaps more importantly, when prerequisite or foundational skills are targeted for intervention supports and mastered, students will obtain the tools necessary to access core instruction and reach math standards (Powell et al., 2013).

KEY INTERVENTION FEATURES FOR STRUGGLING STUDENTS

Unfortunately, there are presently very few standard protocol math intervention packages available for school professionals to use with students at risk for or with weaknesses in math (Fuchs, Fuchs, Powell, et al., 2008; NMAP, 2008). However, common intervention features identified through research offer promising guidelines for creating effective treatment packages. Form 7.1 displays eight essential treatment components that were commonly generated as effective by literature reviews (Baker et al., 2002; Burns et al., 2010; Codding, Burns, & Lukito, 2011; Fuchs, Fuchs, Powell, et al., 2008.; Gersten et al., 2009; Swanson, 2009). The use of these components is intended to be combined into treatment packages, as they do not necessarily result in improved math outcomes when used in isolation (Fuchs, Fuchs, Powell, et al., 2008; Gersten, Chard, et al., 2009; Swanson, 2009). The first two components, explicit and strategy instruction, represent instructional approaches that encompass many of the other key components.

Explicit Instruction

One of the most robust findings to date is that students experiencing challenges with math benefit most when explicit instruction is provided to facilitate skill acquisition (Baker et al., 2002; Fuchs, Fuchs, Powell, et al., 2008; Gersten, Chard, et al., 2009; Swanson, 2009). Explicit instruction involves teacher modeling of rules, concepts, and principles, as well as demonstration of step-by-step plans for solving specific problems. Problem-solving tasks are divided into separate skills and steps that are modeled and practiced. This methodology also incorporates guided practice using teacher-modeled steps, and is followed with daily corrective feedback moving toward a gradual shift increasing students' independent practice. Fundamental to explicit instruction is the use of individually paced instruction, as well as review and maintenance checks to ensure skill mastery (see Chapter 2 for more details).

Strategy Instruction

Strategy instruction incorporates the use of think-alouds to model problem-solving steps, reminders to use particular strategies or procedures to solve problems, step-by-step prompts about the problem-solving process, and multistep process directions. Discussion is predicated on why a strategy is useful to solve a problem, as well as how to apply the strategy and check whether the strategy is working (Swanson, 2009). This form of instruction may also include the use of simple heuristics such as "say, ask, check," which reminds students to read the problem, ask themselves questions about the process of reading the problem, and check their work for each step (Kroesbergen & Van Luit, 2003; Montague, 2008b). The purpose of strategy instruction is to provide and model the use of visual and verbal prompts as a mechanism for students to monitor their own problem solving (Goldman, 1989). Therefore, a central aspect of strategy instruction is explaining the reasoning and process for problem solving along with providing strategy cues to students.

Sequencing Instruction

Providing a carefully constructed sequence of instructional tasks emphasizing absent foundational or prerequisite skills and building mastery in those areas is a consistent recommendation made by experts (Baker et al., 2002; Fuchs, Fuchs, Powell, et al., 2008; Gersten, Beckmann, et al., 2009; Gersten, Chard, et al., 2009; Swanson, 2009). Off-task behaviors increase when difficult tasks are presented and also when too many skills or concepts are presented at one time (Burns & Dean, 2005). Retention of previously introduced skills is better when a small amount of material is presented in one learning occasion. For example, students learning math facts have shown greater retention when instruction focused on learning four new facts in one session (Haegele & Burns, 2015).

Sequencing instruction requires that students' specific skill strengths and weaknesses be identified, and that instruction begins at an appropriate level of challenge that can build upon previous knowledge. Math concepts need to be divided into smaller units according to task analyses or criteria. Students learn each skill to mastery from the earliest unknown skill for the task. In this way, simpler skills and concepts within the sequence are provided first and serve as a foundation for increasingly complex math tasks. For example, students might first learn to add and subtract zero and one or doubles (rule-based facts) before proceeding to two and three, the latter for which greater knowledge of counting principles and strategies are required (Fuchs, Fuchs, Powell, et al., 2008; Woodward, 2006). Research has indicated that learning multiplication facts with 2's (2×5) and 3's (3×4) is easier for students to learn than 6's (6×8) and 7's (7×4), and therefore would be instructed first (Burns, Ysseldyke, Nelson, & Kanive, 2015). With respect to word problems students might be assessed and instructed accordingly on prerequisite skills, such as checking work, basic facts, and multidigit computation before teaching story-problem types (Fuchs, Fuchs, Powell, et al., 2008; Fuchs, Powell, Seethaler, Cirino, Fletcher, et al., 2009).

As students move to mastery of subskill areas, the level of teacher assistance also fades, with students increasing their own management of the learning task. Additionally, the range of examples that represent the broader concept or skill increases as students master foundational skills in order to facilitate generalization (Gersten, Beckmann, et al., 2009; Gersten, Chard, et al., 2009). In essence, within the sequencing of instructional skills and concepts taught, school professionals should be tracking the instructional hierarchy of skill progression so it is known whether students have acquired a skill, become fluent, maintained performance while independently working, and can generalize component skills to broader skill concepts, ideas, and tasks.

Ongoing Progress Monitoring and Feedback

Monitoring student progress using measures that are sensitive to change over time was a clear recommendation offered by the NMAP (2008) given the robust effect that distributing precise student performance data to teachers has on math achievement (Gersten, Beckmann, et al., 2009). Given recommendations that intervention content should be broken down into small components or skill sets and presented sequentially (e.g., Swanson, 2009), progress monitoring in math requires administration of two different measures in order to examine immediate retention and generalized treatment effects. The first represents the specific skills (using subskill mastery measures) targeted for intervention and is administered daily or according to treatment session, and the second measure represents broader grade-level skills and concepts administered weekly, biweekly, or monthly (Hosp & Ardoin, 2008; Gersten, Beckmann, et al., 2009). The National Center on Intensive Intervention (*www.intensiveintervention.org*) provides lists of and reviews for general outcome (grade-level) and mastery (skill-specific) measures that could be used for monitoring progress. Examples of free access to CBM probes that are already created or can be generated electronically are found at *interventioncentral.org* and *www.otiss.net* (OTISS).

In order to assist educators with the link between subskill mastery measures and intervention we provide three tables that include the subskill area, the recommended administration time, and the mastery criteria according to CBA (see Tables 7.2, 7.3, and 7.4). We also have included decision-making charts that help link the assessment data to specific interventions for early numeracy skills and computation (see Figures 7.1 and 7.2, respectively).

Of course, collecting progress monitoring data becomes more informative and effective when it is used to evaluate the success of an intervention, and adjustments are made according to student responsiveness (Baker et al., 2002; Fuchs, Fuchs, Powell, et al., 2008; Gersten, Chard, et al., 2009). School professionals (including interventionists and teachers) should be provided with detailed information on each student's progress, skill strengths, and weaknesses. When sharing these data with general education teachers it is most useful to offer specific ideas for how core instruction can be adjusted to improve student learning (Baker et al., 2002; Gersten, Chard, et al., 2009). Providing students with their progress monitoring data or asking students to track their own performance is also effective and may improve engagement in the learning process (Codding, Chan-Iannetta, et al., 2011; Codding, Chan-Iannetta, et al., 2009; Gersten, Chard, et al., 2009). Peer modeling, assistance, or presentation of procedures and concepts might also be an important form of feedback provided to students (Baker et al., 2002; Gersten, Chard, et al., 2009; Swanson, 2009). This

TABLE 7.2. Subskills for Number Foundations

Early numeracy assessments by skill area	Assessment	Skill	Time	Mastery
Gateway skills: A foundational piece to understanding quantity is acquiring gateway skills. These include counting skills, number recognition, and writing numbers. These skills are needed to support the development of concepts aligned with number sense such as correspondence, cardinality, and quantitative relationships.	Oral counting	Rote counting	1 minute	80 DCPM
	Number identification	Symbol recognition	1 minute	60 DCPM
	Number writing	Symbol production	1 minute	60 DCPM
Number sense: Students develop skills to describe, compare, and manipulate numbers and their associated quantities. Students expand math-related vocabulary to perform and describe these tasks across contexts.	Missing number	Counting from number	1 minute	20 DCPM
	Quantity discrimination	Number comparison	1 minute	20 DCPM
Number combinations: Students combine gateway and number sense skills, and write and solve basic number sentences to represent the manipulation of quantity.	Number combinations: addition	Addition: Sums to 10	1 minute	20 DCPM
	Number combinations: subtraction	Subtraction: Sums from 10	1 minute	20 DCPM

Note. Reprinted with permission from Brian C. Poncy and Gary Duhon. Copyright © 2016.

TABLE 7.3. Subskills for Basic Facts and Procedural Computation

Probe set	Skill	Problem type(s)	Time	Mastery
Basic fact computation: These single-skill probes consist of basic number combinations.	+	$0 + 0$ to $9 + 9$	1 minute	40 DCPM
	−	$0 - 0$ to $18 - 9$ single-digit answers	1 minute	40 DCPM
	×	0×0 to 9×9	1 minute	40 DCPM
	÷	$0 \div 0$ to $81 \div 9$ single-digit answers	1 minute	40 DCPM
Mixed computation: These probes target a single skill (e.g., addition) and combine operations with the targeted skill.	+	Mixed addition	3 minutes	20 DCPM
	−	Mixed subtraction	3 minutes	20 DCPM
	×	Mixed multiplication	3 minutes	20 DCPM
	÷	Mixed division	3 minutes	20 DCPM

Note. Reprinted with permission from Brian C. Poncy and Gary Duhon. Copyright © 2016.

TABLE 7.4. Subskills for Procedural Computation

Skill		Problem type(s)	Time	Mastery
Multidigit addition	+	3 × 3 digit	2 minutes	20 DCPM
	+	2 × 1 digit with regrouping	2 minutes	20 DCPM
	+	3 × 3 digit with regrouping	2 minutes	20 DCPM
Multidigit subtraction	–	3 × 3 digit	2 minutes	20 DCPM
	–	2 × 1 digit with regrouping	2 minutes	20 DCPM
	–	3 × 3 digit with regrouping	2 minutes	20 DCPM
Multidigit multiplication	×	2 × 1 digit	2 minutes	20 DCPM
	×	4 × 2 digit	2 minutes	20 DCPM
	×	4 × 3 digit	2 minutes	20 DCPM
Multidigit division	÷	3 ÷ 1 digit no remainder	2 minutes	20 DCPM
	÷	3 ÷ 1 digit with remainder	2 minutes	20 DCPM
	÷	3 ÷ 1 digit with decimals	2 minutes	20 DCPM

Note. Reprinted with permission from Brian C. Poncy and Gary Duhon. Copyright © 2016.

evidence might imply that using peer modeling, assistance, or feedback during small-group interventions could be beneficial to all students.

Drill, Practice, and Cumulative Review

Providing sufficient, carefully constructed opportunities for practice along with cumulative review in order to facilitate fluency and retention of previously learned concepts and skills is a longstanding and powerful education tradition (Baker et al., 2002; Baroody, Eiland, et al., 2009; Burns et al., 2006; Codding, Burns, et al., 2011; Daly et al., 2007; Fuchs, Fuchs, Powell, et al., 2008; NMAP, 2008; Powell, Fuchs, Fuchs, Cirino, & Fletcher, 2009; Swanson, 2009). One of the best predictors of maintaining math competency into adulthood is quantity of school-based rehearsal and practice (Bahrick et al., 2013). Some experts have suggested that as much as 70% of instructional time should be allocated to practice activities (Binder, 1996). Students who display math weaknesses or have specific math learning disabilities require more opportunities to practice, and these additional practice opportunities result in achievement gains (Burns et al., 2014; Stickney et al., 2012). Development of effective practice opportunities includes (1) the use of materials that match individual student's instructional level, (2) brief but frequent sessions, and (3) material that is sequenced systematically in small sets and according to student progress (Baroody, Eiland, et al., 2009; Burns et al., 2006; Daly et al., 2007; Fuchs, Fuchs, Powell, et al., 2008; Martens & Eckert, 2007).

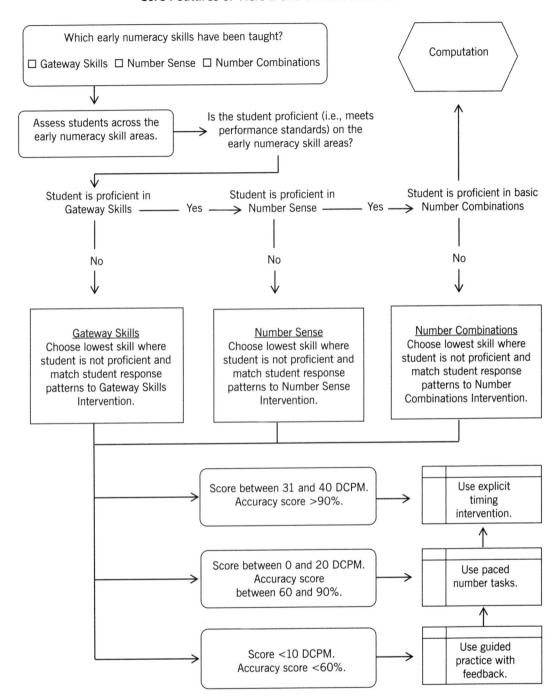

FIGURE 7.1. Flowchart linking early numeracy assessment to intervention. Adapted with permission from Brian C. Poncy and Gary Duhon. Copyright © 2016.

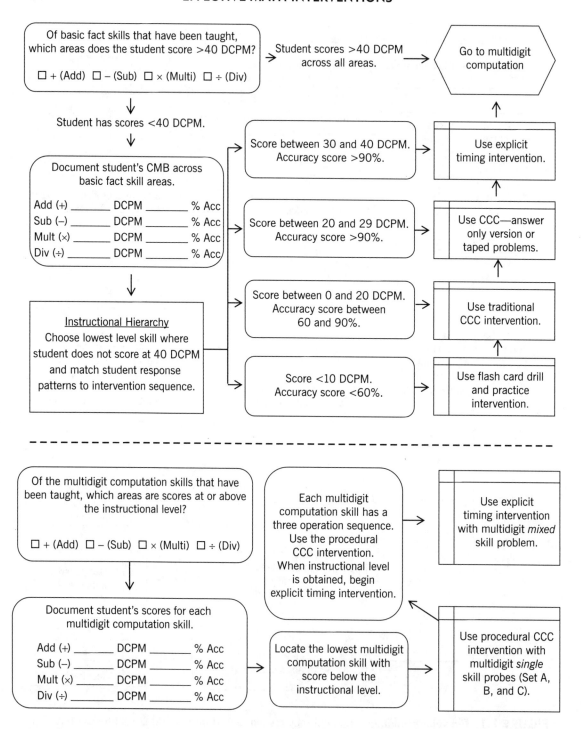

FIGURE 7.2. Flowchart linking computation assessment to intervention. Adapted with permission from Brian C. Poncy and Gary Duhon. Copyright © 2016.

Practice is often described as consisting of four distinct activities—guided practice, drill, practice, and cumulative review—all of which contribute to building acquisition, fluency, maintenance (retention), and generalization (Fuchs, Fuchs, Powell, et al., 2008; Haring & Eaton, 1978). *Guided practice* is often incorporated into interventions and instruction when students are learning a new concept (acquisition stage of skill development; Hudson & Miller, 2006). This form of practice is accomplished when teachers or interventionists lead a practice activity step-by-step as the activity is simultaneously completed by students. While leading the activity, interventionists can verbalize the steps aloud or ask for students to think aloud.

Drill is the practice of individual skills and concepts in isolation (e.g., flash cards) with immediate feedback, errorless learning, and modeling from teachers or peers. Drill is also essential in the acquisition of skill building and may lead to skill fluency because students learn to associate particular problems with their answers and discriminate among problems (Codding, Burns, et al., 2011; Cohen, Servan-Schreiber, & McClelland, 1992; Haring & Eaton, 1978; Symonds & Chase, 1992).

Practice refers to the application of newly acquired knowledge, skills, and concepts in the context of tasks that include previously learned material, such as worksheets containing multiple types of word problems or mixed facts (Daly et al., 2007; Fuchs, Fuchs, Powell, et al., 2008; Haring & Eaton, 1978). When students are working on acquiring new skills or in the early stages of fluency building, practice that incorporates modeling or errorless learning (either student/self- or teacher directed) is necessary (Codding, Burns, et al., 2011). When students are building fluency and working toward retention it is important that students are able to perform the task independently with at least 85% accuracy and at a rate of 14–31 DCPM for grades 2 and 3, or 24–49 DCPM for grades 4 and 5 (Burns et al., 2006, 2010; Gickling & Thompson, 1985). Timed practice with performance feedback on progress toward mastery goal attainment and reinforcement is useful to facilitate fluency as well as retention and generalization (Codding et al., 2007; Codding, Chan-Iannetta, et al., 2009; Rivera & Bryant, 1992).

Cumulative review can take many forms. The purpose is to provide opportunities for the previously subdivided skills and concepts to be combined in order to promote retention and generalization of skills and concepts. Cumulative review might be incorporated into sessions that occur periodically throughout treatment that are devoted to reviewing content combined from two or three previous lessons (Fuchs, Fuchs, & Hollenbeck, 2007; Fuchs, Fuchs, Powell, et al., 2008). Cumulative review activities can also be built into each session, typically at the beginning or end, and consist of review of all previously learned content.

Student Verbalization

Verbalizing thinking may be an important strategy for encouraging students' self-regulation during the problem-solving process (Gersten, Chard, et al., 2009; Swanson, 2009). Students who struggle with math would benefit from explicit instruction that teaches students how to use language to guide problem solving. Therefore, interventionists should foster and model conversations that permit students to explain how they generated their answers or communicate how they are planning to approach solving various types of math problems. Strategy steps for different problem types are usually stated aloud in action terms, such as "Read the problem first, next find the bigger number," and followed by students repeating and completing each step (Kroeger & Kouche, 2006; Tournaki, 2003). In small intervention groups, think-aloud procedures could be modeled by interventionists and practiced by students using choral responding (Codding & Martin, 2016). In their seminal work, Meichenbaum and Goodman (1971) also suggested that modeling of and practice with self-statements such as "Work slowly and follow the steps," help students focus attention to the task, prevent impulsive responding, and manage frustration.

Visual Representation

Strategic use of visual representation along with concrete manipulatives and practice with numerals is important for promoting math knowledge (Flores, 2009, 2010; Gersten, Chard, et al., 2009; Miller & Mercer, 1993b; Mercer & Miller, 1992b; Swanson, 2009). Although the use of manipulatives (e.g., counters, chips, and blocks) to illustrate early math concepts is not new, current recommendations suggest that the same math concept be illustrated sequentially using concrete examples, visual representations, and abstract numerical symbols (Baroody, Bajwa, et al., 2009). For example, Mercer and Miller (1992b) found that students with math learning disabilities benefited from independent number combinations practice with concrete manipulatives an average of three times before practicing the same concept using visual displays (e.g., pictures of objects, tally marks, number lines/paths, arrays, strip diagrams, and/or ten frames). Once students are able to independently and accurately solve problems using visual representations, practice with the numerals is initiated (Flores, 2010). A critical aspect of this progression is that the use of manipulatives is brief and faded in order to advance toward visual representations, which serve as an intermediate step, and then on to abstract symbols (i.e., numerals). The benefits of using visual representations might be most apparent when they are specific rather than general and students are directed to use visual representations that are appropriate for solving different math tasks (Gersten, Chard, et al., 2009). For example, number lines provide a useful conceptual illustration of addition and subtraction by linking counting principles (i.e., counting up and counting down) and magnitude comparisons. Place value can be represented by ten frames or drawings using base-ten principles, and fractions can be illustrated by strip diagrams.

Motivation and Reinforcement

Students with math learning difficulties often experience challenges initiating and persisting with problem solving. Including motivation strategies into an intervention package may help encourage students' active engagement in math activities (Gersten, Beckmann, et al., 2009; NMAP, 2008). Interventionists can provide reinforcement for effort (e.g., how hard a student worked to solve or attempt to solve a problem), persistence (e.g., sticking with a problem-solving task through all the steps), task completion, and/or skill improvement (Gersten, Chard, et al., 2009). Reinforcement might consist of (1) specific praise by using statements such as "I like how you are checking your work and following each problem-solving step" (Schunk & Cox, 1986); (2) tokens or points that are exchanged for prizes from a treasure chest (see Form 7.2; Fuchs et al., 2005; Fuchs, Fuchs, Craddock, et al., 2008); and/or (3) goal setting (Schunk, 1985; Fuchs, Fuchs, Hamlett, Katazaroff, & Dutka, 1997; Fuchs, Fuchs, Karns, et al., 1997; Codding, Chan-Iannetta, et al., 2009; Codding, Chan-Iannetta, et al., 2011).

CONCLUSION

Students experience numerous types of difficulties with whole-number knowledge. We described three central areas—(1) early numeracy, (2) computation, and (3) word-problem solving—that are important to address through carefully constructed interventions. Although there are only a few commercially available math interventions with proven evidence of effectiveness, school professionals can evaluate existing interventions or create their own interventions according to eight key empirically supported features.

Checklist for Evaluating Interventions for Key Evidence-Based Features

	Present	Partially Present	Absent
1. Content is provided using explicit instruction.			
a. Interventionist models rules, concepts, and principles.			
b. Interventionist demonstrates step-by-step plans for problem solving.			
c. Tasks are divided into separate skills or steps and taught accordingly.			
2. Strategy instruction is incorporated.			
a. Instruction includes a discussion of why strategies are helpful for which types of problems.			
b. Interventionist provides reminders and prompts to apply particular strategies or procedures to the problem-solving process.			
c. Interventionist encourages students to check their work and discuss whether the strategy that was applied was effective.			
3. Instruction is sequenced.			
a. Instruction begins at an appropriate level of challenge (e.g., instructional level).			
b. Content is divided into small units that are ordered sequentially targeting prerequisite skills first.			
c. Mastery criteria for each small unit is provided.			
d. Only small amounts of new material are presented each lesson.			
e. Assistance of the interventionist gradually fades as students master each subskill or small unit.			
f. The range of examples increases as prerequisite skills are mastered in order to broaden application of subskills.			
4. Progress monitoring and feedback are embedded.			
a. Student performance on each small unit or subskill is monitored daily (or each session) with an assessment tool sensitive to change.			
b. Grade-level skills are monitored weekly, biweekly, or monthly.			

(continued)

	Present	Partially Present	Absent
c. Criteria for mastery are provided for each type of progress monitoring tool.			
d. Students are given opportunities to track or view their performance.			
e. Recommendations are provided for the interventionist to determine whether students should progress to the next skill or unit, revisit a previous skill or unit, or terminate the intervention.			
f. Troubleshooting recommendations are provided.			
5. Drill, practice, and cumulative review activities are included.			
a. Guided practice is incorporated into lessons when students are learning new material.			
b. Drill (practice of skills in isolation) activities that include errorless learning, modeling, and immediate feedback are incorporated to build accuracy with new material.			
c. Practice that embedded newly learned with previously learned material is included.			
d. Opportunities for timed practice is provided to build fluency.			
e. Cumulative review sessions or activities are incorporated to bridge subdivided skills or concepts.			
6. Student verbalization of the problem-solving process is modeled and encouraged.			
a. Interventionist models and explicitly teaches students how to use verbalizations and language.			
b. Students are given opportunities to practice using verbalizations.			
7. Visual representations are used.			
a. Interventionist teaches students how to use visual representations.			
b. Interventionist provides opportunities for students to use concrete manipulatives, visual representations, and numerals with the same concept.			
c. Visual representations are specific to problem types.			
8. Reinforcement is provided.			
a. Reinforcement is provided for effort, initiation, persistence, or skill improvement.			
b. Reinforcement includes praise, points/tokens, prizes, and/or goal setting.			
c. Interventionist provides specific reinforcement to students consistently.			

FORM 7.2

Five Frames for Reinforcement

5 stickers = trade in for

5 stickers = trade in for

CHAPTER 8

Early Numeracy Interventions

This chapter provides a brief introduction to the meaning of number sense with an emphasis on counting and cardinality, as well as magnitude comparison, followed by descriptions of commercially available or free research-supported interventions.

WHAT IS NUMBER SENSE?

Early numeracy competencies necessary for learning require that students recognize the relationship among numerals (e.g., 8), number words (e.g., *eight*), and the quantities they represent (Geary, 2011b). Number sense is acquired both informally, through interactions with family members and/or caregivers, and formally, via school (Geary, 2013; Gersten & Chard, 1999). There is no one agreed-upon definition of number sense, and some conceptualizations of number sense contain as many as 30 components (Berch, 2005). Box 8.1 summarizes five components of number sense (Geary, 2013; Gersten et al., 2005; Kalchman et al., 2001).

The two central elements of number sense with implications for school-based interventions are strategic counting and magnitude comparison (Gersten, Clarke, & Jordan, 2007; Jordan, Kaplan, Oláh, & Locuniak, 2006). Experts suggest that by age 6 children assemble their knowledge of counting principles and magnitude comparison into a mental number line (Geary, 2011a, 2011b; Kalchman et al., 2001).

BOX 8.1. Definition of Number Sense	
Component	**Example**
The understanding of numerals as symbols (e.g., 1, 2, 3) that map on to quantities.	1 = •; 2 = ••; and 3 = •••.
Fluent and flexible use of numbers.	Easily composes (2 + 2 = 4) and decomposes numbers (5 = 3 + 2, 4 + 1); transitions quickly between quantities and numerals (••• + 2 = 5).
Proficiency with quantity comparisons (e.g., Which is more? Which is less?).	9 > 8; •• < ••••.
Mental representation of numbers.	Knowing that the numeral 3 represents three objects (•••) is systematically ordered between 2 and 4, and represents one more than 2 automatically, perhaps through construction of a mental number line. 0 1 2 3 4 5
Ability to recognize errors or unreasonable solutions to problems.	5 + 6 = 9 cannot be true because 5 + 6 is larger than 10 (5 + 5 + 1 = 10).

Counting and Cardinality

Knowing how to count, understanding the counting principles, and being able to strategically use counting to solve math problems is linked to the development of math reasoning as well as arithmetic performance (Geary, 2011a, 2011b; Gersten et al., 2007). Computation begins with counting (Kilpatrick et al., 2001; Wu, 2011). Addition and multiplication, for example, represent a means to simplify counting. Through counting children understand that each successive number within a string of numbers (e.g., 1, 2, 3, 4, 5) is one more than the previous number (Le Corre & Carey, 2007; Sarnecka & Carey, 2008). Children recognize when given the problem $3 + 1 = x$, for example, that the answer, 4, is the same as the number after 3 when they count aloud ("One, two, three, four. Four comes after three"). This is referred to as the *number-after* rule, which represents a connection between the counting sequence and $n + 1$ number combinations (Baroody, Eiland, et al., 2009). Children who are able to count efficiently and understand the cardinality principle are also able to detect errors in their own counting and make adjustments to fix their mistakes (e.g., Le Corre, Van de Walle, Brannon, & Carey, 2006; Wynn, 1992). Strategic counting extends these counting skills by providing a foundation for the commutative (e.g., 4 + 5 = 5 + 4) and associative (e.g., [2 + 6] + 1 = 2 + [6 + 1]) laws and likely facilitates automaticity with number combinations (Baroody, Eiland, et al., 2009; Jordan et al., 2003a).

Counting Skills

Young children count objects in a collection by assigning them a unique numeral and understanding that the last number they come to is the sum of the collection. There is also evidence that grouping small sets of items occurs spontaneously in young children (Clements, 1999; Le

Corre & Carey, 2007). Even infants can identify a group of up to four items instantly (this is called *subitizing*). When 4- and 5-year-olds are presented with a story problem orally—such as "If you have four cookies and I give you two more, how many do you have all together?"— most children will respond with a number greater than four, although usually not the correct number (Griffin, 2003; Griffin & Case, 1997). These children can recognize that adding items to a set makes it larger than either part, demonstrating some initial understanding of part–whole relationships (Baroody, Eiland, et al., 2009). When large sets of objects are encountered, counting is required to determine how many total objects are present (Jordan et al., 2010). Counting requires children to use one-to-one correspondence to provide number word tags to each object. Children must also understand that number word tags have a stable order such that they can count in order from one, and also know that the last number in the set represents the total number of objects (i.e., cardinality).

Table 8.1 displays core counting skills. Before entering kindergarten, most children understand the basic counting principles (Baroody & Gatzke, 1991; Gelman & Gallistel, 1978):

1. One-to-one correspondence between verbal labels and objects ("one" = •, "two" = ••, and "three" = •••).
2. Stable order such that verbal labels (or tags) "one, two, three" are always represented in that order, with one coming before two, and two coming before three.
3. Cardinality (i.e., knowing that the last number counted in an array represents the total number of items).
4. Automatically recognize the number of items in a set when presented with, for example, an array of dots (•••), and can estimate which number array is larger (•••• vs. ••).

Strategic Counting

Once students understand how to count sequentially, usually by the start of kindergarten, instruction should focus on helping children learn to use various counting strategies (Gersten et al., 2007; Siegler, 1988). Strategic counting tends to unfold in stages for children without math difficulties (see Figure 8.1; Butterworth, 2005; Griffin, 2003). Rudimentary counting strategies such as *counting all* reflect younger children's tendency to solve the problem 2 + 3 by raising two fingers on one hand and three fingers on the other hand, and then counting all objects from one (Butterworth, 2005). *Counting on from first* is more efficient because rather than visualizing both sets of quantities using their fingers, children will start counting from the first addend. In the problem 2 + 3, students will count on from "two" and use their fingers to represent "three, four, five." The *min* strategy, which is also referred to as the *counting on* strategy, represents a more efficient counting strategy that is commonly demonstrated by 5- and 6-year-old children (Griffin, 2003). The min strategy is an essential form of counting during which children, when presented with a problem such as $3 + 2 = x$, recognize the larger quantity (3) and count up by the other addend (2). When the problem is presented in the reverse order, $2 + 3 = x$, children recognize that it is easier

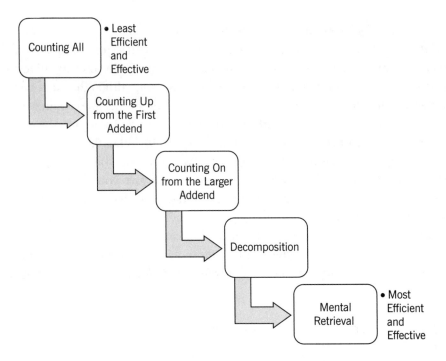

FIGURE 8.1. Pathway to automaticity.

to begin counting from 3. Use of the min strategy requires children to recognize the number of items in a set, determine which of the two numbers is larger, provide the appropriate number word label, be able to count reliably in order from any starting point, and recognize that the subsequent number in a set increases by one (Baroody, Eiland, et al., 2009; Gersten & Chard, 1999; Griffin, 2003). Children can also learn to count up from the subtrahend (5 − 3 = x) to solve subtraction problems (Fuson & Fuson, 1992).

More advanced strategies rely on children combining rules that were previously learned. These strategies might be displayed by children at the end of kindergarten or in first grade (Sarama & Clements, 2009). The *counting down* strategy for subtraction (4 − 1 = x) requires that children start with the larger number and count backward to get the answer, which helps to illustrate the $n − 1$ number combinations. Therefore, children must know the number that comes before a given minuend. *Decomposition* strategies make use of children's knowledge that numbers are made of two parts (part–part–whole relations; Baroody & Gannon, 1984). For example, the *doubles + 1* decomposition strategy encourages children to use their knowledge of previously learned doubles facts (e.g., 2 + 2 = 4) to solve novel problems such as 2 + 3 (e.g., = 2 + 2 + 1; Woodward, 2006). During the *make-ten* strategy, students will solve a complex addition problem, 8 + 9 = x, by separating 8 into its parts (7 + 1) to more easily compute the answer (7 + 1 + 9 = 7 + 10 = 17; Cheng, 2012; Fuson & Kwon, 1992).

The use of number words along with objects is useful to help children practice strategic counting and can also assist them with understanding part–whole relations (Baroody,

Bajwa, et al., 2009). For example, when students are given five counting cubes, they can compose and decompose the cubes to represent different number combinations (e.g., four cubes and one cube is five cubes, five cubes take away one cube is four cubes, two cubes and three cubes is five cubes). Using concrete manipulatives can facilitate children's recognition of common patterns. For example, students may recognize that a number set remains unchanged when no blocks are removed, but the number set increases when two blocks are added.

Children experiencing math difficulties often use immature counting strategies such as guessing or lining up two sets of items, and/or rudimentary counting strategies such as solving an addition problem by counting all the objects from one using their fingers (Mazzocco, Devlin, & McKenney, 2008). Interventionists should make sure that students possess basic counting skills and are able to count on from the larger addend (the min strategy), which is the more efficient form of strategic counting. It is also important that children are able to recognize numerals and match numerals to their quantities so that strategic counting can progress from number words and objects to the use of numerals (Gersten et al., 2007).

Magnitude Comparison

Magnitude comparison builds upon the foundational informal skill subitizing (i.e., automatic recognition of a quantity of objects) and results in discrimination of two sets of objects or pictures of objects. Children subsequently learn to connect numerals to the object or pictorial representation of it—understanding, for example, that seven is bigger than four, and later are able to determine that seven is three greater than four (Gersten & Chard, 1999). Numerical quantity discrimination among numbers that are farther apart (e.g., nine vs. one) is easier for children to recognize initially than those that are closer together (e.g., three vs. four); this phenomenon is known as the *distance effect* (Wilson, Dahaene, Dubois, & Fayol, 2009). Students entering kindergarten may understand numerical quantity comparisons like knowing which numeral is bigger when given a set of two (5, 2), and be able to describe the distance between the numbers ("Five is three bigger than two"); may know only that five is greater than two but not by how many; and may have to use their fingers or objects to determine which numeral is bigger (Claessens et al., 2014; Gersten & Chard, 1999; Siegler, 1988). In essence, children develop a mental number line to represent whole numbers and the relationships between them (Gersten & Chard, 1999; Jordan et al., 2006).

As students progress through early schooling more mental number line representations are generated (e.g., counting by 2's, 5's, 10's), and double-digit number combinations begin to be conceptualized using number lines for 10's and 1's (Kalchman et al., 2001). Some experts suggest that number line estimates for numbers 0–100 and 0–1,000 occur in second and fourth grades, respectively (Siegler & Ramani, 2009). Number line representations in preschool- and elementary school-age children are related to the use of more sophisticated counting strategies and predict performance on arithmetic combinations (Booth & Seigler, 2008).

RESEARCH-SUPPORTED INTERVENTIONS

How early in schooling should math supports be implemented? We previously discussed that if a school is collecting universal screening data, then interventions should be provided shortly after identifying which students fall into the at-risk range. However, for kindergarten students, some experts recommend that math interventions *not be* introduced until midyear in order to appropriately capture the students most in need of additional support (Jordan et al., 2007). This suggestion is rooted in research that shows some children who enter kindergarten with low number knowledge show moderate gains by midyear just by being exposed to the core curriculum (Jordan et al., 2007). In subsequent grades, interventions should begin as soon as a concern is identified through multiple sources of data (e.g., universal screening tools, review of permanent products, teacher interviews).

Unfortunately, there are only a handful of interventions that are available that address early numeracy skills. In the absence of accessibility to the interventions described below, interventionists could generate their own strategies by (1) examining the prerequisite skill list in Table 8.1 to identify the skills to assess and target for intervention and (2) applying the eight recommended intervention components from Chapter 7: (1) explicit instruction; (2) strategy instruction; (3) sequencing instruction; (4) ongoing progress monitoring and feedback; (5) drill, practice, and cumulative review; (6) student verbalization; (7) visual representation; and (8) motivation and reinforcement.

The interventions described below are delivered in four different formats: (1) individual tutoring, (2) small-group tutoring, (3) CAI, or (4) a combination of small-group tutoring and CAI. Recommendations for the amount of time each of these treatments should be administered varies widely from 15 minutes twice weekly for 3 weeks (per student), to 30 minutes daily (small groups of five students) for 15 weeks, or 30 minutes weekly for 30 weeks (per student). Figure 8.2 illustrates the amount of total minutes required to be allocated to the intervention according to our recommendations and considering student group size.

Curriculum content for these interventions falls into two categories. The first category represents intervention programs with a specific focus on one early numeracy foundational skill, such as numerical representations on number lines (see Table 8.2). Also in this category are programs that target specific missing foundational number skills using placement tests. The second category represents the integration of key early number concepts along with broader whole-number knowledge concepts and activities (see Table 8.3). Figure 8.3 illustrates whether these interventions might be applied to students in the acquisition or fluency stages of skill development.

Specific Interventions Targeting Number Foundations

The Great Race

The Great Race (Ramani, Hitti, & Siegler, 2012; Ramani & Siegler, 2008; Siegler & Ramani, 2009) is an intervention that encourages direct instruction of number lines in the form of board games designed in a linear, horizontal format (see Appendix 8.1). The game manual

TABLE 8.1. Counting Skills

Concept	Description	Sample skill hierarchy
Subitizing	• Instantly seeing the total number of objects or pictures presented without counting.	• Instantly recognize a number quantity within 5 when presented in a number array or with objects. • Instantly recognize a number quantity within 10 when presented in a number array or with objects.
Magnitude comparison	• Determining whether one group of objects or a numeral is the same as, less than, or more than another group of objects or a numeral.	• Identify whether objects in one group are <, >, or = to objects in another group. • Identify whether written numerals (e.g., 0–10; 0–20; 0–100; 0–1,000) are <, >, or =. • Identify numbers on the number line when all numbers are presented. • Identify where a number belongs on the number line when the number line is only partially labeled.
Counting	• Stable order. • Learn patterns of number words. • Successive number names refer to larger quantities.	• Verbal counting by 1's from 1 to 20. • Verbal counting forward from a number other than 1. • Verbal counting by 1's from 1 to 30. • Ordinal position counting 1st to 10th. • Skip counting by 10's from 10 to 100. • Verbal counting backward from 10 to 0. • Verbal counting by 1's from 1 to 100. • Skip counting from 2; 5; 100; 1,000. • Verbal counting by 1's from 100 to 999.
Cardinality	• One-to-one correspondence. • Last number in a set is the total number of objects counted.	• Counting one group of visually represented objects (e.g., pictures, drawings, lines). • Counting more than two groups of visually represented objects (e.g., pictures, drawings, lines). • Count up to 20 objects arranged in a row. • Count up to 20 objects arranged in an array. • Count up to 20 objects arranged in a circle. • Count up to 10 objects in a scattered configuration. • Given a numeral from 0 to 20 and count out the corresponding number of objects.
Numeral identification	• Matching the correct number word with the numeral. • Writing numerals. • Matching numerals to quantities.	• Verbally matching the correct number word when given numerals (0–10; 0–20; 0–100). • Writing numerals (0–10; 0–20; 0–100). • Writing the numeral that corresponds to the number of objects presented.
Part–part–whole relations	• Seeing quantities as being made up of two parts. • Putting two parts together (composing). • Separating numbers or sets of quantities into parts (decomposing).	• Put together all possibilities of two sets of objects or pictures for quantities 2–10. • Separate sets of objects or pictures into two parts for quantities 2–10. • Recognize that numbers 11–19 represent one group of 10 and 1, 2, 3, 4, 5, 6, 7, 8, 9 are singles (1's). • Compose and decompose sets of pictures or objects larger than 10 into groups (10's) and singles (1's). • Make 10 using combinations of numerals 1–9.

Note. See the following references for more information: Baroody, Eiland, and Thompson (2009); Cheng (2012); Gersten, Clarke, and Jordan (2007); Sarama and Clements (2006); Stein, Kinder, Silbert, and Carnine (2006).

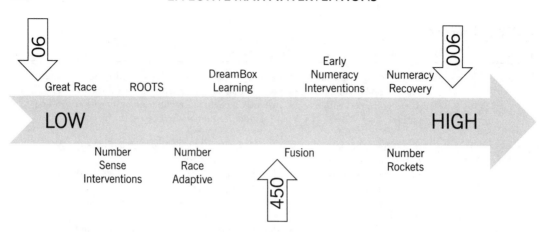

FIGURE 8.2. Intervention intensity considering the ratio of total minutes to the number of students (i.e., total duration the intervention was implemented, in number of minutes, divided by the number of students served simultaneously). For example, Roots is implemented in small groups of 5 for 16 total weeks, 3 times weekly, for 20 minutes each session (16 × 3 = 48 sessions; 48 sessions × 20 minutes each session = 1,045 total minutes; 960 total minutes/5 students = 192 minutes each student).

is available for free at *www.education.umd.edu/HDQM/labs/Ramani/Documents/The%20 Great%20Race_Teacher%20Manual.pdf.* The horizontal box is divided into equal squares that are consecutively numbered from 1 to 10. Each child receives a player piece and begins his or her turn with a spinner divided into two sections labeled with the numerals 1 and 2 to indicate whether he or she moves either one or two spaces along the game board. Game completion ranges from 2 to 4 minutes, permitting the game to be played as many as five times per session. This intervention was designed to be delivered individually between a student and/or a tutor for 15 minutes each session once or twice per week for a total of 2–3 weeks. The small-group version of the intervention includes three students and one tutor, administered 25 minutes per session, with each game lasting between 5 and 7 minutes. Preliminary evidence for this treatment has been illustrated with preschool students and delivered by researchers. The Great Race improved the accuracy of number identification, number line estimation, counting, magnitude comparison, and arithmetic for children who played the game compared with those who did not play the game (Ramani & Siegler, 2008; Siegler & Ramani, 2009). Intervention effects remained after 9 weeks. A variation of this game, called Race to Space, was recently generated for kindergarten students targeting numerals 0–100 arranged on a 10 × 10 matrix according to base-ten construction (Laski & Siegler, 2014). The blue hue of the background color of the game board gradually darkens as the numerals increase, providing a visual cue for number magnitude. The spinner for this game contains five sections labeled with numerals 1–5. The game was played twice per session with each session lasting an average of 25 minutes. Sessions were conducted twice weekly for 2 weeks. Positive effects were generated for number line estimation, numerical position encoding, and correct use of the counting on strategy. Forms 8.1–8.4 provide sample game boards and spinners for The Great Race and Race to Space.

TABLE 8.2. Specific Interventions That Target Number Foundations

	The Great Race	Number Race Adaptive Software	Numeracy Recovery
Treatment component	• Progress monitoring and feedback • Drill, practice, review • Visual representations	• Sequenced instruction • Progress monitoring and feedback • Drill, practice, review • Visual representations • Reinforcement	• Explicit instruction • Sequenced instruction • Progress monitoring and feedback • Drill, practice, review • Visual representations
Level of skill proficiency	• Fluency	• Fluency	• Acquisition
References	• <5 studies • Conducted by program authors	• <5 studies • Conducted by program authors	• <5 studies • Conducted by program authors
Grades	• PreK–K	• PreK–3	• K–2
Target skills	• Counting • Number line • Numeral identification	• Magnitude comparison • Number line • Numeral identification • Number combinations	• Counting • Part–whole • Numeral identification • Number combinations • Problem solving
Interventionist	• Paraprofessional	• Student	• General ed teacher
Effect size	• Moderate	• Small	• Small • Moderate
Cost of materials	• Free	• Free	• Unknown
Reviewed by educational clearinghouses	• No	• No	• No

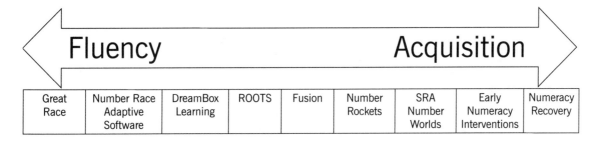

Great Race	Number Race Adaptive Software	DreamBox Learning	ROOTS	Fusion	Number Rockets	SRA Number Worlds	Early Numeracy Interventions	Numeracy Recovery

FIGURE 8.3. Applying interventions to the instructional hierarchy.

TABLE 8.3. Broad Interventions That Target Whole-Number Knowledge

	DreamBox Learning	Early Numeracy Interventions	focusMATH Intensive Intervention	Fusion	Number Rockets	Number Sense Interventions	Roots	SRA Number Worlds with Building Blocks
Treatment component	• Sequenced instruction • Progress monitoring and feedback • Drill, practice, review • Visual representations • Reinforcement	• Explicit instruction • Strategy instruction • Sequenced instruction • Progress monitoring and feedback • Drill, practice, review • Visual representations • Reinforcement	• Explicit instruction • Strategy instruction • Sequenced instruction • Progress monitoring and feedback • Drill, practice, review • Visual representations • Reinforcement	• Explicit instruction • Sequenced instruction • Progress monitoring and feedback • Drill, practice, review	• Explicit instruction • Sequenced instruction • Progress monitoring and feedback • Drill, practice, review • Visual representations • Reinforcement	• Explicit instruction • Sequenced instruction • Drill, practice, review • Visual representations	• Explicit instruction • Sequenced instruction • Progress monitoring and feedback • Drill, practice, review • Visual representations • Reinforcement	• Explicit instruction • Strategy instruction • Sequenced instruction • Progress monitoring and feedback • Drill, practice, review • Visual representations
Level of skill proficiency	• Fluency	• Acquisition	• Acquisition	• Acquisition • Fluency	• Acquisition • Fluency	• Acquisition • Fluency	• Acquisition • Fluency	• Acquisition • Fluency • Generalization
References	• <5 studies • Conducted by program authors	• <5 studies • Conducted by program authors	• <5 studies • Conducted by program authors	• <5 studies • Conducted by program authors	• <5 studies • Conducted by program authors	• <5 studies • Conducted by program authors	• <5 studies • Conducted by program authors	• 5–10 studies • Conducted by program authors
Grades	• K–2	• 1	• K–6	• 1	• 1	• K	• K	• PreK–8
Target skills	• Counting • Number line • Part–whole • Number combinations	• Counting • Magnitude comparison • Part–whole • Number combinations • Problem solving	• Counting • Magnitude comparison • Part–whole • Number combinations • Problem solving	• Number line • Part–whole • Numeral identification • Number combinations • Problem solving	• Counting • Magnitude comparison • Part–whole • Numeral identification • Number combinations	• Subitizing • Counting • Magnitude comparison • Number line • Part–whole • Numeral identification	• Counting • Part–whole • Number combinations	• Subitizing • Counting • Magnitude comparison • Part–whole • Number combinations

					• Number combinations • Problem solving			
Interventionist	• Student	• Para-professional	• Para-professional	• Para-professional	• General ed teacher • Special ed teacher • Math specialist • Para-professional	• University student	• Para-professional	• Para-professional
Effect size	• Small	• Small • Moderate	• Small • Moderate	• Large	• Moderate	• Moderate	• Small	• Moderate • Large
Cost of materials	• Other: $20/student/year	• $150–$300	• Other: $4.60–$33.94/student; teacher manual $84.97–$127.97	• $150–$350	• <$150	• <$150	• $150–$350	• Other: contact sales representative
Reviewed by educational clearinghouse	• What Works Clearinghouse	• National Center on Intensive Intervention	• National Center on Intensive Intervention	• National Center on Intensive Intervention	• Blueprints for Healthy Youth Development • Institute for Education Sciences Regional Education Laboratory • National Center on Intensive Intervention	• None	• National Center on Intensive Intervention	• None

Number Race Adaptive Game

The Number Race Adaptive Game (Wilson et al., 2009; Wilson, Dehaene, et al., 2006; Wilson, Revkin, Cohen, Cohen, & Dehaene, 2006) is a software program, available for free at *http://sourceforge.net/projects/numberrace*, which follows the same conceptual basis as The Great Race. Students are presented with a task, such as number comparison, for which they are required to choose the larger of two quantities of treasures presented symbolically (i.e., numerals or number word) or nonsymbolically (i.e., dot arrays). Following their selection, students receive feedback in all three formats: numeral, number word, and dot array. The program varies in difficulty level, adapting to individual student needs, by alternating numerical distance (e.g., decreasing difference between dot arrays and numerals from large to small), time permitted for response selection, and conceptual complexity (e.g., decrease ratio of nonsymbolic to symbolic information, adding and subtracting quantities). The program was administered for 15 minutes daily per week for 3 weeks; teachers served as supervisors. Preliminary evidence showed improvement in number comparisons compared with a control group but was not maintained (Räsänen, Salminen, Wilson, Aunio, & Dehaene, 2009).

Numeracy Recovery

Numeracy Recovery (Dowker, 2001) is an individualized intervention designed for students ages 5–8 and is available from the author. The intervention was designed to be administered by a classroom teacher once weekly across 30 weeks for 30 minutes per session. Primary classroom teachers were able to administer this intervention by adding other school professionals, such as teaching assistants, into the classroom to work with students who were not receiving the intervention. Core concepts are delivered and practiced through the use of counters, verbalization, object sorting and recording, exposure to and practice with the same problem delivered in different forms, sequenced presentation of a small set of basic facts, and number games. Students do not necessarily receive intervention across the entire sequence of number concepts, but rather the component that a student is missing serves as the target of the intervention, which is determined by results from a numeracy screening tool.

Preliminary research evidence found that students who received this treatment package for 30 weeks demonstrated improvement on three different standardized tests that assessed number skills, number operations, and arithmetic (Dowker, 2007). The intervention authors reported that the positive effects of the intervention were maintained 1 year after the treatment ended. Qualitative feedback from teachers reported enjoying the opportunity to individually work with students and that students enjoyed the intervention.

Broad Interventions Targeting Whole-Number Knowledge

DreamBox Learning

DreamBox Learning© is an online learning program that tailors the computer activities (e.g., games, visual representations, virtual manipulatives) to students' instructional levels. It is available for purchase at *www.dreambox.com*. This program is administered individually for a minimum of 90 minutes weekly via computer technology. Supervision of the program use by an adult is recommended. Although no peer-reviewed articles were located for this intervention, a technical report meeting criteria from What Works Clearinghouse was available (Wang & Woodworth, 2011). This report indicated that students who used Dream-Box Learning outperformed students who did not on a broad measure of math achievement across kindergarten and first grades (Wang & Woodworth, 2011).

Early Numeracy Interventions

This CCSS-aligned intervention, designed by Bryant and colleagues (Bryant et al., 2011; Bryant, Bryant, Gersten, Scammacca, & Chavez, 2008; D. P. Bryant, Bryant, Gersten, Scammacca, Funk, et al., 2008; Bryant, Pfannenstiel, & Bryant, 2014), is available from Psycho-Educational Services (*www.psycho-educational.com/mathematics/#*). It addresses the needs of first-grade students at risk for math difficulties, or other students in elementary school performing at a first-grade level. The intervention package is delivered 3 or 4 days weekly for 25–30 minutes across 19–20 total weeks in small groups of four to five students. This program can be implemented by paraprofessionals, provides a scripted training manual, and requires a half day of formal training. Implementation of the intervention during research studies was good—training occurred before each unit accompanied by weekly follow-up support—technical support can be obtained, if necessary, from Psycho-Educational Services. Students receiving the treatment package outperformed students in the comparison group on targeted measures, including place value, number sequences, and number combinations (adding and subtracting), as well as broader computation measures (Bryant et al., 2011).

focusMATH Intensive Intervention

focusMATH© is commercially available at *www.pearsonschool.com/focusmath*, and is designed to be used in kindergarten through sixth grade to address number sense, computation, and problem-solving skills. This intervention is intended to be delivered individually or in small groups of six to eight students. Intervention implementation is 45–60 minutes per session, three to five times weekly, for 4–6 weeks for each unit workbook. A detailed teacher's manual is required to deliver the intervention, although formal training is not required and no content-specific qualifications are required by interventionists. Preliminary research has been conducted only with third and fifth grades but demonstrated that students receiving this intervention made significant gains in multiplication and division operations in third grade (Styers & Baird-Wilkerson, 2011). In fifth grade, gains were observed in numeration, addition, and subtraction, as well as mental computation and estimation.

Fusion

Fusion (Clarke et al., 2013), also referred to as Whole Number Foundations Level 1, is a recently developed intervention designed for first-grade students who are at risk for math difficulties, and is available for purchase at *https://dibels.uoregon.edu/market/movingup/*

firstfoundation. Treatment sessions are intended to be implemented with small groups of three to five students for 30 minutes across 4 or 5 days each week for a total of 15 weeks. A paraprofessional can implement this intervention by using a scripted manual, two half-day trainings, and ongoing follow-up support. Preliminary evidence found that students receiving this intervention perform better than students who do not on a measure aligned with the program (Clarke, Doabler, Strand Cary, Kosty, Baker, et al., 2014).

Number Rockets

Number Rockets (Fuchs, Paulsen, & Fuchs, n.d.) is a treatment package designed for first grade that includes individual or small-group tutoring and optional computer practice (Mac products only). The program is commercially available at *http://vkc.mc.vanderbilt.edu/ numberrockets*. Treatment sessions are designed to be 40 minutes in length, provided three times weekly for 16 weeks (Fuchs et al., 2005; Fuchs, Fuchs, & Hollenbeck, 2007). Thirty minutes of each session are devoted to tutoring in groups of two to three students, and 10 minutes at the end of each session is reserved for computation practice that may occur using a computer program called Math Flash or with paper and pencil (Fuchs, Hamlett, & Powell, 2003). Certified teachers or paraprofessionals can administer the program using a scripted manual, following participation in one full training; weekly follow-up support is available. Research findings show improvement on targeted measures of performance, including computation, concepts and application, and story problems tasks for students receiving the intervention who outperformed students not receiving treatment (Fuchs et al., 2005).

Number Sense Interventions

The Number Sense Interventions program (Jordan & Dyson, 2014) is designed to be used independently or with the Number Sense Screener™ (Jordan & Glutting, 2012). Number Sense Interventions is aligned with the CCSS and addresses early numeracy topics such as counting to 100, recognizing quantities and numerals, and writing numerals, as well as solving story problems and written equations. It is available for purchase at *http://products. brookespublishing.com/Number-Sense-Interventions-P695.aspx*. This program was developed for use with kindergarteners at risk for math difficulties (Tier 2 within an RTI framework) and contains 24 scripted lessons, photocopied materials, flash cards, charts, and activity sheets. The program is implemented over 8 weeks in 30-minute sessions delivered 3 days weekly in small groups of four students. University undergraduate and graduate students administered the program, making it unclear how feasible it is for typical school professionals to administer. Training was conducted in group sessions and consisted of didactic and practice components. It is unclear how much total time the training required. Results from existing studies demonstrated that students participating in different iterations of the intervention program outperformed students in control groups on measures of number sense, arithmetic fluency, and calculation (Dyson, Jordan, Beliakoff, & Hassinger-Das, 2015; Dyson, Jordan, & Glutting, 2013; Jordan, Glutting, Dyson, Hassinger-Das, & Irwin, 2012).

ROOTS

ROOTS (Clarke, Smolkowski, et al., 2011), also referred to as the Whole Number Foundations Level K, is the kindergarten companion to Fusion. ROOTS targets early numeracy topics such as counting, cardinality, and magnitude comparison and is available for purchase at *https://dibels.uoregon.edu/market/movingup/kfoundation*. The program is designed for use with small groups of students (approximately five) who are determined to be at risk for greater math difficulties. There are 50 total lessons and treatment sessions designed to last 16–20 weeks when two to three sessions are delivered each week. Each treatment session lasts about 20 minutes. Instructional assistants representing a range of educational backgrounds (high school graduates, associate's and bachelors' degrees) and experience (i.e., 1–10 or more years) administered the program, suggesting that a wide range of professionals and paraprofessionals can deliver the program using the scripted lessons and activities. Training constitutes two half-day workshops and ongoing consultation support. Research findings suggest that this intervention benefited students' early math abilities compared with controls; the achievement gap between students receiving ROOTS and their typical peers was reduced (Clarke et al., 2016).

SRA Number Worlds

The SRA Number Worlds© intervention, designed by Sharon Griffin, Douglas Clements, and Julie Sarama, can be purchased from McGraw-Hill at *www.sranumberworlds.com*. It can be implemented in small groups with four to five students and also includes a software supplement called Building Blocks™, with the length of implementation varying between 15 and 60 minutes depending on grade level and format (Griffin & Case, 1997). The curriculum is developmentally sequenced and aligned with the CCSS (Griffin, 2004). Activities include interactive games, verbal prompts, scripted questions, think-alouds, and a variety of visual representations (e.g., thermometer, dial, number line, group of objects, dot patterns). A consideration for use of this program is that training for teachers is intensive (e.g., 3–12 full-day workshops and on-site-designated mentor teacher); preliminary positive results were accomplished with researcher collaboration (Clements & Sarama, 2011; Griffin & Case, 1997).

Research has demonstrated that students who receive SRA Number Worlds improve their number knowledge, strategy use, and generalization of these skills in kindergarten, all of which were retained through second grade (Griffin, 2004; Griffin & Case, 1997). The published research on Building Blocks was effective at the preschool level (Clements & Sarama, 2008). Effects of the program in preschool were maintained only through first grade when a follow-through program was implemented in kindergarten and first grade (Clements, Sarama, Wolfe, & Spitler, 2013). Both aspects of the program were evaluated through extensive field testing and various studies by the authors (e.g., Case, Griffin, & Kelly, 1999; Clements, 2007; Clements et al., 2013; Clements & Sarama, 2007, 2008, 2011; Griffin & Case, 1997; Griffin, Case, & Siegler, 1994; Sarama & Clements, 2004).

CONCLUSION

Number sense is central to whole-number knowledge. We listed key concepts within number sense that are important for students to understand, and serve as important target areas for intervention work. We then described 11 intervention programs that represent (1) individual tutoring, (2) small-group tutoring, (3) CAI, or (4) a combination of small-group tutoring with CAI. Most of these interventions target several aspects of number sense; however, a few of these interventions either target magnitude comparison skills or individualize the intervention to specific student needs. Eight of these intervention programs are commercially available, and two are free with downloadable software or interventionist manuals, and one is available through the author.

APPENDIX 8.1. The Great Race/Race to Space Intervention Brief

CCSS Domain Areas Addressed:

Counting and Cardinality (K)	Operations and Algebraic Thinking (K–5)	Numbers and Operations in Base Ten (K–5)	Measurement and Data (K–5)
☑	☑	☐	☐

Instructional Hierarchy:

Acquisition	Fluency	Maintenance	Generalization	Adaptation
☐	☑	☐	☐	☐

Setting:			**Tier of Support within RTI Framework:**		
Whole-Class	Small-Group	Individual	Universal Prevention	Targeted Intervention	Individualized Intervention
☐	☑	☑	☐	☑	☐

Mediator: ☑ Teacher or Interventionist ☐ Student (with teacher oversight) ☐ Parent

Effectiveness: Moderate effect size.	**Amount of Evidence:** Six peer-reviewed studies between 2008 and 2014.

Acceptability: Not collected.

Brief Description: The Great Race is constructed as a linear board game for preschoolers, and its partner game, Race to Space, is a matrix board game for kindergarteners that is designed to improve numerical identification, use of the counting on strategy, number line estimation, and magnitude comparison.

Materials Required: Game board, spinner, and game pieces.

Training Required: Training of paraprofessionals required 1 hour and consisted of watching a demonstration video of game playing, practice with the game board materials, and acclimation to a manual that included game rules, scripts, and prompts for error correction.

Duration: The Great Race can be implemented from about 15 minutes per occasion when provided individually and anywhere from 20 to 25 minutes per occasion when delivered in a small-group format (three students). Race to Space is implemented individually for 25 minutes. All variations of the game were administered two times weekly. Effects for the game (as evaluated in the research studies) were found after a total of 2 weeks (four sessions) of intervention implementation.

Active Treatment Components: Opportunities to practice, error correction, feedback.

Procedures:

1. Construct the game board by generating 10 horizontally arranged squares of equal size with the numbers 1 to 10 listed in order from left to right. Be sure the word *start* is listed by the numeral 1 and *end* is listed by the numeral 10.
2. Create a game spinner by dividing a circle into two halves; one half should be labeled with the numeral 1 and the other with the numeral 2.
3. Locate items (e.g., tokens, dry beans, beads) that can be used as game pieces. Be sure that items represent different colors or shapes.
4. Allow the student to select his or her token.
5. Tell the student that you and he or she will take turns spinning the spinner and whomever reaches the end first wins.
6. Tell the student that when it is his or her turn he or she should move the token the number of spaces indicated on the spinner (either a 1 or 2).
7. Tell the student to say the number that he or she spun *and* say the numbers on the spaces through which he or she moved (e.g., if the student was on the numeral 5 and spun a 2, he or she should say, "I am on number 5 and I spun a 2, so I will move two spaces. The student should say "6, 7," as he or she moves the token).
8. If the student names the numeral incorrectly, tell the student the correct number(s) and repeat the name(s) while moving the token.

The format of these intervention briefs was based on the Evidence-Based Intervention (EBI) Network at the University of Missouri (*http://ebi.missouri.edu/*).

9. If the student spins a 2 and then moves through the next spaces by saying "1, 2," remind the student to say the names of the number on each space. If that prompt is not effective, then point to the numerals and name them. Have the student repeat the names as you point to the spaces.
10. Repeat the game about five times per 15-minute session.
11. At the end of each session (or at least once weekly) students are administered a brief assessment (e.g., CBM) that is completed individually and scored to monitor progress.

Treatment Variations:

• *Great Race—Small Group:* Designed to be played with three students and a tutor. Each child is permitted a practice turn before the game begins and each student is able to be first at least once during each session. Each game lasts approximately 5–7 minutes and can be repeated at least three times per session.
• *Race to Space:* Designed for use with kindergarteners. Construct the game board by generating a 10 × 10 matrix of squares with the numerals 1 to 100 arranged from the bottom to the top. The numeral 0 should be placed with the word *start* at the bottom left corner of the matrix. Construct a spinner by generating a circle with five sections labeled 1 to 5. Let the students know that the purpose of the game is to learn more about the numbers from 0 to 100. Follow The Great Race rules listed above. Periodically draw the student's attention to his or her position on the game board (e.g., "Wow! You are on 15!").

Selected References:

1. Laski, E. V., & Siegler, R. S. (2014). Learning from number board games: You learn what you encode. *Developmental Psychology, 50*(3), 853–864.
2. Ramani, G. B., Hitti, A., & Siegler, R. S. (2012). Taking it to the classroom: Number board games as a small group learning activity. *Journal of Educational Psychology, 104*(3), 661–672.
3. Ramani, G. B., & Siegler, R. S. (2011). Reducing the gap in numerical knowledge between low- and middle-income preschoolers. *Journal of Applied Developmental Psychology, 32*(3), 146–159.
4. Ramani, G. B., & Siegler, R. S. (2008). Promoting broad and stable improvements in low-income children's numerical knowledge through playing number board games. *Child Development, 79*(2), 375–394.
5. Siegler, R. S., & Ramani, G. B. (2009). Playing linear number board games—but not circular ones—improves low-income preschoolers' numerical understanding. *Journal of Educational Psychology, 101*(3), 545–560.
6. Siegler, R. S., & Ramani, G. B. (2008). Playing linear numerical board games promotes low-income children's numerical development. *Developmental Science, 11*(5), 655–661.

Game Board for The Great Race

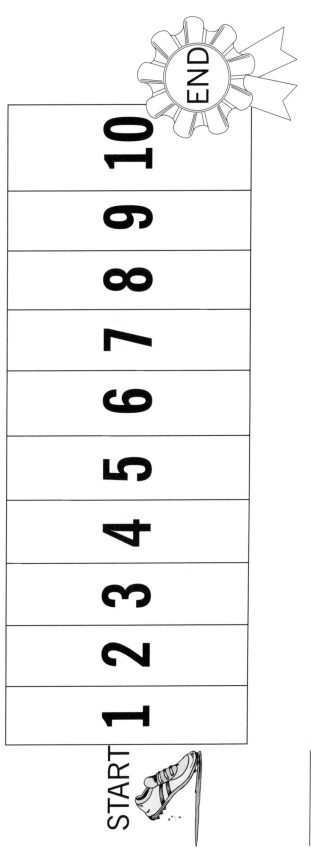

The Great Race

FORM 8.2

Spinner for The Great Race

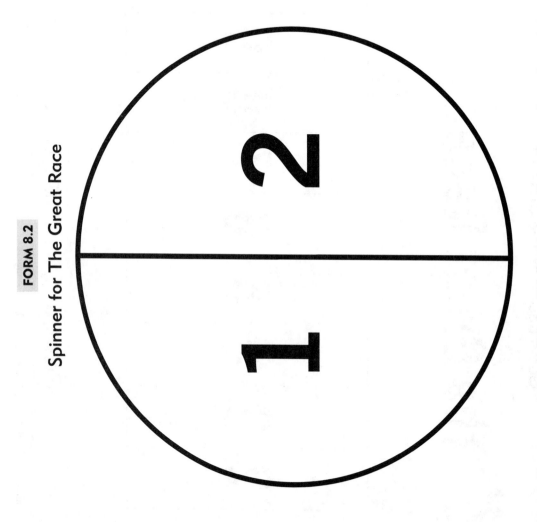

Game Board for Race to Space

Race to Space

91	92	93	94	95	96	97	98	99	100
81	82	83	84	85	86	87	88	89	90
71	72	73	74	75	76	77	78	79	80
61	62	63	64	65	66	67	68	69	70
51	52	53	54	55	56	57	58	59	60
41	42	43	44	45	46	47	48	49	50
31	32	33	34	35	36	37	38	39	40
21	22	23	24	25	26	27	28	29	30
11	12	13	14	15	16	17	18	19	20
1	2	3	4	5	6	7	8	9	10

0
Start

Spinner for Race to Space

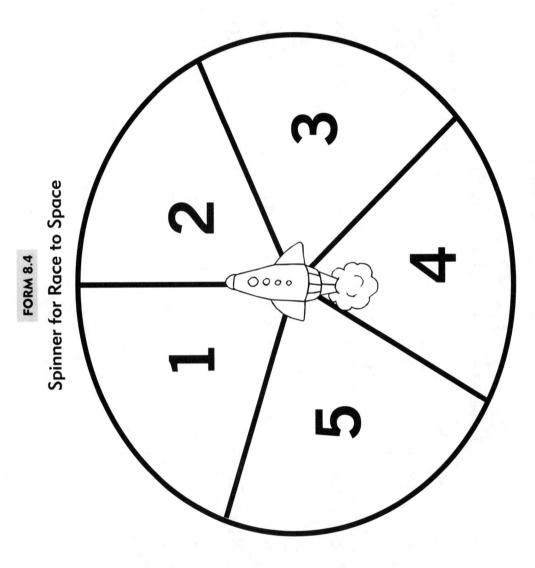

CHAPTER 9

Basic and Complex Computation Interventions

Fluency with basic facts and flexible use of procedures, such as algorithms, to solve complex computation problems represents two key areas of whole-number proficiency (NGA & CCSSO, 2010; NMAP, 2008; Wu, 2011). According to the CCSS, by the end of second grade it is expected that students can automatically (from memory) add and subtract within 20 and know the sums of all single-digit addition facts. By the end of third grade, students are expected to fluently add and subtract numerals within 1,000, using strategies such as mnemonics, algorithms, and mental math that align with knowledge of place value and the base-ten number system (NGA & CCSSO, 2010; NMAP, 2008). Third-grade students are also expected to have memorized all single-digit multiplication facts. These expectations suggest that students will be able to effortlessly recall simple number combinations, a foundational skill, whether those number combinations are presented in isolation or in the context of other more complex math tasks (O'Connell & SanGiovanni, 2011). For example, if students can automatically retrieve 3 + 4, they are more likely to access 30 + 40, 53 + 24, 321 + 452, \$1.30 + \$1.40, and $\frac{3}{9} + \frac{4}{9}$ (Cumming & Elkin, 1999; O'Connell & SanGiovanni, 2011). Likewise, for more complex computation, these expectations suggest that students are able to understand how to solve three-digit addition problems, for example, multiple ways and can quickly and easily apply the most useful strategy to any problem. Table 9.1 displays sample selected skill hierarchies across each operation that describes the conceptual, procedural, and automatic skills and concepts to be learned. This chapter discusses (1) the importance of automatic retrieval of basic facts, (2) the research evidence for interventions to improve automaticity, (3) the importance of multidigit computation, and (4) the research evidence for interventions to improve multidigit computation.

TABLE 9.1. Computation Skill Development

Operation	Skill hierarchy	Concepts	Procedures	Automaticity
Addition	• One-digit facts within 10 • One-digit facts within 20 • Three one-digit numbers less than 10 • Two-digit, no regrouping • Two-digit, with regrouping • Three two-digit numbers • Four two-digit numbers	• Associative and commutative laws of addition • Distributive law • Meaning of the equal sign • Understanding place value	• Use counting (e.g., counting on, skip counting) • Use objects, pictures, arrays, or drawings to represent quantities • Decompose and compose numbers • Rounding and estimation • Use standard algorithms with multidigit numbers	• Fluently add within 5 • Fluently add within 10 • Fluently add within 20 • Sums of all one-digit facts • Fluently add within 100 • Fluently add within 1,000
Subtraction	• One-digit facts to 10 • One-digit facts to 20 • One/two-digit from a two-digit number, no regrouping • One/two-digit from a two-digit number with regrouping • Two/three-digit from a three-digit number, with regrouping	• Distributive law • Meaning of the equal sign • Understanding place value • Relationship between subtraction and addition	• Use counting (e.g., counting on) • Use objects, pictures, arrays, or drawings to represent quantities • Decompose and compose numbers • Rounding and estimation • Use standard algorithms with multidigit numbers	• Fluently subtract within 5 • Fluently subtract within 10 • Fluently subtract within 20 • Fluently subtract within 100 • Fluently subtract within 1,000
Multiplication	• One-digit facts within 100 • 2×1 digit, no regrouping • 2×1 digit, with regrouping • 3×1 digit/4×1 digit • 2×2 digit • Multidigit numbers, no regrouping • Multidigit numbers, with regrouping	• Associative and commutative laws of multiplication • Distributive law • Meaning of the equal sign • Understanding place value • Relationship between addition and multiplication	• Use counting (e.g., skip counting) • Use repeated addition • Use objects, pictures, arrays, or drawings to represent quantities • Decompose and compose numbers • Rounding and estimation • Use standard algorithms with multidigit numbers	• Fluently multiply facts of 0–5 • Fluently multiply facts of 6–12 • Products of all one-digit facts
Division	• One-digit facts within 100 • Two/three-digit dividends and one-digit divisor, no remainder • Two/three-digit dividends and one-digit divisor, with remainder • Three/four-digit dividends and one-digit divisor • Three/four-digit dividends and two-digit divisor	• Distributive law of addition and subtraction • Meaning of the equal sign • Understanding place value • Relationship between multiplication and division • Relationship between subtraction and division	• Use objects, pictures, arrays, or drawings to represent quantities • Use repeated subtraction • Decompose and compose numbers • Rounding and estimation • Use standard algorithms with multidigit numbers	• Fluently divide facts of 0–5 • Fluently divide facts of 6–12

Note. See the following references for more details: NGA and CCSSO (2010); Stein, Kinder, Silbert, and Carnine (2006); Wu (2011).

NUMBER COMBINATIONS:
WHY IS AUTOMATIC RETRIEVAL IMPORTANT?

A central aspect of mastering whole-number knowledge is developing automaticity with basic number combinations across all four operations. Compared with their international peers, U.S. students display lower rates of basic fact fluency (NMAP, 2008). One study demonstrated that as many as 38% of students in first through third grade failed to display automaticity with basic addition and subtraction (Stickney et al., 2012). This finding is problematic because automatic retrieval of basic facts leads to higher general math performance in first and third grades, as well as with high school seniors (e.g., Jordan et al., 2009; Price et al., 2013; Stickney et al., 2012).

A robust finding in the literature is that automatic recall of number combinations is one hallmark indicator of students experiencing challenges in math and is predictive of learning disabilities in third grade (Geary, 2011b; Gersten et al., 2005; Jordan, Hanich, & Kaplan, 2003b; Mazzocco & Thompson, 2005; NMAP, 2008). Students without math learning disabilities recall up to three times as many number combinations as their peers with learning disabilities *even though accuracy is equivalent* (Gersten & Chard, 1999; Hasselbring et al., 1988). Students without basic fact fluency seem to be less able to grasp underlying math concepts, perform procedural computation tasks, solve word problems, or access higher-level math curricula (Fuchs, Fuchs, Compton, et al., 2006; Gersten & Chard, 1999; Jordan, Hanich, & Kaplan, 2003a). This may be because students without automaticity of number combinations (e.g., operands 0–9) appear to direct more cognitive resources (e.g., attention, working memory) to retrieving the solution to basic facts than typically performing peers (Barrouillet & Fayol, 1998; Dehaene, 2011; DeSmedt et al., 2011). This difference likely contributes to the difficulty these students experience when solving more complex computation and problem-solving tasks that require students to access higher-order cognitive processes to be successful (Barrouillet & Fayol, 1998; Dehaene, 2011; DeSmedt et al., 2011; Price et al., 2013).

Students with low number combination fluency also appear to experience greater anxiety for math tasks than students with more fluent skills (Cates & Rhymer, 2003; Throndsen, 2010). Whether it is the additional effort required, anxiety, or a combination of the two, students with poor number combination fluency also tend to engage in less frequent practice with math content and complete fewer math-related tasks (Billington, Skinner, & Cruchon, 2004; Skinner, Belfiore, Mace, Williams, & Johns, 1997).

Acquisition

Explicit instruction containing modeling and immediate error correction are commonly used components for building accurate responding, as are using number lines, concrete and visual representations, and strategic counting (Fuchs, Powell, et al., 2010; Gersten, Chard, et al., 2009; Stokes & Baer, 1977). These strategies are effective for helping students understand concepts that underlie number combinations, such as quantity discrimination, counting, and mental use of number lines, as we discussed in the previous chapter (Gersten et al., 2005; Poncy et al., 2006). Even when students have been exposed to conceptual instruction and activities that build basic skill acquisition, they may still display slow, yet accurate, responding when asked to solve basic number combinations (Haring & Eaton, 1978; Rivera & Bryant, 1992). Explicit opportunities for practice with number combinations are necessary to promote automaticity (Powell et al., 2009; Tournaki, 2003). For students with the lowest rates of automaticity (e.g., 85–100% accuracy, <20 DCPM) the best outcomes occur when drill (i.e., practicing skills or concepts in isolation) and practice with modeling (either embedded within the math task or with teacher/interventionist support) are used (Codding, Burns, et al., 2011). Drill provides students opportunities to practice basic facts in isolation, whereas practice with modeling engages students in self-managed or teacher-directed interventions when they are transitioning between accurate and fluent performance.

It may also be useful, particularly for students who are mastering facts more slowly than expected, to incorporate backup strategies (e.g., Baroody, Bajwa, et al., 2009). Backup strategies refer to the progression we described in Chapter 8 leading from strategic counting to automatic retrieval. When students do not display automatic retrieval, application of one of the earlier strategies might be helpful such as (1) decomposition strategies (e.g., doubling strategies: $6 + 7 = 6 + 6 + 1$); (2) visual representation via number lines, ten frames, or arrays; or (3) strategic counting strategies such as the min strategy (counting up from the larger addend or from the minuend to the subtrahend; Fuchs, Powell et al., 2010; Woodward, 2006). An efficient way to incorporate strategic counting, decomposition, and/or visual representation into drill-and-practice strategies may be to provide students with opportunities to use these strategies with the number combinations students are unable to solve from memory (Fuchs, Powell, et al., 2010). It may also be important to consider the developmental sequence that students often learn basic facts within. For example, early in schooling, students first learn to add and subtract by one (see Figures 9.1 and 9.2).

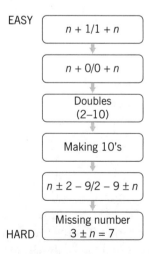

FIGURE 9.1. Sequence of easiest to hardest addition/subtraction facts to learn.

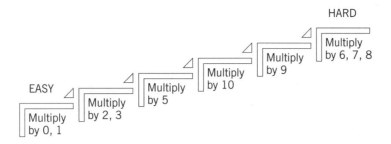

FIGURE 9.2. Sequence of easiest to hardest multiplication facts to learn (see Burns, Ysseldyke, Nelson, and Kanive, 2015 for more details).

Fluency

Fluency refers to high rates of accurate responding—in other words, automatic retrieval of simple number combinations from memory. Strategies to enhance fluency differ from those designed to increase acquisition of number combinations (Codding, Burns, et al., 2011; Codding et al., 2007). For students who have not yet mastered basic number combinations but can perform simple problems accurately (100% accuracy; 20–30 DCPM; Howell & Nolet, 1999), the most effective practice opportunities are those occurring daily and designed to (1) be brief, timed, and novel; (2) provide immediate performance feedback; and (3) support engagement with reinforcement (Daly et al., 2007; Rivera & Bryant, 1992). Fluency-building activities should include a range of facts presented in the context of previously learned items (e.g., worksheets, story/word problems) in order to ensure maintenance and generalization of skills (Codding, Burns, et al., 2011; Haring & Eaton, 1978). These activities should occur daily for 5–10 minutes and vary to promote engagement and motivation (Gersten, Beckmann, et al., 2009; Marzano, Pickering, & Pollock, 2001). Self-managed practice opportunities are also effective ways to improve fluency (Codding, Hilt-Panahon, et al., 2009; Codding, Burns, et al., 2011). For example, in each intervention session, students could choose to engage one of several options such as explicit timing, peer-pair practice with flash cards, high-preference worksheets, or computer-based practice. Interventionists could also preprogram different fluency-building activities sessions on a rotating schedule.

Research-Supported Interventions for Number Combinations

Despite the central role that fluency with number combinations has on later math achievement, there are very few standard protocol interventions that directly support improvement of number combinations beyond first grade. The existing interventions with empirical evidence are listed and described in Tables 9.2 and 9.3. The good news is that there are many simple interventions that have been evaluated in peer-reviewed research articles that focus on improving number combination fluency. In the following section, we describe seven interventions that focus on building automaticity with students in the acquisition and fluency stages of number combination development (see Figure 9.3). Each of these strategies offers direct practice on fact retrieval and has evidence of effectiveness.

TABLE 9.2. Free Interventions That Improve Acquisition of Single- and Multidigit Computation

	Concrete–Representation–Abstract	Incremental Rehearsal	Math to Mastery	Cover–Copy–Compare
Treatment components	• Explicit instruction • Strategy instruction • Sequenced instruction • Progress monitoring and feedback • Drill, practice, review • Visual representations	• Explicit instruction • Sequenced instruction • Progress monitoring and feedback • Drill, practice, review	• Explicit instruction • Progress monitoring and feedback • Drill, practice, review • Reinforcement	• Explicit instruction • Progress monitoring and feedback • Drill, practice, review • Reinforcement
Level of skill proficiency	• Acquisition	• Acquisition • Fluency	• Acquisition • Fluency	• Acquisition • Fluency
References	• 5–10 studies • Conducted by program authors and other research groups	• <5 studies • Conducted by program authors and other research groups	• <5 studies • Conducted by program authors	• >10 studies • Conducted by program authors and other research groups
Grades	• 3–7	• 3–7	• 2 and 3	• 1–10
Target skills	• Multidigit addition • Multidigit subtraction, with regrouping ones, tens, hundreds • Multidigit multiplication, with one- and two-digit multipliers	• Multiplication	• Addition, with and without regrouping	• Addition • Subtraction • Multiplication • Division
Interventionist	• Special ed teacher	• Special ed teacher • Paraprofessional	• Paraprofessional	• Student (monitored by adult)
Effect size	• Large	• Large	• None reported	• Moderate

TABLE 9.3. Free Interventions That Improve Fluency with Number Combinations

	Taped Problems	Explicit Timing	High-Preference/Interspersed Problems
Treatment components	• Progress monitoring and feedback • Drill, practice, review • Reinforcement	• Progress monitoring and feedback • Drill, practice, review	• Progress monitoring and feedback • Drill, practice, review • Reinforcement
Level of skill proficiency	• Fluency	• Fluency	• Fluency • Generalization
References	• >10 studies	• 5–10 studies	• <5 studies
	• Conducted by program authors and other research groups	• Conducted by program authors and other research groups	• Conducted by program authors and other research groups
Grades	• 2–5	• 2–6	• 3–5
Target skills	• Addition (with and without regrouping) • Subtraction • Multiplication • Division	• Addition (single and multidigit) • Subtraction (single and multidigit) • Multiplication (single and multididdigit)	• Addition (multidigit with and without regrouping) • Subtraction (multidigit with and without regrouping)
Interventionist	• General ed teacher • Paraprofessional	• General ed teacher • Paraprofessional	• Paraprofessional • Student (monitored by adult)
Effect size	• Moderate • Large	• None reported	• None reported

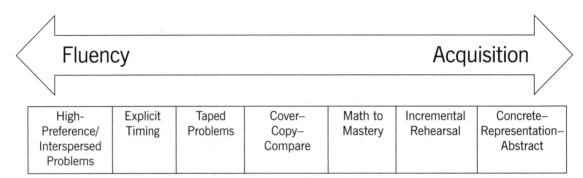

FIGURE 9.3. Identifying interventions along the instructional hierarchy.

Common considerations when using these interventions is to introduce new facts in small sets of no more than 10, use fact families, and define a specific performance criterion for mastery that is achieved *prior to* introducing new facts (Hasselbring et al., 2005; Stein, Silbert, et al., 2016; Woodward, 2006).

Math to Mastery

Math to Mastery (MTM; Doggett, Henington, & Johnson-Gros, 2006) has been examined in three peer-reviewed studies and is a free intervention that can be administered by many school professionals (see Appendix 9.1). Although the existing research has primarily applied MTM with students needing support with addition, the procedures could easily be adapted for the remaining arithmetic operations (Mong, Doggett, Mong, & Henington, 2012; Mong & Mong, 2010, 2012). MTM consists of five simple steps, including (1) direct instruction and guided practice, (2) timed trials, (3) immediate corrective feedback, (4) self-monitoring of performance, and (5) reinforcement. As the name implies, math trials continue until a mastery criterion is achieved (e.g., 40 DCPM) or ten 1-minute trials are completed. The materials required to implement the intervention include a manual of instructions (see Doggett et al., 2006), individually designed worksheets, and a timer. The intervention has been conducted individually in 10-minute sessions, three to five times weekly, for 3–8 weeks. Across the three peer-reviewed studies, all students who participated achieved (1) mastery performance across one to four skills, (2) generalization to multiple skill probes, and (3) retention of performance levels across time.

Cover–Copy–Compare

Cover–copy–compare (CCC; Skinner, Belfiore, et al., 1997) has been examined in over 20 studies, 12 that were analyzed in a meta-analysis (Joseph et al., 2012). It consists of five or six simple steps (depending on the variation that is selected) that students manage themselves, but oversight is provided by an interventionist or teacher (see Appendix 9.2). CCC is most often applied individually, given that it is student managed, but it has also been delivered as a classwide procedure (see Chapter 4). This intervention has been used with all four math operations addressing number combinations, as well as multidigit operations. Specialized worksheets need to be constructed by interventionists or can be generated online by using the Math Worksheet Generator available from Intervention Central (*www.interventioncentral.org/teacher-resources/math-work-sheet-generator*). CCC has been implemented anywhere from 3 to 20 minutes, although most often it is delivered in 5- to 10-minute increments, for two to five sessions per week across 2–16 weeks. Interventionists' responsibilities include (1) determining the target skill, (2) making CCC worksheets and goal charts (if using), (3) training students on CCC procedures, (4) circulating around the classroom to oversee accurate implementation of CCC by students, and (5) providing rewards (if using). Overall, CCC is an effective intervention. Evidence of skill retention, generalization, and acceptability has been found (e.g., Joseph et al., 2012; Poncy, McCallum, & Schmitt, 2010; Poncy & Skinner, 2011).

Flash Card Practice

Flash cards provide students with opportunities to practice simple number combinations in isolation, which is an essential aspect of practice (Burns et al., 2010; Codding, Burns, et al., 2011; Cohen et al., 1992; Symonds & Chase, 1992). Traditional drill often requires that a sequence of items, usually all unknown math facts, be presented by an interventionist with modeling after which students provide oral responses and receive immediate error correction and feedback. However, other forms of flash card practice include interspersing known facts, also referred to as review problems, with the presentation of unknown or new facts. The ratio of unknown to known facts presented in one session has ranged from introducing two new facts and their inverses in one session (Hasselbring, Goin, & Sherwood, 1986), to three new facts (unknown) within a set of 10 facts (seven known; Cooke, Guzaukas, Pressley, & Kerr, 1993; Schnorr, 1989), to one new fact to nine known facts (Burns, 2005). Incorporating some known items is useful, perhaps even necessary, for increasing students' academic engagement and preference for the activity (Cooke et al., 1993; Skinner, Fletcher, Wildmon, & Belfiore, 1996). Students may also have a difficult time learning more than a handful of new math facts in one session given the potential load on working memory and the limited number of contextual cues that are available to trigger solutions for math facts (as opposed to reading or spelling words; Cooke et al., 1993).

INCREMENTAL REHEARSAL

Incremental rehearsal (Burns, 2005) is an individually administered flash card procedure that includes a progression of known to unknown facts beginning with the presentation of one known and one unknown item, and ending with the presentation of 90% known and 10% unknown facts (see Appendix 9.3). Typically, nine trials with each unknown fact are conducted, and a range of three to six unknown facts are presented each session. Incremental rehearsal has been applied with multiplication facts but can easily be adapted for use with all four math operations. It is a free intervention that can be developed using flash cards, a recording sheet, and a stopwatch or kitchen timer. Incremental rehearsal has been implemented for 10–20 minutes per session, twice weekly, for 4–12 weeks. Preliminary research on incremental rehearsal in math has shown it to be effective for improving multiplication fact fluency and accuracy (Burns, 2005; Codding, Archer, & Connell, 2010). Generalization for simple word problems and fractions that did not involve reducing has also been demonstrated (Codding et al., 2010).

Taped Problems

Taped problems (McCallum, Skinner, & Hutchins, 2004) has been examined in 11 peer-reviewed articles. This intervention was designed to be administered individually (Bliss et al., 2010; Carroll, Skinner, Turner, McCallum, & Woodland, 2006; McCallum et al., 2004; Mong & Mong, 2012; Poncy, Skinner, & Jaspers, 2007), but has been adapted for classwide use (see Chapter 4). A variation has been developed that adds contingent reinforcement to the treatment package (McCleary et al., 2011). This free intervention requires students to listen to an audio recording that presents math facts with their answers using varying time-delay procedures (from no delay to a 3- or 4-second delay; see Appendix 9.4). Students record their answers on a worksheet that contains the problems (without the answers) before the answer is provided by the audio recording. The progressive delay sequence is used in order to prevent students from using less inefficient strategies, such as finger counting, to solve problems and encourage automatic mental retrieval. Taped problems has been applied with all math operations, including simple and complex computation problems. The recording and worksheets used with the intervention can be easily developed by school professionals. Taped problems has been implemented (most often) for 8–15 minutes per session, three to five times weekly, for 3–10 weeks.

Evidence has suggested that taped problems is more effective for students in the fluency stage of skill development, and it requires less instructional time than other similar strategies, making it an efficient option (Carroll et al., 2006; Kleinert et al., 2015; Mong & Mong, 2012; Poncy et al., 2007). Retention of fluency gains has been demonstrated on all studies that measured maintenance (over half of all studies) and generalization to facts that represent the inverse of what was taught (e.g., student correctly answers 5 + 3 when only taught 3 + 5).

Explicit Timing

Explicit timing (Van Houten & Thompson, 1976), a simple and free procedure, has been examined in six peer-reviewed articles, and provides students with timed opportunities to practice number combinations interspersed with short intervals where students assess their progress. This intervention has been delivered in small groups and classwide (see Appendix 9.5). It is based on the premise that students who are in the fluency stage of learning benefit from repeated opportunities to practice in novel and interesting ways (Daly et al., 2007; Rivera & Bryant, 1992). Students are provided with a math assignment and are required to mark their progress in 1-minute intervals until they either complete the assignment or until the designated time for the task is finished (e.g., 5–10 minutes of total practice; Codding et al., 2007). By requiring students to briefly stop and circle or underline the problem that was completed during each of these short time intervals, immediate feedback on fluency is provided (i.e., number of problems completed), and progress becomes more salient to the student (Rhymer et al., 2002; Van Houten & Thompson, 1976). The explicit timing procedure that we are describing here does not refer to timed worksheet practice that is conducted for 1 or 2 total minutes, which has also been described as explicit timing, timed practice, or math sprints (e.g., Miller & Hudson, 2007). Explicit timing has been implemented in brief sessions of 3–10 minutes (most often), two to five times weekly, for 4–6 total weeks.

Evidence has suggested that this intervention increases rates of correctly completed problems. It is important that explicit timing be applied at students' instructional levels, because some evidence suggests that students in the acquisition phase of skill development may experience decreases in accurate performance (Codding et al., 2007; Rhymer, Henington, Skinner, & Looby, 1999; Rhymer et al., 2002; Van Houten & Thompson, 1976). Explicit timing may be more effective at increasing rates of responding when the task involves single-digit number combinations as compared with complex number combinations (e.g., 3×3 digit multiplication; Rhymer et al., 2002). Student acceptability for this intervention ranges from moderate to high.

High-Preference/Interspersed Problems

High-preference/interspersed problems has been examined in numerous studies for improving homework and classwork completion rates at the secondary and college levels (e.g., Belfiore, Lee, Vargus, & Skinner, 1997; Johns, Skinner, & Nail, 2000; Lee, Lylo, Vostal, & Hua, 2012). Three peer-reviewed studies have examined the impact of this intervention on math performance of elementary-level students (Hawkins, Skinner, & Oliver, 2005; Montarello & Martens, 2005; Rhymer & Morgan, 2005). High-preference/interspersed problems is a practice procedure useful for students who are building fluency and generalization with complex computation, such as multidigit operations, and consists of substituting target problems with easy, already mastered problems (see Appendix 9.6). Usually, easy problems are inserted at every other problem (one easy problem, one target problem) or every third problem (one easy problem, three target problems). Worksheets can be created using a variety of Web resources including *interventioncentral.org* and *themathworksheetsite.com*. A variation of this intervention is to ask teachers or interventionists to deliver the math problems orally and require students to mentally solve the problem before recording the answer. The purpose of interspersing easy, usually single-digit basic facts, is to encourage students' endurance, persistence, and sustained attention to independent practice tasks. High-preference/interspersed problems can be administered in many formats, including small groups and classwide, given that the activities it is applied to are independently managed by each student. High-preference/interspersed problems has been implemented for 10–15 minutes, three to five times weekly, for a total of 3–5 weeks.

Evidence suggests that this procedure improves initiation and engagement with worksheet practice tasks (Calderhead, Filter, & Albin, 2006; Lee et al., 2012; Skinner, Hurst,

Teeple, & Meadows, 2002). Improvements in written computation performance are greater when easy problems are interspersed at every other problem (1:1 ratio), but when interventionists provide the problem orally, easy problems should be interspersed at every third problem (1:3 ratio; Hawkins et al., 2005). High-preference/interspersed problems is rated as highly acceptable by teachers and students as an effective and appropriate practice strategy. One study demonstrated that although students and teachers preferred high-preference/interspersed problems, performance was better when using the explicit timing intervention (Rhymer & Morgan, 2005). It may be that high-preference/interspersed problems is a useful strategy for students whose motivation or persistence on practice activities are contributing to their lack of automaticity with number combinations.

Academy of MATH

When describing early numeracy interventions (see Chapter 8) we listed several commercially available options that also embed skill development with number combinations. The only additional program available that yields small to moderate effect sizes according to the National Center on Intensive Intervention website is Academy of MATH®. This program is an online intervention tool designed for students in grades 2–12, and addresses computation and word-problem solving along with other math areas consistent with the CCSS. We located one study examining the effectiveness of this program that included students in grades 2–4 (Torlaković, 2011). The intervention is intended to be administered in small groups for 30 minutes per session, three times per week, for 20 total weeks. Paraprofessionals can deliver the intervention and it is recommended that 6 hours of hands-on training with interventionists along with 3 days of on-site mentoring and coaching with students be provided by a certified Academy of MATH implementation specialist before use. The program costs are found on the EPS Literacy and Intervention website at *http:// eps.schoolspecialty.com,* and either a per-school perpetual license or annual per-student subscription is granted.

PROCEDURAL COMPUTATION

Once students have attained automaticity with single-digit facts, they will possess some of the foundational tools necessary for solving complex computation problems that include multiple digits. Other aspects of the whole-number knowledge necessary for solving multidigit computation problems include understanding place value and estimation within the base-ten system. Standard algorithms provide shortcuts to solve complex computation problems—however, students also need to understand the reason these algorithms work. For example, students need to understand that 358 is also represented by 300 + 50 + 8, or, three hundreds, five tens, and eight ones (Thanheiser, 2012; Wu, 2011). By knowing this, students understand that the columns within an algorithm can be computed individually because each adjacent column (moving to the left) is 10 times as great as the previous digit (Thanheiser, 2012). Students should be able to use their number line knowledge to estimate an answer. For example, students should be able to determine that the answer to 358 + 421 is greater than 750 but less than 800. There is a bidirectional relationship between procedural multidigit computation and conceptual understanding, suggesting that knowing algorithms and grasping the underlying concepts appear to be mutually dependent (Fuchs, Geary, et al., 2014; NMAP, 2008; Wu, 2011).

There are relatively few intervention strategies with empirical support that emphasize place value instruction. We describe below how the concrete–representation–abstract (CRA) sequence of instruction has been used in the literature to improve conceptual and procedural understanding of multidigit computation problems. This intervention is most appropriate for students in the acquisition stage of skill development. Although not empirically validated, we have created a variation of CCC that teaches students how to apply the traditional regrouping algorithm and also includes visual cues that facilitate self-monitoring of intervention steps (see Form 9.1). This version of CCC is appropriate for students transitioning from the acquisition to fluency stage of learning.

CRA Sequence

Six peer-reviewed studies have applied CRA (Mercer & Miller, 1992b) instruction to multidigit computation (Flores, 2009, 2010; Flores, Hinton, & Strozier, 2014; Mancl, Miller, & Kennedy, 2012; Miller & Kaffer, 2011; Peterson, Mercer, & O'Shea, 1988). It is a free intervention procedure, and interested educators should also access the materials from Mercer and Miller (1992; see Appendix 9.7). This scripted set of 10–16 lessons includes three lessons that focus on concrete manipulatives using base-ten blocks before practicing the same concept using similar visual displays over three lessons. Visual displays consist of squares to represent hundreds, long lines to represent tens, and short lines to represent ones. The remaining lessons focus on computing multidigit problems using numerals with a mnemonic (i.e., DRAW, RENAME; see Box 9.1). The sequence for each lesson maintains the same process: (1) demonstration, (2) guided practice, and (3) independent practice. Student progress is monitored and charted. Intervention sessions are generally conducted individually for 30 minutes, three to four times weekly across 12 weeks. Special education teachers have generally provided the intervention, so it is unclear whether other school staff might be able to implement the procedure with fidelity.

BOX 9.1. Mnemonics to Support Multidigit Problem Solving

DRAW	RENAME
D = **D**iscover the sign.	**R** = **R**ead the problem.
R = **R**ead the problem.	**E** = **E**xamine the ones column.
A = **A**nswer or draw and check.	**N** = **N**ote the ones in the ones column.
W = **W**rite the answer.	**A** = **A**ddress the tens column.
	M = **M**ark the tens in the tens column.
	E = **E**xamine and note the hundreds; exit with a quick check.

Note. For more details, see Flores, Hinton, and Strozier (2014) and Miller and Kaffar (2011).

Across peer-reviewed studies, all students made improvements in accurately solving multidigit computation that was maintained after the intervention period ended, and in some cases, student improvement transferred to word-problem solving. Students and teachers also reported liking the intervention, with acceptability ratings ranging from good to excellent.

CONCLUSION

Automaticity with basic facts and procedural fluency with more complex computation problems are core aspects of whole-number knowledge. We described nine simple and free ways to improve students' proficiency with computation. This chapter's appendices and a form provide brief intervention protocols, as well as sample materials that can be used to implement these interventions.

APPENDIX 9.1. Math to Mastery Intervention Brief

CCSS Domain Areas Addressed:			
Counting and Cardinality (K)	Operations and Algebraic Thinking (K–5)	Numbers and Operations in Base Ten (K–5)	Measurement and Data (K–5)
☐	☑	☑	☐

Instructional Hierarchy:				
Acquisition	Fluency	Maintenance	Generalization	Adaptation
☑	☑	☐	☐	☐

Setting:			Tier of Support within RTI Framework:		
Whole-Class	Small-Group	Individual	Universal Prevention	Targeted Intervention	Individualized Intervention
☐	☐	☑	☐	☐	☑

Mediator: ☑ Teacher or Interventionist ☐ Student (with teacher oversight) ☐ Parent

Effectiveness: Socially significant performance gains evident for all nine participants across three of three studies.	**Amount of Evidence:** Three peer-review studies between 2010 and 2012.

Acceptability: Collected in two studies (Mong & Mong, 2010, 2012); satisfaction ratings were modestly to highly acceptable among students.

Brief Description: Math to Mastery is a teacher-directed instructional approach where students are individually administering the intervention.

Materials Required: Individualized worksheets, goal charts or graphs, kitchen timer or stopwatch.

Training Required: Interventionists can use a manual to administer the five-step procedure (Doggett et al., 2006). Training may be needed on using CBA to determine the skill that should be targeted for intervention.

Duration: Math to Mastery is implemented for 10 minutes per occasion, three to five times weekly, for a total of 3–8 weeks depending on the number of skills targeted for intervention.

Active Treatment Components: Demonstration, opportunities to practice, timed trials, error correction and feedback, self-monitoring progress, social reinforcement (praise).

Procedures:

1. Determine the skill or skills that will be used for the intervention according to CBA or computer-adapted assessments. The earliest prerequisite skill that is not mastered in the sequence for each math operation should be targeted.
2. Interventionist demonstrates how to complete each math problem on the worksheet while the student follows along on his or her own copy.
3. Student practices each problem on the worksheet in 1-minute trials until mastery (32 DCPM) is attained or 10 (1-minute) trials are completed.
4. Interventionist follows along while student is working marking errors and giving immediate corrective feedback.
5. After each 1-minute trial the interventionist computes the digits correct and errors, and offers lots of praise for effort and performance.
6. Students chart their performance at the end of each 1-minute trial.
7. At the end of each session (or at least once weekly) all students are administered a brief assessment (e.g., CBA), which is completed individually and scored to monitor progress on the target skill.
8. Once every other week or monthly a multiple-skill CBM probe is administered to progress monitor for generalization.

Selected References:

1. Doggett, R. A., Henington, C., & Johnson-Gros, K. N. (2006). *Math to Mastery: A direct instruction remedial math intervention designed to increase student fluency with basic math facts.* Unpublished manuscript, Mississippi State University.

The format of these intervention briefs was based on the Evidence-Based Intervention (EBI) Network at the University of Missouri (*http://ebi.missouri.edu/*).

2. Mong, M. D., Doggett, R. A., Mong, K. W., & Henington, C. (2012). An evaluation of the math to mastery intervention package with elementary school students in a school setting. *Journal of Evidence-Based Practices for Schools, 13,* 61–78.

3. Mong, M., & Mong, K. W. (2010). Efficacy of two math interventions for enhancing fluency with elementary students. *Journal of Behavioral Education, 19,* 273–288.

4. Mong, M. D., & Mong, K. W. (2012). The utility of brief experimental analysis and extended intervention analysis in selecting effective mathematics interventions. *Journal of Behavioral Education, 21,* 99–118.

APPENDIX 9.2. Cover–Copy–Compare Intervention Brief

CCSS Domain Areas Addressed:

Counting and Cardinality (K)	Operations and Algebraic Thinking (K–5)	Numbers and Operations in Base Ten (K–5)	Measurement and Data (K–5)
☐	☑	☑	☐

Instructional Hierarchy:

Acquisition	Fluency	Maintenance	Generalization	Adaptation
☑	☑	☐	☐	☐

Setting: / **Tier of Support within RTI Framework:**

Whole-Class	Small-Group	Individual	Universal Prevention	Targeted Intervention	Individualized Intervention
☑	☐	☑	☑	☑	☑

Mediator: ☐ Teacher or Interventionist ☑ Student (with teacher oversight) ☐ Parent

Effectiveness: Moderate effect size. Socially significant classwide performance gains evident in five of seven studies.	**Amount of Evidence:** Twenty-two peer-reviewed studies between 1993 and 2012.

Acceptability: Collected in three studies (Codding et al., 2007, 2009; Grafman & Cates, 2010); satisfaction ratings were modestly to highly acceptable among students. Teachers preferred the six-step version to the traditional five-step version (Grafman & Cates, 2010).

Brief Description: CCC is an interventionist-/teacher-monitored student-directed instructional approach. This procedure may work best when students monitor their own performance, set goals, and are provided rewards for task engagement and improved math computation fluency.

Materials Required: CCC worksheet and grid, goal charts or graphs, reward menu and reward items, kitchen timer or stopwatch.

Training Required: Students need to be trained on the five- or six-step CCC procedure by teachers, which can be done usually in one brief 10- or 15-minute session. Teacher training may be needed on using CBA to determine the skill that should be targeted for classwide intervention.

Duration: The CCC procedure can be implemented anywhere from 3–20 minutes per occasion, two to five times weekly, for a total of 2–16 weeks, depending on the number of skills targeted for intervention.

Active Treatment Components: Modeling, opportunities to practice, error correction, feedback, goal setting and charting (optional), rewards (optional).

Procedures:

1. Determine the skill or skills that will be used for the intervention according to the average class performance according to CBA or computer-adapted assessments. The earliest prerequisite skill that is not mastered in the sequence for each math operation should be targeted.
2. Interventionist establishes a set amount of time for the CCC session (e.g., 3–10 minutes).
3. Interventionist models the five- or six-step procedure and demonstrates using practice examples.
4. Interventionist distributes CCC materials (i.e., worksheet, index card).
5. Students are instructed to look at each math problem and the corresponding answer located on the left side of the CCC worksheet. Students may choose to whisper the problem and answer to themselves.
6. Students are instructed to cover the problem with the answer on the left side of the CCC worksheet with their hand, index card, or by folding the page.
7. Students write the problem and the answer on the right side of the page. Some CCC worksheets are designed so the problem is already written, and the student is only responsible for recording the answer.
8. Students uncover the problem with the answer.
9. Students compare their written response with the model. If the student's response matches the model, the student proceeds to the next problem on the left side of the page. If the student's response does not match the model, the student corrects his or her mistake before moving on to the next problem.

10. At the end of each session (or at least once weekly) students are administered a brief assessment (e.g., CBM), which is completed individually and scored to monitor progress. For classwide applications, class scores are averaged to determine whether the skill has been mastered and a new skill can be introduced.

Treatment Variations:

- Adding a sixth step (modified CCC): After students look at the model provided with the problem and the answer, students are instructed to copy the problem and answer next to the model as a practice step. Then students follow the same procedures described above by covering the model and copied problem, recording the problem and answer from memory, and comparing the written response with the model.
- Answer only: Worksheets are constructed so that partially completed problems are presented following the model problem. Students are required to use the CCC procedure to record the answer only.
- Verbal: Rather than using written responses, students verbally state the problem and the answer.
- Verbal and written: Students are required to write and verbally state the problem and the answer after viewing the model problem.
- Goal setting and charting: Students score their own performance on the weekly (or session-based) assessment of the target skill and record their scores on a chart or graph.
- Rewards: Group contingencies are provided according to either task engagement or academic performance criteria, or both. Rewards are administered to the entire class when the class has made the teacher-determined criteria.

Selected References:

1. Ardoin, S. P., Witt, J. C., Connell, J. E., & Koenig, J. L. (2005). Application of a three-tiered response to intervention model for instructional planning, decision making, and the identification of children in need of services. *Journal of Psychoeducational Assessment, 23*, 362–380.
2. Codding, R. S., Hilt-Panahon, A., Panahon, C. J., & Benson, J. L. (2009). Addressing mathematics computation problems: A review of simple and moderate intensity interventions. *Education and Treatment of Children, 32*, 279–312.
3. Codding, R. S., Shiyko, M., Russo, M., Birch, S., Fanning, E., & Jaspen, D. (2007). Comparing mathematics interventions: Does initial level of fluency predict intervention effectiveness? *Journal of School Psychology, 45*, 603–617.
4. Grafman, J. M., & Cates, G. L. (2010). The differential effects of two self-managed math instruction procedures: Cover, copy, and compare versus copy, cover, and compare. *Psychology in the Schools, 47*, 153–165.
5. Poncy, B. C., McCallum, E., & Schmitt, A. J. (2010). A comparison of behavioral and constructivist interventions for increasing math-fact fluency in a second-grade classroom. *Psychology in the Schools, 47*, 917–930.
6. Poncy, B. C., & Skinner, C. H. (2011). Combining class-wide cover, copy, and compare with an interdependent group contingency to enhance addition-fact fluency in a first-grade classroom. *Journal of Applied School Psychology, 25*, 244–269.
7. Poncy, B. C., Skinner, C. H., & McCallum, E. (2012). A comparison of class-wide taped problems and cover, copy, and compare for enhancing mathematics fluency. *Psychology in the Schools, 49*, 744–755.
8. Skinner, C. H., Belfiore, P. J., Mace, H. W., Williams, S., & Johns, G. A. (1997). Altering response topography to increase response efficiency and learning rates. *School Psychology Quarterly, 12*, 54–64.

APPENDIX 9.3. Incremental Rehearsal Intervention Brief

CCSS Domain Areas Addressed:		
Counting and Cardinality	Operations and Algebraic Thinking	Numbers and Operations in Base Ten
☐	☑	☑

Instructional Hierarchy:				
Acquisition	Fluency	Maintenance	Generalization	Adaptation
☑	☑	☐	☐	☐

Setting:			Tier of Support within RTI Framework:		
Whole-Class	Small-Group	Individual	Universal Prevention	Targeted Intervention	Individualized Intervention
☐	☐	☑	☐	☐	☑

Mediator: ☑ Teacher or Interventionist   ☐ Student (with teacher oversight)   ☐ Parent

Effectiveness: Large average effect size.	**Amount of Evidence:** Two peer-reviewed studies (2005 and 2010).

Acceptability: Unknown—no data collected.

Brief Description: Teacher-directed instructional approach.

Materials Required: Flash cards, individualized worksheets, kitchen timer or stopwatch.

Training Required: About 2 hours of training is required for the IR procedure and another 2 hours for CBA to monitor progress.

Duration: IR is implemented for 10–20 minutes per occasion, twice weekly, for a total of 4–12 weeks.

Active Treatment Components: Modeling, prompting, opportunities to practice, error correction and immediate feedback.

Procedures:

1. Determine the skill that will be used for the intervention according to CBA or computer-adapted assessments. The earliest prerequisite skill that is not mastered in the sequence for each math operation should be targeted.
2. Conduct a fact assessment before each intervention session. All math facts for the targeted skill are randomly shuffled and presented one at a time. Any fact the student does not answer correctly within 2–3 seconds is considered incorrect. Place incorrect responses in one pile (unknowns), and correct responses in a separate pile (knowns). Record which facts are unknown.
3. From the pile of known facts, select nine flash cards to use throughout the intervention session.
4. Select the first unknown fact from the pile of unknown flash cards and verbally state the number combination with the answer.
5. Ask the student to orally restate the number combination and the answer that you just modeled. If the student provides an incorrect response, repeat step 4.
6. Present the first known fact from the nine selected flash cards to the student and ask the student to say the number combination with the answer.
7. Present the first unknown fact a second time and ask the student to say the number combination and answer.
8. Present the first known fact again followed by the second known fact from the nine selected known flash cards and ask the student to say the number combinations and answers.
9. Continue with the progression described in steps 5–8, adding one new known fact each trial, so that the first unknown fact (U1) is practiced nine times and all nine known facts (K1–9) are practiced after the unknown fact is presented (last trial = U1 followed by K1, K2, K3, K4, K5, K6, K7, K8, K9).
10. Once the sequence is completed (steps 5–9), the first unknown fact becomes the first known fact and the ninth known fact is removed.
11. Repeat steps 4–10 for the second unknown fact from the unknown flash card pile.
12. The number of unknown facts practiced each session will vary (usually between three and six). When three errors occur while rehearsing one fact, IR practice should be stopped.

13. At the end of each session (or at least once weekly) all students are administered a brief assessment (e.g., CBA), which is scored to monitor progress on the target skill.
14. Once every other week or monthly a multiple-skill CBM probe is administered to progress monitor for generalization.

Selected References:

1. Burns, M. K. (2005). Using incremental rehearsal to increase fluency of single-digit multiplication facts with children identified as learning disabled in mathematics computation. *Education and Treatment of Children, 28*, 237–249.
2. Burns, M. K., Zaslofsky, A., Kanive, R., & Parker, D. (2012). Meta-analysis of incremental rehearsal using phi coefficients to compare single-case and group designs. *Journal of Behavioral Education, 21*, 185–202.
3. Codding, R. S., Archer, J., & Connell, J. (2010). A systematic replication and extension of using incremental rehearsal to improve multiplication skills: An investigation of generalization. *Journal of Behavioral Education, 19*, 93–105.

APPENDIX 9.4. Taped Problems Intervention Brief

CCSS Domain Areas Addressed:		
Counting and Cardinality	Operations and Algebraic Thinking	Numbers and Operations in Base Ten
☐	☑	☑

Instructional Hierarchy:				
Acquisition	Fluency	Maintenance	Generalization	Adaptation
☐	☑	☐	☐	☐

Setting:			Tier of Support within RTI Framework:		
Whole-Class	Small-Group	Individual	Universal Prevention	Targeted Intervention	Individualized Intervention
☑	☑	☑	☑	☑	☑

Mediator: ☑ Teacher or Interventionist   ☐ Student (with teacher oversight)   ☐ Parent

Effectiveness: Moderate to large average effect size.	**Amount of Evidence:** 10 peer-reviewed studies between 2004 and 2012.

Acceptability: Collected across four studies using a Likert scale. Teachers indicated high acceptability; student acceptability ranged from moderate to high.

Brief Description: Teacher-mediated instructional approach using prerecorded audio prompts.

Materials Required: Audio recorder with cassette tape (or MP3 player), taped problems worksheet, kitchen timer or stopwatch, headphones (optional), incentives (optional).

Training Required: None indicated; training on CBA to monitor progress may be needed.

Duration: Implemented 3–15 minutes per occasion, three to five times weekly, for a total of 3–10 weeks.

Active Treatment Components: Opportunities to practice, errorless learning, progressive time delay, and immediate feedback.

Procedures:

1. Determine the skill that will be used for the intervention according to CBA or computer-adapted assessments. Skills that fall in the instructional range (minimum of 85% accuracy; 14–31 DCPM for grades 1–3; 24–49 for grades 4 and 5) are best for matches for this intervention.

2. Consider dividing the target skill into sets of 10–20 problems that are presented one set at a time, introducing a new set only after the previous set of problems has been mastered.

3. Construct a worksheet with a list of problems, excluding the answer, that represent each set. Be sure to number each problem.

4. Create the cassette tape using the audio recorder. State the problems that align with each problem set worksheet in order, using the numbers on the worksheet. New problems should be stated 3 seconds following reading the answer to the previous problem. Each problem in the problem set will be read four times total. The first time through, record each problem in the same order as the worksheet with the answer (no delay, begin with problem and answer). The second time through the problem set, record each problem with a 3-second delay between reading the problem and answer. The third time through, read the problem and then state the answer using a 2-second delay. The fourth time through, read the problem and state the answer using a 1-second delay.

5. Inform the students that they will be listening to a tape with problems and answers, and ask them to follow along with the tape on their worksheet. Tell them to try and "beat the tape" by writing the answer to each problem before the answer is provided by the tape. Tell them to correct any mistakes as needed.

6. At the end of each session (or at least once weekly) all students are administered a brief assessment (e.g., CBA), which is scored to monitor progress on the target skill.

7. Once every other week or monthly a multiple-skill CBM probe is administered to progress monitor for generalization.

Treatment Variations:

- During classwide applications teachers should walk around the room to monitor student engagement with the TP procedure and accuracy with the implementation.
- An interdependent group contingency can be added to the TP intervention by averaging class performance on problem sets and comparing the performance with the previous week. If the class average improved, each student in the class can receive a reward such as pencils, erasers, stickers, lunch with the teacher, or a class party.

Selected References:

1. McCallum, E., Skinner, C. H., & Hutchins, H. (2004). The taped-problems intervention: Increasing division fact fluency using a low-tech self-managed time-delay intervention. *Journal of Applied School Psychology, 20,* 129–147.
2. McCallum, E., Skinner, C. H., Turner, H., & Saecker, L. (2006). The taped-problems intervention: Increasing multiplication fact fluency using a low-tech, classwide, time-delay intervention. *School Psychology Review, 35,* 419–434.
3. McCleary, D. F., Aspiranti, K. B., Skinner, C. H., Foster, L. N., Luna, E., Murray, K., et al. (2011). Enhancing math fact fluency via taped problems in intact second- and fourth-grade classrooms. *Journal of Evidence-Based Practices for Schools, 12,* 179–201.

APPENDIX 9.5. Explicit Timing Intervention Brief

CCSS Domain Areas Addressed:

Counting and Cardinality	Operations and Algebraic Thinking	Numbers and Operations in Base Ten
☐	☑	☑

Instructional Hierarchy:

Acquisition	Fluency	Maintenance	Generalization	Adaptation
☐	☑	☐	☐	☐

Setting: / **Tier of Support within RTI Framework:**

Whole-Class	Small-Group	Individual	Universal Prevention	Targeted Intervention	Individualized Intervention
☑	☑	☐	☑	☑	☐

Mediator: ☑ Teacher or Interventionist ☐ Student (with teacher oversight) ☐ Parent

Effectiveness: None reported.

Amount of Evidence: Six peer-reviewed studies between 1976 and 2007.

Acceptability: Collected across two studies using a Likert scale. Student acceptability ranged from moderate to high.

Brief Description: Teacher-mediated instructional approach.

Materials Required: Worksheets, kitchen timer or stopwatch.

Training Required: Written directions provided; training on CBA to monitor progress may be needed.

Duration: Implemented 3–30 minutes per occasion, two to five times weekly, for a total of 4–6 weeks.

Active Treatment Components: Timed opportunities to practice and feedback.

Procedures:

1. Determine the skill that will be used for the intervention according to CBA or computer-adapted assessments. Skills that fall in the instructional range (minimum of 85% accuracy; 14–31 DCPM for grades 1–3; 24–49 for grades 4 and 5) are best for matches for this intervention.
2. Provide students with worksheets on the target skill area and inform them how much time they will have to practice. Usually, practice is brief in nature, ranging from a task that can be completed within 3–10 minutes.
3. Tell students how long they will be working for and you will be stopping them at each minute to see their progress. Tell students to begin working and start the stopwatch or kitchen timer.
4. Using a kitchen timer or a stopwatch, stop the students at 1-minute intervals. Say, "Please stop and circle [or underline] the problem that you are working on or just finished. Then put your pencils in the air and wait until I say 'Begin.'"
5. When all students' pencils are in the air, say "Begin." Be sure the students either finish the problem they were working on when they stopped, or if they finished the problem, be sure students work on the subsequent problem on the worksheet.
6. Repeat steps 4 and 5, stopping students at every 1-minute interval until the total time for the task is over.
7. At the end of each session, provide students with an answer key, ask students to trade papers, or show the answers on an overhead projector or use a PowerPoint presentation. Ask students to score their papers. These data can be used to monitor progress on the target skill.
8. Once every other week or monthly a multiple-skill CBM probe is administered to progress monitor for generalization.

Selected References:

1. Codding, R. S., Shiyko, M., Russo, M., Birch, S. Fanning, E., & Jaspen, D. (2007). Comparing mathematics interventions: Does initial level of fluency predict intervention effectiveness? *Journal of School Psychology, 45,* 603–617.
2. Rhymer, K. N., Henington, C., Skinner, C. H., & Looby, E. J. (1999). The effects of explicit timing on mathematics performance in second-grade Caucasian and African American students. *School Psychology Quarterly, 14,* 397–407.
3. Van Houten, R., & Thompson, C. (1976). The effects of explicit timing on math performance. *Journal of Applied Behavior Analysis, 9,* 227–230.

APPENDIX 9.6. High-Preference/Interspersed Problems Intervention Brief

CCSS Domain Areas Addressed:		
Counting and Cardinality	Operations and Algebraic Thinking	Numbers and Operations in Base Ten
☐	☑	☑

Instructional Hierarchy:				
Acquisition	Fluency	Maintenance	Generalization	Adaptation
☐	☑	☑	☑	☐

Setting:			Tier of Support within RTI Framework:		
Whole-Class	Small-Group	Individual	Universal Prevention	Targeted Intervention	Individualized Intervention
☐	☑	☐	☐	☑	☐

Mediator: ☐ Teacher or Interventionist   ☑ Student (with teacher oversight)   ☐ Parent

Effectiventess: None reported.	**Amount of Evidence:** Three peer-reviewed studies (2005).

Acceptability: Two studies collected student and teacher acceptability; ratings were high.

Brief Description: Student-managed approach.

Materials Required: Specialized worksheets.

Training Required: Not described. Teachers may require 2 hours for CBA to monitor progress.

Duration: HPI is implemented for 10–15 minutes per occasion, 3–5 days per week, for a total of 3–5 weeks.

Active Treatment Components: Opportunities to practice.

Procedures:

1. Determine the skill that will be used for the intervention according to CBA or computer-adapted assessments. Skills that fall in the instructional range (minimum of 85% accuracy; 14–31 DCPM for grades 1–3; 24–49 for grades 4 and 5) are best matches for this intervention.
2. Create worksheets that include the target skill and intersperse a one-digit × one-digit (basic fact) in the same area of operation (addition, subtraction, multiplication, or division) as the target skill.
3. It is recommended that the single-digit facts be assessed using CBA to be sure that these facts fall in the mastery range of performance for students (above 31 [grades 1–3] or 50 [grades 4 and 5] DCPM).
4. Simple single-digit problems should be interspersed into target skill worksheets every other problem (one easy problem, one target problem).
5. Distribute worksheets to students and set a kitchen timer or stopwatch for 10 minutes. When 10 minutes have been completed, tell students to stop working.
6. Collect and score the worksheets, provide an answer key, and have students score their own worksheet, or have them exchange papers and score their peer's worksheet.
7. At the end of each session (or at least once weekly), all students are administered a brief assessment (e.g., CBA), which is scored to monitor progress on the target skill.
8. Once every other week or monthly a multiple-skill CBM probe is administered to progress monitor for generalization.

Treatment Variations:

- Students can be provided this intervention orally by an interventionist who reads the problems on the worksheet aloud. Students can be provided with a worksheet with space to record their answer and may or may not include the problem. Students are asked to listen to the problem being presented, solve the problem mentally, and record their answer on the worksheet. Interventionists should permit students 20 seconds to solve the target problem before moving on to the next problem and 4 seconds for the easy problem.

Selected References:

1. Hawkins, J., Skinner, C. H., & Oliver, R. (2005). The effects of task demands and additive interspersal ratios on fifth grade students' mathematics accuracy. *School Psychology Review, 34,* 543–555.
2. Montarello, S., & Martens, B. K. (2005). Effects of interspersed brief problems on students' endurance at completing math work. *Journal of Behavioral Education, 14,* 249–266.

3. Rhymer, K. N., & Morgan, S. K. (2005). Comparison of the explicit timing and interspersal interventions: Analysis of problem completion rates, student preference, and teacher acceptability. *Journal of Behavioral Education, 14,* 283–303.

4. Skinner, C. H., Hurst, K. L., Teeple, D. F., & Meadow, S. O. (2002). Increasing on-task behavior during mathematics independent seat-work in students with emotional disturbance in interspersing additional brief problems. *Psychology in the Schools, 39,* 647–659.

APPENDIX 9.7. Concrete–Representation–Abstract Intervention Brief

CCSS Domain Areas Addressed:

Counting and Cardinality (K)	Operations and Algebraic Thinking (K–5)	Numbers and Operations in Base Ten (K–5)	Measurement and Data (K–5)
☐	☑	☑	☐

Instructional Hierarchy:

Acquisition	Fluency	Maintenance	Generalization	Adaptation
☑	☐	☐	☐	☐

Setting: | | | **Tier of Support within RTI Framework:** | | |

Whole-Class	Small-Group	Individual	Universal Prevention	Targeted Intervention	Individualized Intervention
☐	☐	☑	☐	☐	☑

Mediator: ☑ Teacher or Interventionist ☐ Student (with teacher oversight) ☐ Parent

Effectiveness: Large effect sizes computed across two different studies.	**Amount of Evidence:** Six peer-reviewed studies between 1988 and 2014.

Acceptability: Collected in three studies (Flores, 2010; Flores et al., 2014; Miller & Kaffer, 2011); satisfaction ratings were high among students and teachers.

Brief Description: CRA is a teacher-directed instructional approach where students are individually administering the intervention.

Materials Required: Ten to 16 scripted lessons, learning sheets, place-value mats, student notebooks, base-ten blocks, goal charts or graphs.

Training Required: Training may be required on the scripted lessons and use of the materials.

Duration: CRA is implemented for 30 minutes per occasion, three to four times weekly, for a total of 12 weeks depending on the number of skills targeted for intervention.

Active Treatment Components: Demonstration, guided practice, independent practice, feedback on progress.

Procedures:

1. Determine the skill or skills that will be used for the intervention according to CBA or computer-adapted assessments. The earliest prerequisite skill that is not mastered in the sequence for each math operation should be targeted.
2. At the end of each session (or at least once weekly), all students are administered a brief assessment (e.g., CBA), which is completed individually and scored to monitor progress on the target skill.
3. Once every other week or monthly a multiple-skill CBM probe is administered to progress monitor for generalization.
4. Demonstrate how to solve math problems using base-ten manipulatives. Interventionists solve the problem using a physical demonstration with the manipulatives but also think aloud. Interventionists should engage students by asking questions without having students solve the problems.
5. The interventionist and students take turns completing the steps of the problem-solving process using the base-ten manipulatives.
6. The students complete the problems independently with the base-ten manipulatives.
7. The interventionist reviews the lesson activities.
8. After three lessons using the base-ten manipulatives, steps 4–7 are repeated but students draw pictures instead of using the base-ten manipulatives. Teach students to draw pictures of problems using images similar to the base-ten manipulatives. For example, 1's are short tally marks, 10's are represented by long lines, and 100's are represented by squares.
9. After three lessons using drawings to depict problem solving, steps 4–7 are repeated using numerals instead of drawings, and also applying the mnemonic RENAME (Read the problem, Examine the one's column, Note the ones in the one's column, Address the ten's column, Mark the ten's column, Examine and note the hundreds' column) or DRAW (Discover the sign, Read the problem, Answer or draw and check, and Write the answer).

Treatment Variations:

- Show students' progress monitoring data by using a graph that contains an aimline with the students' target goal at the start of each session (Flores et al., 2014).
- Word-problem-solving practice is included as a transfer activity and students use the mnemonic FAST RENAME (Find what you are solving for, Ask yourself "What are the important parts of the problem," Set up the numbers, Tie down the sign; Miller & Kaffer, 2011).

Selected References:

1. Flores, M. M. (2010). Using the concrete–representational–abstract sequence to teach subtraction with regrouping to students at risk for failure. *Remedial and Special Education, 31,* 195–207.
2. Flores, M. M., Hinton, V., & Strozier, S. D. (2014). Teaching subtraction and multiplication with regrouping using the concrete–representational–abstract sequence. *Learning Disabilities Research and Practice, 29,* 75–88.
3. Miller, S. P., & Kaffar, B. J. (2011). Developing addition with regrouping competence among second graders with mathematics difficulties. *Investigations in Mathematics Learning, 4,* 24–49.

Procedural Cover–Copy–Compare

Target Behavior

Procedural Cover–Copy–Compare (P-CCC) was designed to be used with a student who can fluently complete basic fact skills (>40 DCPM) but is unable to complete multidigit computation problems above 20 DCPM. This pattern of responding is indicative of a student who lacks the procedural skill set needed to apply his or her prior knowledge of fact skills. P-CCC is a multicomponent intervention that incorporates teacher demonstration, guided practice using visual cues, independent practice, and performance feedback with reteaching (if needed). This same instructional sequence can be used across all skills (i.e., +, −, ×, ÷). The combination of these approaches integrates modeling, cueing, and feedback to encourage errorless learning, but also fades supports so students independently apply and practice the taught procedural skills.

Materials

P-CCC Teacher Script with matched multidigit computation probe, P-CCC Implementation Checklist, pencil, timer (optional).

P-CCC Procedures: Teacher

1. Teacher training: Read OTISS-Math Computation Packet and watch P-CCC training clips.
2. Select skill (+, −, ×, ÷) and obtain subskill probe sets A, B, and C for that skill. Begin using the P-CCC intervention with set A, then set B, and last, set C (move to next skill when student scores >20 DCPM with 90% accuracy across 3 days).

Multidigit Computation Subskill Probes

	Skill	Set	Problem type(s)	Time	Mastery
Multidigit addition	+	A	3 × 3 digit	2 minutes	20 DCPM
	+	B	2 × 1 digit with regrouping	2 minutes	20 DCPM
	+	C	3 × 3 digit with regrouping	2 minutes	20 DCPM
Multidigit subtraction	−	A	3 × 3 digit	2 minutes	20 DCPM
	−	B	2 × 1 digit with regrouping	2 minutes	20 DCPM
	−	C	3 × 3 digit with regrouping	2 minutes	20 DCPM
Multidigit multiplication	×	A	2 × 1 digit	2 minutes	20 DCPM
	×	B	4 × 2 digit	2 minutes	20 DCPM
	×	C	4 × 3 digit	2 minutes	20 DCPM
Multidigit division	÷	A	3 ÷ 1 digit, no remainder	2 minutes	20 DCPM
	÷	B	3 ÷ 1 digit, with remainder	2 minutes	20 DCPM
	÷	C	3 ÷ 1 digit, with decimals	2 minutes	20 DCPM

(continued)

3. Implement P-CCC intervention.
   a. Have relevant materials organized and ready (P-CCC script and implementation checklist, multidigit computation probe, and score key)
   b. Give student probe, document date, record start/end time.
   c. Read script to demonstrate procedures, model completion using visual cues.
      • Scripts are included for each of the three subskills across +, −, ×, and ÷.
   d. Have student complete problem and verbally describe procedures. Provide feedback as needed and repeat until student accurately completes problem.
   e. Have student complete problems containing visual cues.
      • Provide behavior-specific praise as needed.
   f. Have student complete remaining problems (no visual cues).
      • Problems on second page will require student to discriminate when and when not to use the taught procedure (monitor carefully).
   g. After student finishes, present student with scoring key. Review completed probe and provide student with feedback on accuracy. Provide error correction and reteaching as necessary.
      • Progress monitor and incorporate self-graphing with reward as needed.

P-CCC Procedures: Student

1. Student records information on daily probe (name, date, start/end time).
2. Student watches and listens to teacher, who completes the first problem, describes procedures, and defines the purpose of visual cues.
3. Student completes problem and verbally describes procedures to teacher with support of visual cues (teacher provides feedback and reteaching as needed). Repeat as needed.
4. Student completes problems independent of teacher using visual cues.
5. Student completes problems independent of both teacher and visual cues, and discriminates when and when not to use taught procedure.
6. Student receives feedback (teacher-led review of score key) on accuracy of performance and corrects inaccurate problems using step 2.

Addition Subskill Set A: 3 × 3 Digit without Regrouping

Teacher Script

"Today we are going to work on some bigger, multidigit addition problems. Your packet contains two pages. On the first page, you will find four rows of problems. The first two rows have lines that show columns that you can use with the multidigit problems. For example, on the first problem, you start by adding ____ + ____ in the ones column, then move to the tens column and add ____+____. Last, you move to the hundreds column and compute ____ + ____.

"The rest of the problems on the first and second rows have lines to show the columns, but the last two rows have multidigit problems without the columns but you do them in the same way. For example, on the first problem of the third row, begin with the ones column and add ____+____, then move to the tens column and add ____+____, and finish with ____+____ in the hundreds column. The second page has problems but no lines. Work as fast as you can to correctly complete all the problems. After you are done, raise your hand and we will check your work to see how many you answered correctly! Are there any questions?"

P-CCC Multidigit Addition Worksheet A

3 6 2 + 5 3 5	4 2 6 + 4 5 3	6 3 4 + 3 5 4	2 4 3 + 5 4 5
4 2 6 + 4 5 3	3 6 2 + 5 3 5	2 4 3 + 5 4 5	6 4 3 + 3 4 5
346 + 543	436 + 453	623 + 355	236 + 553
453 + 436	364 + 534	355 + 623	253 + 536

(continued)

Addition Subskill Set B: 2 + 1 Digit with Regrouping

Teacher Script

"Today we are going to work on some multidigit addition problems that require regrouping. Your packet contains two pages. On the first page, you will find four rows of problems. The first two rows each has two problems in bold with the answer. I am going to explain how to get the answer, then you will cover it and do the problem next to it by yourself. As you complete the problem, I want you to tell me what you are doing to solve the problem. If you are unsure or do something incorrectly, I will help you. When you can correctly complete a problem and describe your steps, I will have you complete rows 3 and 4 by yourself. Let's start.

"Locate the first problem and point to the ones column. You start by adding this column (____ + ____) to get an answer of ____. You can only write down one number in this column (in this case, a ____) so you have to carry the 1. To do this, you move the 1 to the box in the next column and carry the 1 and place it in the box above the ____. Please point to the box. Now locate the number in the tens column and then add the 1 that was carried to get ____. You write down ____ to get an answer of ____.

"Now cover the problem and answer with this piece of paper and attempt the problem next to it. As you are working the problem, I want you to tell me what you are doing. If you are unsure or do something incorrectly, I will help you. When you are finished, uncover the problem, and we will see if your answer is correct. If you can't do the problem correctly or you need my help, I will help you with the steps and I will have you do the next problem and tell me what you are doing. When you can get the right answer without my help, I will have you complete rows 3 and 4 by yourself. These problems have boxes to remind you to carry. If you need help or are unsure what to do, raise your hand and I will help you. After you are done we will check your work to see how many you answered correctly! If you miss any, we will correctly work the problem! Let's start."

(continued)

P-CCC Addition 2 + 1 Digit with Regrouping Worksheet B

□ **66** **+ 9** **75**	□ 66 + 9	□ **84** **+ 7** **91**	□ 84 + 7
□ **97** **+ 5** **102**	□ 97 + 5	□ **78** **+ 2** **80**	□ 78 + 2
□ 59 + 2	□ 65 + 6	□ 78 + 3	□ 39 + 4
□ 47 + 6	□ 27 + 7	□ 95 + 9	□ 16 + 9

CHAPTER 10

Word-Problem Solving

Word-problem solving is one of the most common and complex forms of mathematical problem solving, and as noted earlier, appears to be the most challenging for students according to teacher reports (D. P. Bryant et al., 2000; Jonassen, 2003). Word-problem solving requires integration of many aspects of math knowledge that can be summarized into two primary phases: (1) problem representation and (2) problem solution (Boonen, van Wesel, Jolles, & van der Schoot, 2014). Problem representation refers to determining the underlying situation that is embedded within the text, and consists of understanding math language, identifying relevant information, disregarding irrelevant information, locating missing information, and creating a mental representation or model of the word problem. Problem solution refers to planning how to solve the problem and executing the plan for solving the problem by developing a plan to solve the problem, employing the appropriate procedural strategies to carry out the plan, solving the problem using the correct math operations, and checking and monitoring the work (Desoete, Roeyers, & De Clercq, 2003; Fuchs, Fuchs, Compton, et al., 2006; Montague, 2008b).

Students experiencing difficulties in math struggle solving word problems because they tend not to (1) understand the story problem language, (2) select the appropriate algorithm to solve the problem, (3) execute the step-by-step plan required to solve the problem, (4) self-monitor the problem-solving process, and/or (5) generalize the strategies they have learned to novel word problems (Bryant et al., 2000; Gersten, Beckmann, et al., 2009; Shin & Bryant, 2015).

Historically, curricula have reduced instruction of word-problem solving to the identification of key terms or syntax rather than understanding the underlying structure of the word problem itself (Jitendra, Griffin, Deatline-Buchman, & Sczesniak, 2007). Unfortunately, emphasis on key terms alone—such as underlining the words *combined* or *all together* to signal addition or *how many are left* to signal subtraction as the necessary operation to solve the word problem—is often inaccurate and fails to promote deeper conceptual understanding (NMAP, 2008). Requiring students to spontaneously draw a picture representing a word problem has also been shown to be an ineffective strategy because students have difficulty independently generating a picture without direct instruction (Boonen et al., 2014; van Garderen, Scheuermann, & Jackson, 2012). Even when a picture is generated, the drawing tends to contain the objects or people described in the story rather than the underlying model required to solve the problem.

Current recommendations emphasize providing instruction in elementary school using schemas (e.g., diagrams or spatial layouts) across the word-problem types in elementary school. For addition and subtraction word problems, the three major types are (1) change, (2) group/total, and (3) compare/difference (Fuchs, Seethaler, et al., 2008; Powell, 2011; Zhang & Xin, 2012; Zheng, Flynn, & Swanson, 2012). For multiplication and division, there are

BOX 10.1. Word-Problem Types		
Word-Problem Type	**Definition**	**Example**
Change	The word problem contains a time element and three parts: beginning, change, and ending. A story is presented where the starting quantity is either increased or decreased to end with a new ending quantity.	There were five green frogs in the pond. Two orange frogs hopped into the pond. How many frogs are in the pond now?
Group/total	Two distinct groups/subsets combine to form a larger group/superset.	There were eight frogs in the pond. Some of the frogs were orange and five frogs were green. How many orange frogs were in the pond?
Compare/difference	Compare two quantities to determine the relationship between the numbers.	There are five green frogs and three orange frogs in the pond. How many more green frogs are in the pond than orange frogs?
Equal groups	Describes a number of equal units with the unit rate, number of units, or the product serving as the unknown quantity.	Four friends went to see a movie. The total ticket price was $36. How much does each ticket cost?
Multiplicative comparison	Compares two quantities and includes a compare statement that describes one quantity (comparison) as a part of the other quantity (referent).	Mason sold four cups of lemonade at his lemonade stand on Friday. On Saturday, he sold eight times as many cups of lemonade. How many cups of lemonade did he sell on Saturday?

Note. Based on Fuchs, Seethaler, et al. (2008); Jitendra, DiPipi, and Perron-Jones (2002); Jitendra, Griffin, Deatline-Buchman, and Sczesniak (2007); Powell (2011); and Xin (2008).

two major word-problem types: (1) equal groups and (2) multiplicative comparison (Jitendra, DiPipi, & Perron-Jones, 2002; Xin, 2008). See Box 10.1 for word-problem type definitions and examples. The idea is that by understanding the underlying problem structure, students will be able to solve most word problems they encounter (Cooper & Sweller, 1987; Powell, 2011). In addition, metacognitive strategies that use mnemonics or heuristics to organize problem-solving steps are recommended (see Box 10.2), such as FOPS (Jitendra, 2007) and RUN (Fuchs, Fuchs, Powell, et al., 2008).

The language associated with word-problem solving might be simplified by providing a review of math terms and definitions that the student will be encountering during word-problem-solving practice. Once terms have been reviewed more generally, unknown words within a word problem can be discussed, and students can be encouraged to replace unfamiliar contexts or terms with familiar words (Woodward et al., 2012). For example, the word *defective* could be replaced with the phrase *not working,* or the name given to a character in the word problem could be replaced by the name of a person familiar to the student. If students have little experience with a term, changing the term to represent a familiar experience is also recommended.

It is important to provide students with explicit instruction in word-problem solving and introduce them to a gradually increasing range of problem difficulty starting with simple one-step problems and moving toward complex multistep word problems. A sample sequence for skill development is provided in Table 10.1.

BUILDING WORD-PROBLEM-SOLVING INTERVENTIONS

Unfortunately, there are only a handful of commercially available standard protocol programs that directly teach word-problem solving and few peer-reviewed interventions that are consistently investigated. The good news is that an effective problem-solving intervention can be created from nine key instructional components that have been shown to improve the word-problem-solving accuracy of students who have math disabilities (Zheng et al., 2012). It is possible, however, that building an intervention from these elements could be less effective for students who experience both reading and math difficulties (Zheng et al., 2012). Table 10.2 describes each of these core components.

BOX 10.2. FOPS and RUN Mnemonics	
FOPS	**RUN**
1. **F**ind the problem type.	1. **R**ead the problem.
2. **O**rganize, using the diagram.	2. **U**nderline the question.
3. **P**lan to solve the problem.	3. **N**ame the problem type.
4. **S**olve the problem.	

TABLE 10.1. Sample Skill Sequence for Word Problems

Operation	Word-problem skill hierarchy	Word-problem type hierarchy
Addition and subtraction	• Solve one-step word problems within 10 • Solve one-step word problems within 20 • Solve one-step word problems within 20, with unknowns in all positions using a symbol to represent the unknown number • Solve one-step word problems within 20 that require adding three numbers, with unknowns in all positions using a symbol to represent the unknown number • Solve one-step word problems within 100, with unknowns in all positions using a symbol to represent the unknown number • Solve two-step word problems within 100, with unknowns in all positions using a symbol to represent the unknown number • Solve multistep word problems	• Total/group • Change • Compare
Multiplication and division	• Solve one-step word problems within 100, with unknowns in all positions using a symbol to represent the unknown number • Solve two-step word problems within 100, with unknowns in all positions using a symbol to represent the unknown number • Solve multistep word problems • Solve multistep word problems, with remainders	• Equal groups • Multiplicative comparison

Note. Hierarchies for skill and problem type are listed from least to most difficult.

RESEARCH-SUPPORTED INTERVENTIONS

Several research syntheses have indicated that there are three major intervention types that improve students' word-problem solving: (1) schema instruction and representation techniques, (2) cognitive strategy instruction (CSI), and (3) CAI (Xin & Jitendra, 1999). All three intervention approaches have strong effects with the most benefit observed when these strategies are applied to simple (e.g., one-step) as compared with complex (three or more steps) word problems (Xin & Jitendra, 1999; Zhang & Xin, 2012). The largest effects were found for schema instruction and representation techniques, followed by CSI, and the least effective, although still strong, was CAI (Zhang & Xin, 2012). It is possible that CAI is most appropriate for students in the fluency range of instruction, whereas schema instruction and CSI would be applicable for students in the acquisition stage of learning. However, in Chapter 5 we described ways to evaluate CAI programs that might be appropriate for students in the acquisition stage of learning. See Table 10.3 for a description of three commercially available programs that represent schema instruction and CSI.

TABLE 10.2. Nine Key Instructional Components to Address Word-Problem Solving

Treatment component	Description
Advanced organizer	• Learning objectives are provided to students before instruction begins. • Information is provided to direct students' attention on aspects of instruction before instruction ensues. • Student is asked to look over materials before instruction begins.
Control difficulty or processing demands of tasks	• Material is presented that matches each student's instructional level. • Progress monitoring is used to assess students' mastery of skills and/or knowledge. • The interventionist provides instructional assistance as necessary. • Prompts and cues are gradually faded as students' independent learning improves.
Elaboration	• Concepts are explained or additional information on a concept is provided, as needed, by the interventionist. • Explanations of procedures are repeated.
Explicit practice	• Opportunities for drill and practice are provided. • Interventionists provide daily (or session-specific) feedback on student performance. • Practice is distributed across sessions and is brief. • Sequenced weekly and monthly review of previously presented material is provided.
Questioning	• Instructor and student engage in question-and-answer exchange of ideas (e.g., Socratic dialogue). • Students are encouraged to ask questions. • Interventionist asks process-related question (e.g., "Did you follow the FAST DRAW steps?")
Sequencing	• Instruction is broken down into small steps or components. • Problem-solving tasks are divided into smaller, short, sequential activities.
Skill modeling	• Interventionist models skills and concepts.
Strategy cues	• Reminders are given to use strategies or steps. • Step-by-step prompts or process guidance is given. • Interventionist verbalizes the steps or procedures while solving a problem. • Interventionist uses "think-aloud" models.
Task reduction	• Tasks are broken down into smaller skill sets, steps, or components (e.g., task analysis). • Each skill set is mastered according to a predetermined criterion before moving to a new skill set.

Note. Based on Zheng, Flynn, and Swanson (2012).

TABLE 10.3. Commercially Available Word-Problem-Solving Programs

	Solving Math Word Problems	Pirate Math	Solve It!
Treatment components	• Explicit instruction • Strategy instruction • Sequenced instruction • Progress monitoring and feedback • Drill, practice, review • Visual representations	• Explicit instruction • Strategy instruction • Sequenced instruction • Progress monitoring and feedback • Drill, practice, review • Visual representations • Reinforcement	• Explicit instruction • Strategy instruction • Sequenced instruction • Progress monitoring and feedback • Drill, practice, review • Visual representations • Reinforcement
Level of skill proficiency	• Acquisition	• Acquisition • Fluency • Generalization	• Acquisition
Peer-reviewed references	• > 10 studies • Conducted by program authors	• 5–10 studies • Conducted by program authors	• 5–10 studies • Conducted by program authors
Grades	• 1–8	• 2 and 3	• 5–12
Target skills	• Addition • Subtraction • Multiplication • Division	• Addition • Subtraction • Multiplication • Division	• Addition • Subtraction • Multiplication • Division
Interventionist	• General ed teacher • Special ed teacher • Math specialist	• Paraprofessional	• General ed teacher • Special ed teacher
Effect size	• Large	• Large	• Large
Cost of materials	• <$150	• <$150	• <$150
Reviewed by educational clearinghouses	• None	• National Center on Intensive Intervention	• What Works Clearinghouse

Schema Instruction and Representation Techniques

Representation techniques include the use of diagramming, manipulatives, verbalization, and mapping. A diagram has been defined as the visual representation of information within a spatial layout that illustrates the parts of a word problem, as well as how those parts go together (Diezman & McCosker, 2011; van Garderen, 2007). Word problems can be represented through a number of different types of diagrams, including line diagrams, part–whole diagrams, circle or bar diagrams, tree diagrams, networks, and matrices. Each of these diagrams is useful for solving specific types of problems. For example, networks and line diagrams are used to determine order or sequence; matrices and tables are used to represent relationships between sets; hierarchies or tree diagrams are used to depict diverging and converging paths; and part–whole, circles, or bar diagrams are used to illustrate connections between parts of a group or a whole (van Garderen & Scheuermann, 2014). Unfortunately, without explicit instruction on how to use diagrams, students with learning disabilities construct less effective diagrams and are less likely to know how and why using a diagram is helpful for word-problem solving (e.g., van Garderen & Scheuermann, 2014; van Garderen et al., 2012). Students benefit from instruction that describes (1) what a diagram is, (2) why a diagram is useful (i.e., identify what the problem is asking, track work while problem solving, check the answer), (3) when to use a diagram (i.e., understand what the problem is asking, organize information, determine the steps, check the answer), (4) which type of diagram to use and why, (5) how to create a diagram (i.e., should be brief, uses codes and symbols that are easy to recall, is not necessarily realistic, only selective pieces of information are included), and (6) how to use a diagram (i.e., track thinking, revise, change diagrams, and matching the diagram to the problem). Appendix 10.1 describes a procedure for teaching students to use diagrams for word-problem solving.

Recently, representation techniques have focused on the use of diagrams to directly teach underlying structures of word problems to students at risk for or with learning disabilities in math (e.g., Fuchs, Seethaler, et al., 2008; Jitendra & Hoff, 1996). One specific technique that has considerable empirical support is referred to as schema instruction. Using the word-problem classification system, schema instruction teaches students to recognize whether they are presented with a change, group/total, or compare/difference problem. Any of the three pieces of information from each problem type may be missing, and the problem can be solved using the remaining two pieces of given information. Once students identify the problem type, they use a corresponding schematic diagram to translate the problem from words into numerical sentences that are subsequently solved. In this way, schema instruction facilitates the translation of word problems into mental representations, as well as combines conceptual understanding with procedural knowledge. Explicit modeling of strategy steps, explanation, modeling, and elaboration with think-alouds and practice are also incorporated.

It is recommended that schema instruction be strategically faded over time to promote students' independent problem solving when given novel word problems111 (Jitendra et al., 2007). Schema instruction is also more effective for at-risk students when paired with general classroom instruction (Fuchs, Fuchs, Craddock, et al., 2008). Adding a motivation component to schema instruction may be useful within a small-group tutoring format. Praise and rewards could be directed toward student persistence, contemplation and generation of different solutions, and engagement in self-regulation activities. Figure 10.1 illustrates an example of one type of schema instruction. The following two commercially available programs use schema instruction to teach word-problem solving.

Solving Math Word Problems: Teaching Students with Learning Disabilities Using Schema-Based Instruction

This program, created by Jitendra (2007), is available from PRO-ED (*www.proedinc.com*) and is appropriate for students in grades 1–8. It has two variations: (1) addition and subtraction (21 lessons), and (2) multiplication and division (13 lessons). Units are organized around four problem-solving types and sessions range from 30 to 60 minutes each and are often used three times weekly (Powell, 2011). The program includes a scripted manual and a CD-ROM. Solving Math Word Problems is designed to be implemented in classes, small groups, or individually. Students are taught to identify the problem-solving schema and represent word problems using the appropriate diagram. A four-step strategy, FOPS, is taught to students, and direct modeling of the problem-solving process is provided with think-alouds. Scaffolding is used so that students gradually attain more independence with problem solv-

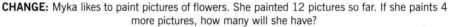

CHANGE: Myka likes to paint pictures of flowers. She painted 12 pictures so far. If she paints 4 more pictures, how many will she have?

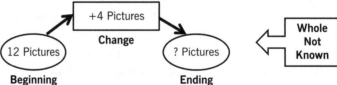

GROUP: There are 75 different flavors of ice cream. Socs has 35 flavors. How many flavors of ice cream are not at Socs?

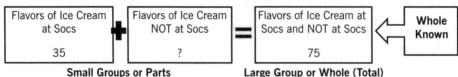

COMPARE: Logan saw a pine tree in the forest. Later, he saw a maple tree that was 9 feet tall. The maple tree was 5 feet shorter than the pine tree. How tall is the pine tree?

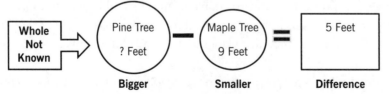

FIGURE 10.1. Examples of three types of story problems and their schematic diagrams. Adapted from Jitendra et al. (2013). Copyright © 2013 SAGE Publications. Adapted by permission.

ing. After completing the diagram, a mathematical equation is recorded and then the problem is solved. Visual diagrams, overhead modeling, reference guides, answer sheets, student pages, and progress monitoring measures are incorporated into the program.

Pirate Math Individual Tutoring

The Pirate Math program (e.g., Fuchs, Powell, et al., 2009) is available from the authors and can be ordered online at *kc.vanderbilt.edu/pals/pdfs/pirate_math.pdf*). It is designated for use with second- and third-grade students, and is designed to be implemented individually. (The corresponding classwide version is described in Chapter 4.) The program consists of both basic word-problem solving, as well as direct computation practice organized into four units. The first unit teaches counting strategies for basic math facts, two-step computation procedures, and solving algebraic equations. The remaining three units provide explicit instruction on three problem-solving types using schema-broadening instruction and the mnemonic RUN (see Box 10.2). Schema-broadening instruction contains the same features as schema-based instruction, and also includes lessons that directly teach students to classify and solve problem types when supplied with word problems that contain novel features (e.g., different format, additional questions, unfamiliar wording, graphic displays) in order to improve transfer to untaught problems (Powell, 2011). Each treatment session is 25–30 minutes in length, delivered three times weekly, for a total of 16 weeks. A scripted manual that contains templates for necessary instructional materials is provided. Training is recommended as 1 full day by the program creators, as well as ongoing weekly follow-up support by school or district-level staff.

Cognitive Strategy Instruction

Strategy instruction or CSI integrates cognitive strategies and processes (i.e., step-by-step problem-solving) with metacognitive strategies and processes (self-regulation of the application of the problem-solving steps; Montague, Enders, & Dietz, 2011). CSI requires the interventionist to (1) explain the plan for *how* to solve a word problem; (2) provide verbal modeling, questioning, and demonstration of the plan steps; (3) offer prompts and cues to use the plan; and (4) demonstrate problem solving through cognitive modeling with think-aloud procedures (Montague, 2008b).

For example, Case, Harris, and Graham (1992) taught students a five-step strategy: (1) read the problem; (2) look for the key words and circle them, (3) draw the problem using pictures, (4) write the corresponding math problem in sentence format, and (5) write the answer. Commonly, cognitive strategies are taught using a heuristic—such as FAST DRAW or SAY, ASK, CHECK—that is incorporated within the instructional routine (i.e., plan for problem solving; see Table 10.4 for specific examples).

Thinking aloud allows an interventionist to illustrate the problem-solving and decision-making process for each type of word problem instructed. By describing this process in a step-by-step fashion, interventionists can help students connect the word problem to the visual or schematic representation (Gersten, Beckman, et al., 2009). In addition, it might

TABLE 10.4. Sample Cognitive Strategy Instruction Techniques

Peer-reviewed reference	Instructional routine	Mnemonic or heuristic	Sample application
Montague, M. (2008). Self-regulation strategies to improve mathematical problem solving for students with disabilities. *Learning Disability Quarterly, 31,* 37–44.	1. Read the word problem for understanding. 2. Paraphrase using your own words. 3. Visualize a picture or diagram. 4. Hypothesize a plan to solve the problem. 5. Estimate the answer. 6. Compute the answer. 7. Check to see if you followed the plan.	1. SAY: Self-instruction 2. ASK: Self-questioning 3. CHECK: Self-monitoring	1. Read the word problem for understanding. SAY: "Read the problem. If I don't understand, I will read the problem a second time." ASK: "Did I read and understand the problem?" CHECK: Make sure I understand the problem as I solve it. 2. Paraphrase using your own words. SAY: "Underline the key information and put into my own words." ASK: "Did I underline the key information? What is the question?" CHECK: Make sure the question matches the information I underlined.
Cassel, J., & Reid, R. (1996). Use of a self-regulated strategy intervention to improve word problem-solving skills of	1. Problem definition: Determine what you have to do. 2. Planning: Determine how to solve the problem.	FAST DRAW	F: Find and highlight the question; write the label for the operation and problem type. A: Ask what the parts of the problem are and circle the numbers needed to solve it.

students with mild disabilities. *Journal of Behavioral Education, 6,* 153–172.

3. Strategy use: FAST DRAW will help you remember how to solve the word problem.
4. Self-monitoring: Be sure to check off the steps as you complete them.
5. Self-evaluation: Ask yourself if you are following the plan and if what you are doing makes sense.
6. Self-reinforcement: Give yourself praise for following the steps and/or for correcting a mistake.

S: Set up the problem by writing and labeling the numbers.
T: Tie down the sign by rereading the problem and deciding which operation to use.
D: Discover the sign by rechecking the problem.
R: Read the number problem.
A: Answer the number problem.
W: Write the answer and check to see if it makes sense.

Pfannenstiel, K. H., Bryant, D. P., Bryant, B. R., & Porterfield, J. A. (2015). Cognitive strategy instruction for teaching word problems to primary-level struggling students. *Intervention in School and Clinic, 50,* 291–296.

1. Inspect and find clues
2. Plan and solve
3. Retrace

1. Read the problem.
2. Underline the question.
3. Circle important words and numbers.
4. Cross out irrelevant information.
5. Write an equation.
6. Draw a picture.
7. Write the inverse equation.
8. Revisit the picture and count again.
9. Check to see if the question was answered.

1. Inspect and find clues.
   a. Read the problem.
   b. Underline the question.
   c. Circle important words and numbers.
   d. Cross out irrelevant information.
2. Plan and solve.
   a. Write the equation.
   b. Draw a picture.
3. Retrace.
   a. Revisit the picture and count again.
   b. Check to see if the question was answered.

be helpful for students to practice thinking aloud after the interventionist has modeled the process for them. Thinking aloud should include an explanation of (1) how the type of problem was identified based on math concepts, (2) why a certain visual representation or schema might be appropriate for the problem type identified, (3) how to represent the information in the problem visually while demonstrating, (4) the steps for solving the problem while demonstrating, and (5) self-regulation and checking completed work (Woodward et al., 2012).

Metacognitive strategies are the self-regulation statements students are taught to use throughout the problem-solving process to monitor their own performance and facilitate active engagement (Montague, 2008b; Rosenzweig, Krawec, & Montague, 2011). In Figure 10.2, we describe four common self-regulation strategies that can be applied to word-problem solving: (1) self-questioning, (2) self-instruction, (3) self-monitoring, and (4) self-evaluation. An example of self-questioning would be when the student asks him- or herself, "What type of problem is this? How do I know?" Self-instruction would be represented by self-statements such as "FAST DRAW will help me remember the steps I need to follow to solve the problem." An example of a self-monitoring statement might be "I set up the problem by writing and labeling the numbers so I can check off this step." A statement representing self-evaluation might be "Did I complete all the steps? I will go back and check." Below, we describe two programs that apply CSI to word-problem solving.

Math Scene Investigator

Math Scene Investigator (MSI; Pfannenstiel, Bryant, Bryant, & Porterfield, 2015) is a CSI procedure applied to word-problem solving for children in early elementary grades that was constructed as part of another commercially available program, the Early Numeracy Intervention Program (Bryant, Pfannenstiel, & Bryant, 2014). Appendix 10.2 describes the step-by-step procedures for applying MSI to word-problem solving. This program asks students to assume the role of detective and to use MSI as a tool to solve a word problem. Students are trained on how to use the three-step MSI procedure across 2–3 days before assuming more independence with the strategy. One peer-reviewed study describes this procedure, but no studies have systematically evaluated this intervention when used separately from the Early Numeracy Intervention Program.

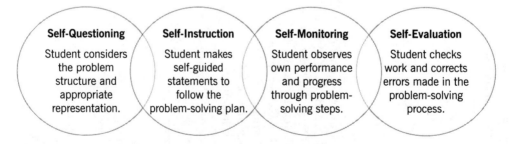

FIGURE 10.2. Self-regulation strategies.

Solve It!: A Practical Approach to Teaching Mathematical Problem Solving Skills

Solve It! (Montague, 2003) is commercially available from Exceptional Innovations (*www. exinn.net/solve-it*). It is designed for students with and without learning disabilities in the upper elementary as well as secondary grades, although most of the research evidence for this intervention is at the middle school level. The instructional guide, which also includes a CD-ROM, contains scripted lessons and all the necessary instructional materials for applying CSI. An implementation guide for facilitators was also developed to support accurate instruction (Montague, 2008a), and 3 full days of professional development have been provided to instructors (Montague, Enders, & Dietz, 2011). When the program was embedded into core instruction, it was administered three times weekly for the first week and once weekly thereafter from October until the end of the school year. For students with math learning disabilities, the program led to performance that was commensurate with typically performing peers. However, after a few weeks, booster lessons were needed to maintain problem-solving performance, and improvement did not transfer to gains on high-stakes testing (Montague, 1997; Montague et al., 2011).

CONCLUSION

Word-problem solving is a complex skill. Students benefit from explicit instruction on word-problem-solving techniques, particularly those that emphasize the underlying structure of the word problem. This chapter describes how schema instruction and CSI can be used to improve word-problem-solving skills for students who are struggling within this area of math. The chapter's appendices provide protocols for using these techniques with students, whereas the tables and figures provide further guidelines on how to use and apply these procedures.

APPENDIX 10.1. "Draw-It" Word-Problem-Solving Cycle Intervention Brief

CCSS Domain Areas Addressed:

Counting and Cardinality (K)	Operations and Algebraic Thinking (K–5)	Numbers and Operations in Base Ten (K–5)	Measurement and Data (K–5)
☐	☑	☑	☐

Instructional Hierarchy:

Acquisition	Fluency	Maintenance	Generalization	Adaptation
☑	☐	☐	☐	☐

Setting: / **Tier of Support within RTI Framework:**

Whole-Class	Small-Group	Individual	Universal Prevention	Targeted Intervention	Individualized Intervention
☐	☑	☑	☐	☑	☑

Mediator: ☐ Teacher or Interventionist   ☑ Student (with teacher oversight)   ☐ Parent

Effectiveness: The percentage of word problems solved correctly increased across problem types and was maintained with three students. | **Amount of Evidence:** One empirical study.

Acceptability: A student satisfaction questionnaire was provided, and suggested students were satisfied with the strategy.

Brief Description: The "draw-it" problem-solving cycle intervention uses cognitive strategy instruction to teach students about diagramming as a process and then to solve word problems using diagramming.

Materials Required: Word problems; note card, poster, or other visual with the four main steps illustrated; checklist containing specific steps for using the procedure.

Training Required: Unspecified.

Duration: Usually 35 minutes per session delivered two to four times per week.

Active Treatment Components: Interactive modeling (model while students work the strategy), guided practice, error correction, feedback.

Procedures:

1. Determine the word-problem types that student(s) need assistance learning. The earliest prerequisite skill that is not mastered in the sequence should be targeted. It is recommended that one word-problem type be taught at a time. Once students have mastered the problem type, then interventionists can teach students the next word-problem type.
2. Interventionist may want to create visual reminders of the problem-solving process such as cards or posters that illustrate the four main steps, as well as a checklist that contains the seven actions associated with the four main steps.
3. Interventionist introduces the first main step to solve the selected word-problem type: *Orient.* Students should be directed to complete the following three actions while the interventionist models them: (1) read the problem, (2) organize the information from the problem, (3) construct a diagram of the problem. Interventionist then teaches students to apply the ASK, DO, CHECK routine.
   a. Read the problem:
      i. ASK: Students ask themselves, "What does the problem tell me?"
      ii. DO: Students discuss the problem.
      iii. CHECK: Students ask themselves, "Are there words I do not understand or know?"
   b. Organize the information:
      i. ASK: Students ask themselves, "What information is known? What information is missing?"
      ii. DO: Students discuss known and unknown information.
      iii. CHECK: Students ask themselves, "Do I have all the information I need?"

The format of these intervention briefs was based on the Evidence-Based Intervention (EBI) Network at the University of Missouri (*http://ebi.missouri.edu/*).

   c. Construct a diagram
      i. ASK: Students ask themselves, "How can I represent the quantities and relationships in the problem? Which diagram should I draw?"
      ii. DO: Students discuss the different diagram options.
      iii. CHECK: Students ask themselves, "Does my diagram match the problem?"
4. Interventionist introduces the second main step to solve the selected word-problem type: *Plan to solve the problem*. Students should be directed to complete the following two actions while the interventionist models them: (1) connect how to solve the problem, and (2) evaluate the plan.
   a. Connect how to solve the problem:
      i. ASK: Students ask themselves, "What steps do I need to solve the problem?"
      ii. DO: Students discuss the steps.
      iii. CHECK: Students ask themselves, "Do my steps match my diagram and the problem?"
   b. Evaluate the plan:
      i. ASK: Students ask themselves, "Will these steps help me answer the question?"
      ii. DO: Students discuss how the steps are connected to solving the problem.
      iii. CHECK: Students ask themselves, "Do I know an easier way to solve the problem? Do I need a different diagram?"
5. Interventionist introduces the third main step to solve the selected word-problem type: *Execute the plan*. Students should be directed to complete the following two actions while the interventionist models them: (1) construct a mathematical sentence, and (2) compute the answer.
   a. Construct a mathematical sentence:
      i. ASK: Students ask themselves, "How do I set up the problem?"
      ii. DO: Students discuss.
      iii. CHECK: Students ask themselves, "Are the quantities the same as my diagram and the problem? Did I use the operations I planned to use? Did I follow the steps I planned to use?"
   b. Compute the answer:
      i. ASK: Students ask themselves, "Have I correctly computed the answer?"
      ii. DO: Students discuss.
      iii. CHECK: Students ask themselves, "Did I do everything I needed to do?"
6. Interventionist introduces the fourth main step to solve the selected word-problem type: *Check the answer*.
      i. ASK: Students ask themselves, "Does my answer make sense?"
      ii. DO: Students discuss.
      iii. CHECK: Students ask themselves, "Is everything right? Do I need to go back and ask for help?"
7. At the end of each session (or at least once weekly), students are administered a brief assessment (e.g., CBM), which is completed individually and scored to monitor progress on word-problem solving.

Selected References:

1. van Garderen, D. (2007). Teaching students with LD to use diagrams to solve mathematical word problems. *Journal of Learning Disabilities, 40,* 540–563.
2. van Garderen, D., & Scheuermann, A. M. (2014). Diagramming word problems: A strategic approach for instruction. *Intervention in School and Clinic, 50,* 282–290.

APPENDIX 10.2. Math Scene Investigator Intervention Brief

CCSS Domain Areas Addressed:			
Counting and Cardinality (K)	Operations and Algebraic Thinking (K–5)	Numbers and Operations in Base Ten (K–5)	Measurement and Data (K–5)
☐	☑	☑	☐

Instructional Hierarchy:				
Acquisition	Fluency	Maintenance	Generalization	Adaptation
☑	☐	☐	☐	☐

Setting:			Tier of Support within RTI Framework:		
Whole-Class	Small-Group	Individual	Universal Prevention	Targeted Intervention	Individualized Intervention
☐	☑	☑	☐	☑	☑

Mediator: ☐ Teacher or Interventionist   ☑ Student (with teacher oversight)   ☐ Parent

Effectiveness: No studies evaluated the MSI intervention in isolation without being part of the Early Numeracy Intervention Program.	**Amount of Evidence:** One study evaluating the entire Early Numeracy Intervention Program of which MSI is a part. No studies could be located evaluating MSI alone.

Acceptability: Informal teacher reports indicated that students using MSI solved word problems faster than those who did not use MSI (Pfannenstiel et al., 2015).

Brief Description: MSI is a cognitive strategy used to help elementary-level students solve various types of word problems. MSI is introduced to students as a tool to solve a mystery and the students play the role of a detective.

Materials Required: Word problems, poster or worksheet with MSI steps and actions.

Training Required: Students need to be trained on the three main steps that are aligned with nine actions across the steps. Training should be provided across 2 or 3 days with the interventionist providing modeling and ample examples. It is recommended that the first two steps are provided on the first training day and the final step introduced on the second training day after reviewing the first two steps.

Duration: Unknown.

Active Treatment Components: Preview/engage prior knowledge (provide lesson goal and connect to previously learned skills), interactive modeling (model while students work the strategy), guided practice, error correction, feedback.

Procedures:

1. Determine the word-problem types that student(s) need assistance learning. The earliest prerequisite skill that is not mastered in the sequence should be targeted. It is recommended that one word-problem type be taught at a time. Once students have mastered the problem type, then interventionists can teach students the next word-problem type using the MSI strategy.

2. Interventionist may want to create cards, worksheets, or posters that illustrate the actions associated with each of the three main steps so that students have a visual reminder of the problem-solving process.

3. Interventionist introduces the first main step to solve the selected word-problem type: *Inspect and Find Clues.* Students should be directed to complete the following four actions while the interventionist models them: (a) read the problem, (b) underline the question and state the unit, (c) circle important information (i.e., the key numbers), and (d) cross out irrelevant (distractor) words.

    a. The interventionist should read the word problem aloud with the student.

    b. Interventionist should prompt the student to find the important question and have the student state the question aloud before writing it down.

    c. Interventionist should ask the student what information should be circled.

    d. Interventionist should ask the student if there is information that is not needed that should be crossed out.

4. Interventionist introduces the second main step to solve the selected word-problem type: *Plan and Solve*. Students should be directed to complete the following two actions while the interventionist models them: (a) write the equation $(2 + 3 = 5)$, and (b) draw a picture to solve the problem. Students are directed to draw circles to represent the problem.
   a. Interventionist prompts the student to write the equation by asking the student what information is known (e.g., the whole number and one part; two small parts).
   b. Interventionist asks the student what math operation is required $(+, -, \times, \div)$ and how the student knows which operation to choose.
5. Interventionist introduces the third main step to solve the selected word-problem type: *Retrace*. Students should be directed to complete the following three actions while the interventionist models them: (a) write the inverse equation, (b) recount picture drawn, and (c) check to see whether the question was answered. Students are directed to check their work by writing the inverse equation $(5 - 3 = 2)$ and checking the picture to be sure it matches the problem and the equation.
   a. Interventionist asks student to retrace by writing the equation and reminding the student what information is known. The interventionist should prompt the student to count the dots on the picture to see if the question was answered.
   b. Interventionist asks the student to check the answer by writing the equation using the opposite operation.
6. At the end of each session (or at least once weekly) students are administered a brief assessment (e.g., CBM), which is completed individually and scored to monitor progress on word-problem solving.

Selected References:

1. Bryant, D. P., Bryant, B. R., Roberts, G., Vaughn, S., Hughes, K., Porterfield, J., et al. (2011). Early numeracy intervention program for first-grade students with mathematics difficulties. *Exceptional Children, 78*, 7–23.
2. Bryant, D. P., Pfannenstiel, K. H., & Bryant, B. R. (2014). *Early Numeracy Intervention Program.* Austin, TX: Psychoeducational Services.
3. Pfannenstiel, K., H., Bryant, D. P., Bryant, B. R., & Porterfield, J. A. (2015). Cognitive strategy instruction for teaching word problems to primary-level struggling students. *Intervention in School and Clinic, 50*, 291–296.

CHAPTER 11

Evaluating Student Progress
and Making Intervention Adjustments

What happens once an intervention is implemented and student progress is being monitored on a weekly, semiweekly, or monthly basis? Recommendations from the National Center on Response to Intervention suggest that progress monitoring data are reviewed every 6–10 weeks by school-based intervention/problem-solving teams or grade-level teams (*www. rti4success*; *www.intensiveintervention.org*). Making data-based decisions on whether a student is making adequate progress toward a predetermined goal is an essential part of intervention implementation. Graphic displays are often the most useful ways to visually evaluate outcomes and are available from most data management systems (e.g., aimsweb™, iSTEEP, mCLASS®: Math). It is also possible to create your own data management system using Microsoft Excel. The focus of this chapter is (1) collecting and graphing intervention data, (2) setting goals, (3) ensuring that intervention implementation is adequate, and (4) adjusting an intervention according to the progress being made toward a goal.

COLLECTING AND GRAPHING INTERVENTION DATA

As a first step, it is ideal if student performance data on the tool you will be using for progress monitoring is collected before the intervention is implemented. This is referred to as baseline, or performance under typical conditions. Baseline data are collected until at least 3 data points have been obtained (Cooper, Heron, & Heward, 2007). Once baseline data are collected, goals can be established using mid- or end-of-year benchmarks from a universal screening tool or by using nationally normed rates of improvement (often provided by the developers of the progress monitoring tool). For simplicity, Figures 11.3–11.6 illustrate a goal line, also referred to as the aim line (dashed line on the graphs), selected based on the fluency criterion of 40 DCPM (Howell & Nolet, 1999). More specifics on goal setting can be found at the National Center on Response to Intervention website (*www.rti4success.org*).

Educators or problem-solving teams should evaluate student data to determine whether the intervention provided was (1) successful, (2) not successful, or (3) successful but very resource intensive (Barnett, Daly, Jones, & Lentz, 2004; Gersten, Beckmann, et al., 2009; Shapiro, 2011). Success can be determined by evaluating whether the student is progressing toward his or her goal. One simplistic way to evaluate these data is to examine whether the four most recent consecutive data points are above the goal line, on the goal line, or below the goal line (Codding & Connell, 2008). If student data are above or on the goal line, then the intervention could be considered successful (option 1). If student data are below the goal line, the intervention is not successful (option 2).

The third consideration is whether the resources required (i.e., effort, materials, personnel, and time) are so demanding that it is not feasible to support the student solely through the general education program. In other words, the student may benefit from individualized services that are more easily rendered through special education. How intensity is defined with respect to effort, materials, personnel, and time will be school and district specific (Barnett et al., 2004). For example, an interventionist might be implementing an intervention accurately (all steps are provided), consistently, and with high quality. In addition, the student's general education teacher employs effective classroom management strategies during core math instruction, provides opportunities for students to practice computation and word-problem solving, and reserves a portion of the designated math instructional time to differentiated activities according to students' skill needs. Despite all of these supports, the student's performance may not be improving.

As another example, let's assume a student is receiving the most comprehensive intervention available within the school system. This intervention program and the delivery of the intervention have been adjusted several times following team meetings. Consequently, intervention supports are provided on a daily basis for 100 minutes at the student's instructional level (which is commensurate with two grades below the grade of record). Although the student is making progress at a slow and steady rate, school personnel are unable to maintain this level of support and believe that greater than 100 minutes per day might be required for the student to adequately access the core curriculum. In both of the examples we described, it might be appropriate for the team to consider whether special education services are warranted.

BASIC CONSIDERATIONS
PRIOR TO ADJUSTING/CHANGING INTERVENTION SUPPORTS

Before a problem-solving or grade-level team can make data-based decisions about student progress, the presence of two basic implementation components needs to be assessed. Figure 11.1 provides a flowchart illustrating the action steps that a school-based team can take before evaluating RTI. In this diagram, student response to the intervention provided can

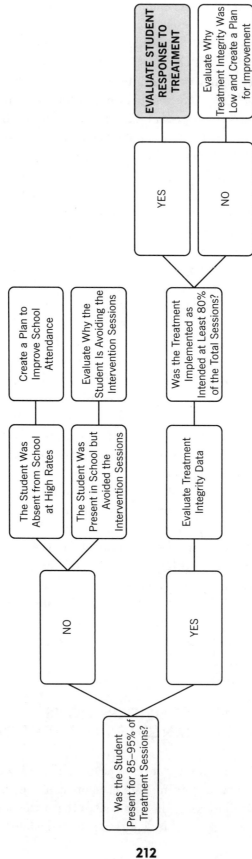

FIGURE 11.1. Basic considerations to make before intervention data can be evaluated.

212

be evaluated only after it is determined that (1) student attendance was adequate and (2) the intervention was implemented as intended (i.e., treatment integrity or procedural fidelity).

Determine Whether the Student Was Present for Most (e.g., 85–95%) of the Intervention Sessions

This recommendation implies that attendance data are recorded during all intervention sessions. Accordingly, the interventionist should also record the start and end time of each intervention session (Barnett et al., 2004; Hardman, McDonnell, & Welch, 1997). Clearly, if the student has high absentee rates, then evaluation of progress on the intervention is inappropriate and the team should focus on developing a plan to ensure the student attends school on a regular basis. However, if the student is present in school but not attending intervention sessions, then more information is needed to determine why the student is not attending the sessions. Student avoidance of intervention sessions may be an indicator to the team that a different intervention approach is needed, and student input should be gathered to make an appropriate decision on how best to support him or her.

Collect and Evaluate Treatment Integrity Data

Put simply, treatment integrity is the extent to which an intervention is implemented as planned or described within an intervention protocol (Gresham, 1989; Yeaton & Sechrest, 1981). If an intervention is not implemented the way it was planned, then it is very difficult to determine whether the intervention is working. More specifically, the evaluation of treatment integrity implies that interventionists are provided with training on how to deliver an intervention (Sanetti & Kratochwill, 2009). There are numerous ways that an intervention may not be implemented as intended within the everyday constraints of the school system. Students may not have had access to the appropriate amount of treatment—that is, the intervention may not be delivered for the total duration recommended per session or for the recommended number of sessions per week. Or it may be that students may not have had access to all components of the intervention—for example, in order to deliver the intervention in the time allocated, the interventionist may need to eliminate one or two intervention steps. A third possibility that can be more difficult to capture is that the interventionist is delivering all of the steps, but the quality of implementation may not match the intervention developers' expectations.

Standard protocol interventions, or interventions with empirically validated scripted treatment protocols, offer the advantage of improving the likelihood that an interventionist will deliver the treatment with high quality (Gresham, 2007). Standard protocol interventions are typically purchased in a prepackaged format containing all necessary intervention and training materials. However, simple interventions with only a few critical steps can also elicit high levels of treatment adherence (Erchul & Martens, 2010). School-based teams can script intervention protocols and provide training to interventionists that include instruction, modeling, role play with immediate feedback, and *in vivo* coaching with performance feedback (Barnett et al., 2014; Ehrhardt, Barnett, Lentz, Stollar, & Reifin, 1996;

Joyce & Showers, 2003). For this book, we have generated intervention briefs that include procedural steps that could be used as intervention scripts and adapted to create treatment integrity checklists (see Chapters 2, 4, 8, 9, and 10).

Treatment integrity data can be collected through (1) direct observation of intervention implementation, (2) review of permanent products generated from intervention delivery, or (3) through interventionists' self-reports of completed steps (DiGennaro Reed & Codding, 2014). *Direct observations* of the implementation of an intervention can be conducted by any school professional using an intervention protocol or script that has been modified to create a checklist. School professionals can observe the intervention being implemented *in vivo* or by watching a video and use the checklist to identify steps that were implemented fully as written, partially as written, or not at all (Codding, Feinberg, Pace, & Dunn, 2005). *Permanent products* require the collection of materials that result from implementing the intervention. *Self-reports* often take the form of the interventionist indicating on the treatment protocol or checklist whether he or she implemented the step completely, partially, or missed a step. Most experts suggest that more than one measure of treatment integrity be collected because each method differs in its ability to capture both adherence and quality of implementation (Barnett et al., 2014; Sanetti & Collier-Meek, 2014). Although self-report may be the easiest data to gather, it is also the least accurate and is not recommended as the only measure of treatment integrity (Noell, 2008; Sanetti & Kratochwill, 2009). Form 11.1 provides an implementation evaluation planning guide that school professionals and teams can use to organize the collection of treatment integrity data.

ADJUSTING INTERVENTIONS ACCORDING TO PROGRESS MONITORING DATA

Once it is determined whether the intervention is successful (performance meets or exceeds the goal) or not successful (performance falls below the goal), problem-solving or grade-level team members should consider one of six options for adjusting an intervention: (1) change the intervention dose (more or less), (2) adjust the target skill, (3) change the assistance provided (more or less), (4) change student groupings, (5) change or modify the intervention, and/or (6) remove the intervention (Barnett et al., 2004; Daly et al., 2007; Gersten, Beckman, et al., 2009; Shapiro, 2011). We have organized each of these options according to whether student performance is exceeding the goal, meeting the goal, or is below the goal (little/no improvement or slow improvement; see Figure 11.2). Below we describe each of these options using a series of case examples.

Performance Exceeds the Goal Line

Case Example 1

After 6 weeks of intervention, Ainsley's performance exceeds the expected goal established when she began receiving additional supports (see Figure 11.3). The school-based or grade-level team should consider several options for how to continue to support Ainsley's math

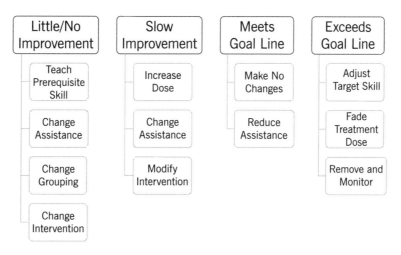

FIGURE 11.2. Adjusting interventions according to the data.

progress: (1) adjust the target skill, (2) fade the dose of treatment, or (3) remove intervention supports and monitor progress. Below we provide several examples of how school-based teams may weigh the different options.

ADJUST THE TARGET SKILL

Ainsley might continue to benefit from additional intervention support, but the skill area targeted for the intervention could be changed. Let's suppose Ainsley has mastered all addition and subtraction basic fact families. If Ainsley continues to be behind on grade-level skills, according to broader computation tests, teacher reports of Ainsley's progress in the

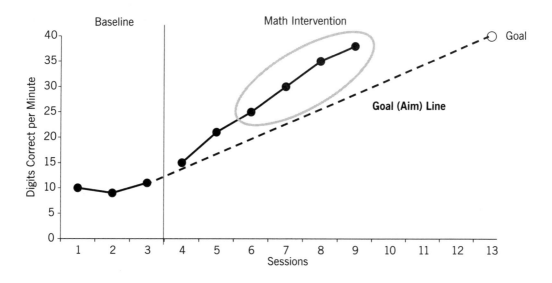

FIGURE 11.3. Performance above (exceeding) the goal line: Ainsley.

classroom, and/or her ability to access grade-level curriculum, the team may conclude that Ainsley would continue to benefit from intervention supports but change the target skill to multidigit computation.

LOWER THE TREATMENT DOSE

The frequency (or dose) of treatment implementation could be faded if a student is making adequate progress. If Ainsley was receiving intervention support four times weekly for 30 minutes, the team could decide to reduce intervention implementation to twice weekly for 30 minutes. Progress monitoring would continue as usual, and the team would be evaluating the data to ensure that Ainsley is continuing to make progress on the target skill or maintain the goal-level performance.

REMOVE INTERVENTION SUPPORTS AND MONITOR PROGRESS

The team could choose to remove the intervention supports if all evidence suggests that Ainsley's math performance is commensurate with her grade-level peers. Once Ainsley's math performance has reached mastery levels according to CBA or computer-adaptive testing (CAT)—and this level of performance is consistently maintained—the intervention supports could then be removed. In order to ensure that Ainsley's success continues and the team's hypothesis is correct, it will be important for Ainsley's performance to be monitored using CBA or CAT on a monthly basis for least 3 months.

Performance Meets the Goal Line

Case Example 2

According to Figure 11.4, after 6 weeks of intervention, Rowan's performance is progressing as expected (her performance matches the goal line). The team should consider the following two options to continue to support Rowan's math progress: (1) make no intervention changes, or (2) reduce the level or type of assistance provided.

MAKE NO CHANGES

As a first option, the team might consider continuing the intervention exactly as is (making no changes), particularly if self-report data from the interventionist and direct observations of the intervention being implemented demonstrate consistency and accuracy of administration.

REDUCE THE ASSISTANCE PROVIDED

The level of assistance provided by the interventionist could also be altered (Barnett et al., 2004; Daly et al., 2007). Assume the team originally determined that Rowan was in the acquisition stage of skill development for addition sums to 10. The level of interventionist

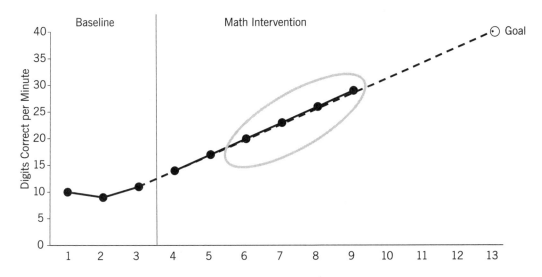

FIGURE 11.4. Performance meeting the goal line: Rowan.

assistance is naturally greater in this phase of skill development. For example, the interventionist might have initially provided modeling, guided practice, immediate error correction, and reinforcement on each isolated number combination presented. However, when recently presented with flash cards representing number combinations with sums to 10, Rowan exhibits perfectly accurate performance. This might suggest that the interventionist can fade the less intensive modeling and feedback, and instead generate more opportunities for Rowan to practice independently.

Performance Is below the Goal Line

Case Examples 3 and 4

According to Figures 11.5 and 11.6, respectively, both Mason and Declan exhibit performance that is below expected levels. Mason's data illustrate that he is progressing but at a rate slower than anticipated. Declan's data illustrate that he is making very little improvement and his performance is not matching the rate of progress anticipated. The school-based team should consider several options for how to continue to support the math progress of Mason and Declan. For Mason, it may be most appropriate to consider increasing the dose of the intervention, changing the level of assistance, and/or modifying the intervention. For Declan, the team might consider changing the target skill, level of assistance, student grouping, or intervention.

INCREASE THE TREATMENT DOSE

According to a panel of experts commissioned by the Institute of Education Sciences (IES), math interventions should be provided 20–40 minutes daily, four to five times per week (Gersten, Beckmann, et al., 2009). Distributing brief learning and practice opportunities

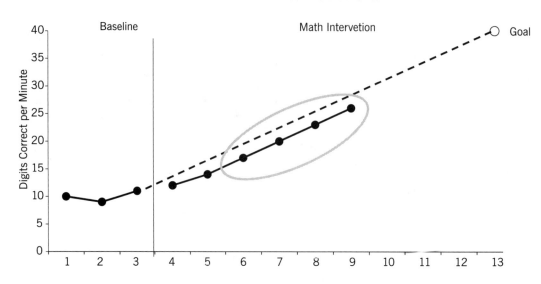

FIGURE 11.5. Performance below the goal line (slow improvement): Mason.

over time improves retention of math skills, particularly for simple tasks (Rohrer & Taylor, 2006). In a study comparing the same math intervention delivered four times weekly, twice weekly, or once weekly, students receiving the intervention four times weekly performed better on computation outcomes than students in the other two groups (Codding & Van-DerHeyden, 2014). Therefore, if Mason is exhibiting slow progress, it might be important to increase the number of intervention sessions provided weekly or the duration of each session to meet the IES recommendations.

If Mason is receiving the intervention daily for 40 minutes, consistent with the IES recommendations, another consideration is reviewing how many opportunities Mason has

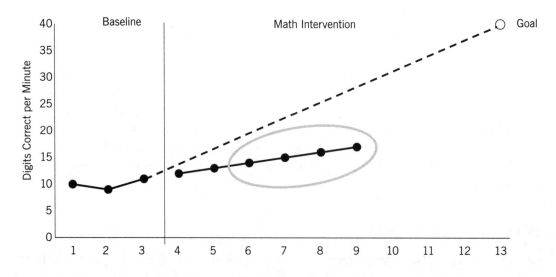

FIGURE 11.6. Performance below the goal line (little improvement): Declan.

to practice various target math skills during each intervention session (Codding & Lane, 2015; Daly et al., 2007). The amount of time students are spending engaging in active practice tasks can be computed and increased. IES recommendations suggest that students receiving intervention supports in all grades practice basic math facts (as one example) for 10 minutes every intervention session (Gersten, Beckmann, et al., 2009).

INCREASE ASSISTANCE

One reason for a student's lack of progress might be that not enough assistance, or *not enough of the appropriate level and type of assistance,* is provided for the student to accurately and efficiently engage in the math task (Daly et al., 2007). Let's assume during treatment sessions the interventionist observes Declan guessing the answers for most of the addition number combinations. When he does use a counting strategy, he only counts all numbers starting from one. When presented with the addition problem $5 + 3 = x$, Declan holds up both of his hands and begins counting from one. In this scenario, it might be useful if the interventionist administered a CRA assessment to further assess the student's understanding of addition concepts in order to provide the appropriate type of assistance required (Allsopp et al., 2008; Lembke et al., 2012).

Within a CRA assessment, the interventionist arranges for the student to solve addition problems using manipulatives such as counting beans, blocks, marbles (concrete); pictures of objects or drawings (representation); and numbers and symbols (abstract). Problems would be formatted in such a way that students were required to express the answer or recognize the answer from several choices (see Table 11.1). The use of receptive (choose the correct problem solution) and expressive (create the solution) tasks allows the interventionist to determine what the conceptual breakdown for the problem-solving task may be and then arrange intervention strategies accordingly.

During the CRA assessment, a student might be given 10 addition problems to solve at each level (concrete, representation, abstract) with five problems representing receptive

TABLE 11.1. CRA Assessment Example

	Receptive	Interventionist-created choices	Expressive	Student answers
Concrete	Point to the sets of blocks that total nine.	▢▢▢▢ ▢▢▢▢▢ ▢▢▢▢ ▢▢▢	There are four blocks on the table. How many more are needed to make seven?	▢▢▢▢
Representation	Circle the picture that totals five.	••••• + •• •••• + •	Using dots, draw the problem 6 + 2.	•••••• + ••
Abstract	Circle the addition problem that equals 10.	5 + 2 = 4 + 6 = 5 + 4 = 8 + 3 =	Solve the addition problem 7 + 8.	15

questions and five problems representing expressive questions. Accuracy of the answers could be used to interpret student performance across each of the levels and receptive and expressive categories. For example, five out of five correct answers (100%) would indicate mastery, three or four out of five correct (60–80%) answers would indicate the instructional level, and two or fewer out of five (<60%) might indicate the frustration level of performance (Allsopp et al., 2008).

A student could perform in the mastery range for both receptive and expressive addition problems using concrete objects such as blocks. However, for questions involving visual representations, the same student falls in the instructional range when answering receptive questions, and in the frustration range on expressive questions. Given this example, the target areas for intervention might include increasing opportunities for the student to practice solving receptive problems using visual representations (fluency stage of the instructional hierarchy) and receiving direct instruction and guided practice (acquisition stage of the instructional hierarchy) on addition problems requiring the student to draw the solution to a problem.

CHANGE STUDENT GROUPINGS

When no or slow progress is observed, the student might benefit from participating in a different student grouping (Gersten, Beckmann, et al., 2009). A student's intervention group could be changed to one that targets a prerequisite skill that is needed to access the material provided in the current grouping. It is also possible that the student might benefit from participating in a smaller group, such as moving from a group of six to a group of three, but keeping the target skill the same.

CHANGE OR MODIFY THE INTERVENTION

Changing or modifying an intervention is another option when a student is making slow or no progress. Important considerations for implementing a different intervention or modifying an existing intervention should include whether (1) the intervention has been implemented accurately, (2) the recommended schedule of intervention delivery was applied, and (3) the correct target skill has been identified. One approach to modifying an intervention is to add components to the intervention to improve student outcomes (Barnett et al., 2004). For example, if Mason was showing slow gradual progress using the CCC intervention, performance feedback with goal setting could be added to highlight for Mason whether he is meeting his goal.

If the team is not observing student progress, then changing the intervention may be warranted. One way to create an individualized intervention that is student specific is through the use of brief experimental analysis (BEA). BEA is a procedure during which two or more intervention strategies are delivered to the student in a predetermined sequence and evaluated to determine which strategy or combination of strategies might yield the best outcomes (Chafouleas, Riley-Tillman, & Eckert, 2003). The strategies selected to compare are empirically supported and typically represent a hypothesized reason for the student's difficulties (e.g., Barnett et al., 2004; Codding, Baglici, et al., 2009; Mong & Mong, 2012). Each strategy is implemented anywhere from one (abridged BEA) to three occasions, across two to three 20-minute sessions (Daly, Witt, et al., 1997; Chafouleas et al., 2003). To evaluate outcomes, the same target skill must be assessed (e.g., addition and subtraction fact families) using alternate forms of the same measure that are equivalent. Common types of outcome measures in math include CBA probes, problem sets, or workbook materials. The objective for conducting a BEA is to identify the strategies that produce the largest outcomes and/or provide an empirical basis for recommending the implementation of a strategy or combination of strategies. In order to evaluate outcomes, a multielement single-case design with a mini-reversal/withdrawal is implemented (Jones & Wickstrom, 2002). The most effective treatment is one that is considered to be apparent during visual analysis, usually representing 20–50% above baseline (i.e., math performance without any intervention support).

In the area of math, BEA has often been employed to identify an appropriate strategy or combination of strategies to improve number combination fluency (Codding, Baglici, et al., 2009; Duhon et al., 2004; Gilbertson, Witt, Duhon, & Dufrene, 2008; Mong & Mong, 2012; VanDerHeyden & Burns, 2009). The strategies that have been tested in the literature have represented either skill or performance (i.e., motivation) deficits and included use of CCC, explicit timing, MTM, taped problems, constant time delay, performance feedback, goal setting, and reinforcement contingent on performance. The order of these strategies can be implemented according to the adult assistance required (i.e., least to most) or to test the reasons for the students' lack of success. Figure 11.7 represents a hypothetical example of a BEA. For this BEA, the following strategies were tested: MTM (acquisition problem), explicit timing (fluency problem), interspersal of easy and instructional-level math problems (persistence problem), a break card (a card that can be traded in for a brief break from an activity contingent on engaging in the activity for an established period of time; avoidance problem), and contingent reinforcement (motivation problem). Eight total lessons were conducted and these lessons were 5 minutes each. Following each lesson, a CBA probe was administered to measure improvement. Two lessons were conducted in one session lasting

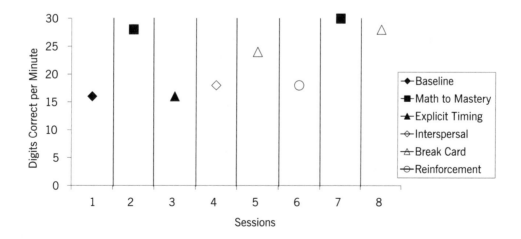

FIGURE 11.7. Abridged brief experimental analysis.

a total of 20 minutes; in all, four 20-minute sessions were conducted with the student. The last session included implementing the two best-performing strategies a second time.

These data suggest that MTM and access to a break card were the most effective strategies, comparatively, and each strategy resulted in improved DCPM over baseline. Using these findings, the school professional or interventionist would recommend to the team that these strategies (alone or combined in a treatment package) could improve student performance over time. Notice that the outcome of a BEA was a *recommendation* about what strategies or combination of strategies could be most effective if implemented with the student.

TEACH PREREQUISITE SKILLS

Slow or absent improvement in math performance may also occur because the skill targeted for intervention support is too difficult. If students are making a large number of errors, then it might be most appropriate to adjust the target skill by teaching prerequisite skills (Daly et al., 2007). Error analysis, flexible interviewing, and fact assessments can all be used to determine the learning gap a student is experiencing and identify the appropriate skill(s) or concept(s) to teach through intervention strategies.

CONDUCT AN ERROR PATTERN ANALYSIS

In Chapter 3, we made recommendations that once a student is identified as at risk during schoolwide screening of grade-appropriate math skills and concepts, additional data (e.g., performance on specific skills such as fact families, 2×2 digit addition without regrouping, or word-problem solving) should be collected using computer-adapted technology or CBA in order to identify the student's pattern of strengths and weaknesses (survey-level assessment or skills analysis). However, if these additional data were not collected prior to providing initial intervention supports, school professionals are encouraged to do so when student performance is not meeting intervention expectations in order to identify the lowest skill in the skill sequence that has not been mastered.

Even with this additional data collection, the target for instruction may still be inappropriate, so it might be useful to conduct an error pattern analysis (e.g., Allsopp et al., 2008; Dennis, Calhoon, Olson, & Williams, 2014). Because students struggling in math tend to make consistent, persistent, and systematic errors, an error pattern analysis can be used to further assess students' academic needs (Dennis et al., 2014; Woodward & Howard, 1994).

An error pattern analysis consists of the following steps (Dennis et al., 2014): (1) identify key early numeracy, computation, or application skills that are difficult; (2) create an error analysis chart; (3) administer CAT or CBA tests targeting those skills; (4) score the materials by evaluating the common error patterns; and (5) record errors made on the error analysis chart. This type of analysis might be particularly useful for multidigit computation or word problems that consist of many different component skills. Form 11.2 provides a sample error analysis chart for multidigit addition and subtraction. Once the specific type of error pattern is identified, intervention supports can be provided accordingly and progress on those error patterns can be evaluated over time until improvement is observed.

CONDUCT A FACT ASSESSMENT

Having students practice solving math problems in the context of word problems, complex computations (multidigit problems), or mixed-skill worksheets offers an important mechanism through which students retain, maintain, and generalize basic fact families (Codding, Burns, et al., 2011; Daly et al., 2007). These contexts are most representative of naturally occurring encounters of basic facts in everyday life and in more advanced school-based math learning. However, should students exhibit slow or little progress when solving simple math facts in these contexts, it might be useful for interventionists to provide drill-based instructional strategies that include opportunities to practice basic facts individually (e.g., Codding, Burns, et al., 2011). A fact assessment can be conducted to determine which facts students are automatically able to recall from memory (Fuchs et al., 2009). Students are expected to respond to the presented math fact within 3 seconds.

Materials needed to conduct the fact assessment include flash cards representative of all four basic arithmetic operations and a worksheet to record the results (Form 11.3). Interventionists should present each flash card (e.g., 6×7) and provide the student with 3 seconds to respond. If the student responds with the correct answer *within* 3 seconds, the fact is considered known. The fact is considered unknown if the student (1) provides the incorrect answer *within* 3 seconds, (2) does not respond *within* 3 seconds, or (3) provides the correct answer *after* 3 seconds. With the set of unknown facts, the interventionist could also determine whether students are able to employ backup strategies, such as *counting up* on the number line or *doubles + 1* (e.g., $7 + 8 = 7 + 7 + 1$) to determine the correct answer.

INTERVIEW STUDENTS

Asking students *how* they plan to or *why* they solved a problem using a particular strategy can provide useful information regarding students' conceptual and procedural understanding of math tasks (Allsopp et al., 2008; Ginsburg, 2009). It is possible that students may record the correct answers to tasks but not have conceptual understanding. It could also be that students know only a portion of the steps required to solve a problem. There are four ways students can be interviewed (Ginsburg, 2009):

1. The interventionist can ask a student to verbally explain how he or she solved, or plans to solve, a math problem.
2. The interventionist can ask a student to play the role of the teacher and demonstrate for the interventionist how the problem was solved using paper and pencil, visual representations, or concrete objects.
3. The interventionist can demonstrate each step of a problem and after solving each step ask the student to explain why a particular strategy or set of strategies was used to solve the step.
4. While the interventionist is demonstrating the steps used to solve a problem, he or she can purposefully make an error and ask the student to identify the error and explain the correct procedure.

The first and second methods for interviewing can easily be conducted before or after progress monitoring is employed. The third and fourth methods for interviewing are more applicable during the course of intervention implementation or instruction (e.g., guided practice or reviewing a math concept). These interviews can be performed individually or in small groups; however, it might be easier to identify specific gaps in understanding when individual interviews are conducted. Educators should be encouraged to ask follow-up questions to students as necessary and permit students to illustrate their thinking and mathematical reasoning through drawings or by using concrete objects (Ginsburg, 2009).

CONCLUSION

Evaluating student response to an intervention requires that data be collected and evaluated in a systematic way. Graphing progress monitoring data can be useful to make decisions on whether or how to adjust an intervention. Before considering evaluation of the data, school-based teams are encouraged to evaluate the quality and accuracy of the implementation of the intervention, as well as student absentee rates. Once those data have been evaluated, teams can use the graphs to determine whether student performance is above, at, or below the goal line. We described six different options for changing or adjusting interventions. For some of these options, we reviewed different assessment methods that can help educators refine the reason for students' math difficulties to better match the treatment to students' needs. If *student assistance* is to be increased, then conducting a CRA assessment might be warranted. If *changing the intervention* is to be considered, then school-based teams might conduct a brief experimental analysis, which is simply a way to test the effectiveness of different possible intervention strategies. If *missing prerequisite skills* is the reason a student is not responding to the intervention, then either an error analysis of concepts or skills might be useful, or a fact assessment could be conducted.

Treatment Implementation Evaluation Planning Guide

Intervention Strategy, Package, or Program	Training Administered?	Intervention Protocol or Script Available?	Intervention Integrity Data to Be Collected	Person Who Will Collect Integrity Data	Frequency of Treatment Integrity Data Collection
	☐ YES by program author(s) ☐ YES by school professional: _____ ☐ YES by electronic media or video ☐ NO	☐ YES ☐ NO	☐ Direct observation ☐ Permanent products ☐ Self-report checklist ☐ Interview with interventionist		☐ Daily ☐ Every other day ☐ Every intervention session ☐ Weekly ☐ Semiweekly ☐ Monthly
	☐ YES by program author(s) ☐ YES by school professional: _____ ☐ YES by electronic media or video ☐ NO	☐ YES ☐ NO	☐ Direct observation ☐ Permanent products ☐ Self-report checklist ☐ Interview with interventionist		☐ Daily ☐ Every other day ☐ Every intervention session ☐ Weekly ☐ Semiweekly ☐ Monthly
	☐ YES by program author(s) ☐ YES by school professional: _____ ☐ YES by electronic media or video ☐ NO	☐ YES ☐ NO	☐ Direct observation ☐ Permanent products ☐ Self-report checklist ☐ Interview with interventionist		☐ Daily ☐ Every other day ☐ Every intervention session ☐ Weekly ☐ Semiweekly ☐ Monthly

Error Analysis Chart: Multidigit Computation (Addition and Subtraction)

Student Name: _____   Intervention Employed: _____

Type of Error	Sample Error Description	Week 1	Week 2	Week 3	Week 4
Math fact (single-digit computation errors)	Simple arithmetic errors: $\begin{array}{r} 28 \\ +51 \\ \hline 68 \end{array}$ $\begin{array}{r} 35 \\ +76 \\ \hline 112 \end{array}$ $\begin{array}{r} 689 \\ -133 \\ \hline 546 \end{array}$ $\begin{array}{r} 12 \\ \times 11 \\ \hline 131 \end{array}$	☐ Yes ☐ No Example:	☐ Yes ☐ No Example:	☐ Yes ☐ No Example:	☐ Yes ☐ No Example:
Procedural (misapplication or lack of knowledge of procedural steps)	Regrouping: $\begin{array}{r} 529 \\ +264 \\ \hline 783 \end{array}$ $\begin{array}{r} 76 \\ +28 \\ \hline 94 \end{array}$ $\begin{array}{r} 44 \\ +56 \\ \hline 910 \end{array}$	☐ Yes ☐ No Example:	☐ Yes ☐ No Example:	☐ Yes ☐ No Example:	☐ Yes ☐ No Example:
	Borrowing (adds 10 but fails to change columns to the left): $\begin{array}{r} 132 \\ -27 \\ \hline 115 \end{array}$	☐ Yes ☐ No Example:	☐ Yes ☐ No Example:	☐ Yes ☐ No Example:	☐ Yes ☐ No Example:

(continued)

Type of Error	Sample Error Description	Week 1	Week 2	Week 3	Week 4
Procedural *(continued)*	Subtracting smaller from larger numbers: 75 − 49 — 34	☐ Yes ☐ No Example:	☐ Yes ☐ No Example:	☐ Yes ☐ No Example:	☐ Yes ☐ No Example:
	Problems borrowing across 0: 109 − 26 — 123	☐ Yes ☐ No Example:	☐ Yes ☐ No Example:	☐ Yes ☐ No Example:	☐ Yes ☐ No Example:
Visual–spatial/visual monitoring (misreading numbers, column alignment, or inadequate spacing of written work)	Number misalignment: 93010 − **325** — 60510	☐ Yes ☐ No Example:	☐ Yes ☐ No Example:	☐ Yes ☐ No Example:	☐ Yes ☐ No Example:
Switch (difficulty switching between two or more operations)	Addition to subtraction: 57 23 + 42 − 16 — — 99 39	☐ Yes ☐ No Example:	☐ Yes ☐ No Example:	☐ Yes ☐ No Example:	☐ Yes ☐ No Example:

227

Note. Error types were generated from Raghubar, Cirino, Barns, Ewing-Cobbs, Fletcher, and Fuchs (2009).

Fact Assessment Worksheet

Number Combination	Correct (answer provided within 3 seconds)	Incorrect	Backup strategies (resolves errors using one or more strategies)
		☐ Wrong answer ☐ No response ☐ Correct answer after 3 seconds	☐ Counting up/on _____ ☐ Doubles + 1 _____ ☐ Decomposition _____
		☐ Wrong answer ☐ No response ☐ Correct answer after 3 seconds	☐ Counting up/on _____ ☐ Doubles + 1 _____ ☐ Decomposition _____
		☐ Wrong answer ☐ No response ☐ Correct answer after 3 seconds	☐ Counting up/on _____ ☐ Doubles + 1 _____ ☐ Decomposition _____
		☐ Wrong answer ☐ No response ☐ Correct answer after 3 seconds	☐ Counting up/on _____ ☐ Doubles + 1 _____ ☐ Decomposition _____
		☐ Wrong answer ☐ No response ☐ Correct answer after 3 seconds	☐ Counting up/on _____ ☐ Doubles + 1 _____ ☐ Decomposition _____
		☐ Wrong answer ☐ No response ☐ Correct answer after 3 seconds	☐ Counting up/on _____ ☐ Doubles + 1 _____ ☐ Decomposition _____

CHAPTER 12

Conclusion

Quantitative literacy and the math proficiency of students in the United States is a matter of national concern. Despite the importance of math for making everyday life decisions and actions, historically less emphasis has been placed on the promotion of math proficiency. Although still in its infancy, there is enough literature available to offer recommendations for effectively supporting students' math development in schools. That is particularly the case for content that aligns with two areas within the CCSS for Mathematics: (1) number operations in base-ten and (2) operations and algebraic thinking.

In this book, we focused on how school professionals can use data and the instructional hierarchy to promote whole-number knowledge. By collecting meaningful data on key number concepts—such as early numeracy skills, computation, and word-problem solving, and assessing what skills and concepts students have mastered, are working toward (instructional level), and are unknown (frustration)—school professionals can make informed decisions about what instructional and intervention strategies are most useful to employ with students. Figure 12.1 provides a summary of how data were described in this book and can be used to identify the classrooms and students who are at risk for greater math difficulties.

This process begins by screening all students in a school to assess the overall health of math instruction (Chapter 3). Should school-level outcomes fall below expectations, the first step may be to address core instruction. Central to improvements in math outcomes is the implementation of an effective core curriculum and research-supported instructional principles that permit all students, regardless of ability, to access the core curriculum (Chapter 2). This means that empirically supported curriculum should be provided daily during scheduled intervals of time, effective instructional design principles be employed (i.e., blending teacher- and student-directed activities, using differentiated instruction, providing explicit instruction), classroom management systems be incorporated, and supplemental activities (i.e., peer tutoring, cooperative learning groups) be embedded into daily routines.

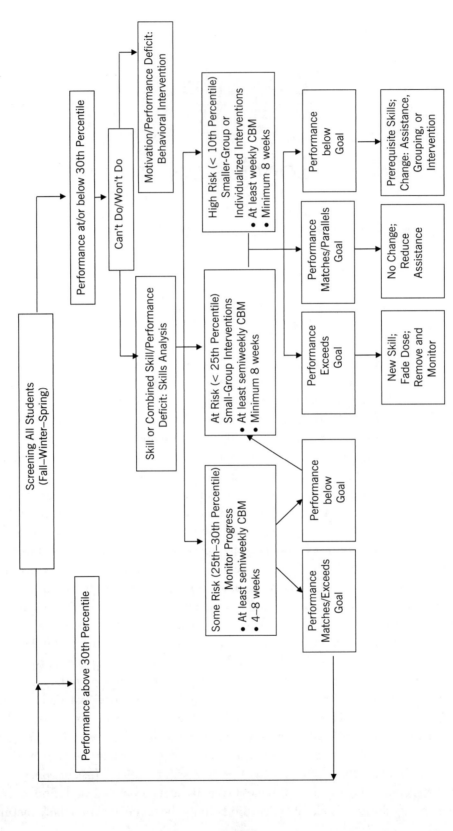

FIGURE 12.1. Instructional decision making. Adapted from Codding and Connell (2008). Copyright © 2008 Taylor & Francis. Adapted by permission.

230

Should classes of students fall below expectations, the peer-reviewed literature offers simple interventions in the areas of computation and word-problem solving that can be provided to bolster skill weaknesses experienced by whole classes of students (Chapter 4). We described the current status of and uses for CAI (Chapter 5) at both the classwide and student levels, as well as how to improve motivation, engagement, and persistence in the math learning of all students (Chapter 6).

For students who fall at or below the 30th percentile on universal screening measures, or those identified through high-stakes assessments and teacher referrals, there are a number of research-supported strategies that educators and school professionals can use to generate treatment packages that will likely improve math outcomes for students at risk for or with math disabilities (Chapter 7). By conducting a can't do/won't do assessment, further information about students' needs can be gathered to determine whether a combination of motivational- and skill-based strategies should be employed. Additionally, collecting more specific data on students' skill strengths and weaknesses (i.e., skills analysis) using CBA or CAT can facilitate homogeneous groupings of students with similar needs. By comparing these data to one of the criteria we described (see Chapter 3), educators and school professionals can target the level of skill proficiency that students are experiencing: acquisition, fluency, maintenance, generalization, and adaptation. Then, packaged interventions or empirically supported intervention strategies can be employed that match students' level of skill proficiency. In Chapters 8–10, respectively, we describe the available empirical evidence and provide protocols for interventions that target early numeracy, computation, and word-problem-solving skills and concepts. These interventions can be delivered to small groups of students or individually; student progress should be monitored on a regular basis. Finally, Chapter 11 describes how students' response to math interventions can be evaluated and adjusted to meet students' needs.

Throughout this book we provided figures, diagrams, flowcharts, checklists, intervention protocols, Web resources, and intervention materials to promote the use of data and the instructional hierarchy (i.e., skill proficiency stages: acquisition, fluency, maintenance, generalization, and adaptation) to inform educators' choice and use of empirically supported intervention packages and strategies.

References

References marked with an asterisk (*) indicate studies included in the meta-analysis (Chapter 5).

Adelman, C. (2006). *The toolbox revisited: Paths to degree completion from high school through college.* Washington, DC: U.S. Department of Education, Office of Education. Available at *www2.ed.gov/rschstat/research/pubs/toolboxrevisit/toolbox.pdf.*

Agodini, R., Harris, B., Thomas, M., Murphy, R., Gallagher, L., & Pendleton, A. (2010). *Achievement effects of four early elementary school math curricula: Findings for first and second graders* (Report submitted to the U.S. Department of Education, Institute of Education Sciences). Princeton, NJ: Mathematica Policy Research.

Allsopp, D. H., Kyder, M. M., Lovin, L., Gerreston, H., Carson, K. L., & Ray, S. (2008). Mathematics dynamic assessment: Informal assessment that responds to the need of struggling learners in mathematics. *Teaching Exceptional Children, 40,* 6–16.

Ancker, J. S., & Kaufman, D. (2007). Rethinking health numeracy: A multidisciplinary literature review. *Journal of the American Medical Informatics Association, 14,* 713–721.

Andersson, U. (2008). Mathematical competencies in children with different types of learning difficulties. *Journal of Educational Psychology, 100,* 48–66.

APA Presidential Task Force on Evidence-Based Practice. (2006). Evidence-based practice in psychology. *The American Psychologist, 61,* 271–285.

Archer, K., Savage, R., Sanghera-Sidhu, S., Wood, E., Gottardo, A., & Chen, V. (2014). Examining the effectiveness of technology use in classrooms: A tertiary meta-analysis. *Computers and Education, 78,* 140–149.

Ardoin, S. P., & Daly, E. J., III. (2007). Close encounters of the instructional kind: How the instructional hierarchy is shaping instructional research 30 years later. *Journal of Behavioral Education, 16,* 1–6.

Ardoin, S. P., Witt, J. C., Connell, J. E., & Koenig, J. L. (2005). Application of a three-tier response to intervention model for instructional planning, decision-making and the identification of children in need of services. *Journal of Psychoeducational Assessment, 23,* 362–380.

Aspiranti, K. B., Skinner, C. H., McCleary, D. F., & Cihak, D. F. (2011). Using taped-problems and reinforcement to increase addition-fact fluency in a general education first-grade classroom. *Behavior Analysis in Practice, 4,* 25–33.

Attewell, P., & Domina, T. (2008). Raising the bar: Curricular intensity and academic performance. *Educational Evaluation and Policy Analysis, 30,* 51–71.

Axtell, P. K., McCallum, R. S., Bell, S. M., & Poncy, B. (2009). Developing math automaticity using a classwide fluency building procedure for middle school students: A preliminary study. *Psychology in the Schools, 46,* 526–538.

Baglici, S. P., Codding, R. S., & Tryon, G. (2010). Extending the research on tests of early numeracy: Longitudinal analyses over two years. *Assessment for Effective Intervention, 35,* 89–102.

Bahrick, H. P., Hall, L. K., & Baker, M. K. (2013). *Life-span maintenance of knowledge.* New York: Psychology Press.

Baird, G. L., Scott, W. D., Dearing, E., & Hamill, S. K. (2009). Cognitive self-regulation in youth with and without learning disabilities: Academic self-efficacy, theories of intelligence, learning vs. performance goal preferences and effort attributions. *Journal of Social and Clinical Psychology, 28,* 881–908.

Baker, S., Gersten, R., & Lee, D. S. (2002). A synthesis of empirical research on teaching mathematics to low-achieving students. *Elementary School Journal, 103,* 51–73.

Bandura, A. (1997). *Self-efficacy: The exercise of control.* New York: Freeman.

Barnett, D., Hawkins, R., McCoy, D., Wahl, E., Shier, A., Denune, H., et al. (2014). Methods used to document procedural fidelity in school-based intervention research. *Journal of Behavioral Education, 23,* 89–107.

Barnett, D. W., Daly III, E. J., Jones, K. M., & Lentz Jr., F. E. (2004). Response to intervention: Empirically based special service decisions from single-case designs of increasing and decreasing intensity. *Journal of Special Education, 38,* 66–79.

Baroody, A. J., Bajwa, N. P., & Eiland, M. (2009). Why can't Johnny remember the basic facts? *Developmental Disabilities Research Reviews, 15,* 69–79.

Baroody, A. J., Eiland, M., & Thompson, B. (2009). Fostering at-risk preschoolers' number sense. *Early Education and Development, 20,* 49.

Baroody, A. J., & Gannon, K. E. (1984). The development of the commutativity principle and economical addition strategies. *Cognition and Instruction, 1*(3), 321–339.

Baroody, A. J., & Gatzke, M. R. (1991). The estimate of set size by potentially gifted kindergarten-age children. *Journal for Research in Mathematics Education, 22,* 59–68.

Barrouillet, P., & Fayol, M. (1998). From algorithmic computing to direct retrieval: Evidence from number and alphabetic arithmetic in children and adults. *Memory and Cognition, 26,* 355–368.

Batsche, G., Elliott, J., Graden, J. L., Grimes, J., Kovaleski, J. F., Prasse, D., et al. (2006). *Response to intervention: Policy considerations and implementation.* Alexandria, VA: National Association of State Directors of Special Education.

Belfiore, P. J., Lee, D. L., Vargas, A. U., & Skinner, C.

H. (1997). Effects of high-preference single-digit mathematics problem completion on multiple-digit mathematics problem performance. *Journal of Applied Behavior Analysis, 30,* 327–330.

Berch, D. B. (2005). Making sense of number sense: Implications for children with mathematical disabilities. *Journal of Learning Disabilities, 38,* 333–339.

Berch, D. B., & Mazzocco, M. M. M. (Eds.). (2007). *Why is math so hard for some children?: The nature and origins of mathematical learning difficulties and disabilities.* Baltimore: Brookes.

Best Evidence Encyclopedia. (n.d.). Mathematics/elementary. Retrieved from *www.bestevidence.org/math/elem/top.htm.*

Billington, E. J., Skinner, C. H., & Cruchon, N. M. (2004). Improving sixth-grade students' perceptions of high-effort assignments by assigning more work: Interaction of additive interspersal and assignment effort on assignment choice. *Journal of School Psychology, 42,* 477–490.

Binder, C. (1996). Behavioral fluency: Evolution of a new paradigm. *The Behavior Analyst, 19,* 163–197.

Bishop, M. J., & Santoro, L. E. (2006). Evaluating beginning reading software for at-risk learners. *Psychology in the Schools, 43*(1), 57–70.

Black, P., & Wiliam, D. (1998). Inside the black box: Raising standards through classroom assessment. *Phi Delta Kappan, 80,* 139–148.

Blankenship, C. S. (1985). Using curriculum-based assessment data to make instructional management decisions. *Learning Disability Quarterly, 25,* 59–76.

Bliss, S. L., Skinner, C. H., McCallum, E., Saecker, L. B., Rowland-Bryant, E., & Brown, K. S. (2010). A comparison of taped problems with and without a brief post-treatment assessment on multiplication fluency. *Journal of Behavioral Education, 19,* 156–168.

Bochniak, J. S. (2014). *The effectiveness of computer-aided instruction on math fact fluency* (doctoral dissertation). Retrieved from ProQuest Dissertations & Theses Global (Order No. 3665364). (*)

Boekaerts, M., Pintrich, P. R., & Zeidner, M. (Eds.). (2000). *Handbook of self-regulation.* San Diego, CA: Academic Press.

Boonen, A. J. H., van Wesel, F., Jolles, J., & van der Schoot, M. (2014). The role of visual representation type, spatial ability, and reading comprehension in word problem solving: An item-level analysis in elementary school children. *International Journal of Educational Research, 68,* 15–26.

Booth, J. L., & Siegler, R. S. (2008). Numerical magnitude representations influence arithmetic learning. *Child Development, 79,* 1016–1031.

Bowman-Perrott, L., Davis, H., Vannest, K., Williams, L., Greenwood, C., & Parker, R. (2013). Academic benefits of peer tutoring: A meta-analytic review of single-case research. *School Psychology Review, 42,* 39–55.

Brophy, J., & Good, T. L. (1986). Teacher behavior and student achievement. In M. C. Wittrock (Ed.), *Handbook of research on teaching* (3rd ed., pp. 328–375). New York: Simon & Schuster.

Brown, A. L. (1981). Metacognitive development in reading. In R. Spiro, B. Bruce, & W. Brewer (Eds.), *Theoretical issues in reading comprehension* (pp. 453–482). Hillsdale, NJ: Erlbaum.

Bryant, B. R., Bryant, D. P., Kethley, C., Kim, S. A., Pool, C., & You-Jin, S. (2008). Preventing mathematics difficulties in the primary grades: The critical features of instruction in textbooks as part of the equation. *Learning Disability Quarterly, 31,* 21–35.

Bryant, D. P., Bryant, B. R., Gersten, R., Scammacca, N., & Chavez, M. M. (2008). Mathematics intervention for first- and second-grade students with mathematics difficulties: The effects of tier 2 intervention delivered as booster lessons. *Remedial and Special Education, 29,* 20–32.

Bryant, D. P., Bryant, B. R., Gersten, R., Scammacca, N., Funk, C., Winter, A., et al. (2008). The effects of tier 2 intervention on first-grade mathematics performance of first-grade students who are at risk for mathematics difficulties. *Learning Disability Quarterly, 31,* 47–63.

Bryant, D. P., Bryant, B. R., & Hammill, D. D. (2000). Characteristic behaviors of students with LD who have teacher-identified math weaknesses. *Journal of Learning Disabilities, 33,* 168–177.

Bryant, D. P., Bryant, B. R., Roberts, G., Vaughn, S., Pfannenstiel, K. H., Porterfield, J., et al. (2011). Early numeracy intervention program for first-grade students with mathematics difficulties. *Exceptional Children, 78,* 7–23.

Bryant, D. P., Pfannenstiel, K. H., & Bryant, B. R. (2014). *Early Numeracy Intervention Program.* Austin, TX: Psychoeducational Services.

Buchik, J. C. (2009). *Increasing student learning of mathematics facts through online computer-assisted instruction* (master's thesis). Retrieved from ProQuest Dissertations & Theses Global (Order No. 1471004). (*)

Burns, M. K. (2005). Using incremental rehearsal to increase fluency of single-digit multiplication fact with children identified as learning disabled in mathematics computation. *Education and Treatment of Children, 28,* 237–249.

Burns, M. K., Appleton, J. J., & Stehouwer, J. D. (2005). Meta-analysis of response-to-intervention research: Examining field-based and research-implemented models. *Journal of Psychoeducational Assessment, 23,* 381–394.

Burns, M. K., Codding, R. S., Boice, C., & Lukito, G. (2010). Meta-analysis of acquisition and fluency math interventions with instruction and frustration level skills: Evidence for a skill-by-treatment interaction. *School Psychology Review, 39,* 69–83.

Burns, M. K., & Dean, V. J. (2005). Effect of acquisition rates on off-task behavior with children identified as learning disabled. *Learning Disability Quarterly, 28,* 273–281.

Burns, M. K., Deno, S., & Jimerson, S. R. (2007). Toward a unified model of response to intervention. In S. R. Jimerson, M. K. Burns, & A. M. VanDerHeyden (Eds.), *The handbook of response to intervention: The science and practice of assessment and intervention* (pp. 428–440). New York: Springer.

Burns, M. K., Kanive, R., & DeGrande, M. (2012). Effect of a computer-delivered math fact intervention as a supplemental intervention for math in third and fourth grades. *Remedial and Special Education, 33,* 184–191. (*)

Burns, M. K., Peters, R., & Noell, G. H. (2008). Using performance feedback to enhance implementation fidelity of the problem-solving team process. *Journal of School Psychology, 46,* 537–550.

Burns, M. K., VanDerHeyden, A. M., & Jiban, C. L. (2006). Assessing the instructional level for mathematics: A comparison of methods. *School Psychology Review, 35,* 401–418.

Burns, M. K., & Ysseldyke, J. E. (2009). Reported prevalence of evidence-based instructional practices in special education. *Journal of Special Education, 43,* 3–11.

Burns, M. K., Ysseldyke, J. E., Nelson, P. M., & Kanive, R. (2015). Number of repetitions required to acquire single-digit multiplication math facts for elementary students. *School Psychology Quarterly, 30*(3), 398–405.

Burns, M. K., Zaslofsky, A., Kanive, R., & Parker, D. (2012). Meta-analysis of incremental rehearsal using phi coefficients to compare single-case and group designs. *Journal of Behavioral Education, 21,* 185–202.

Butterworth, B. (2005). The development of arithmetical abilities. *Journal of Child Psychology and Psychiatry, 46,* 3–18.

Butterworth, B. (2010). Foundational numerical capacities and the origins of dyscalculia. *Trends in Cognitive Science, 14*(12), 534–541.

Calderhead, W. J., Filter, K. J., & Albin, R. W. (2006). An investigation of incremental effects of interspersed math items on task-related behavior. *Journal of Behavioral Education, 15,* 51–65.

Cameron, J., Banko, K. M., & Pierce, D. (2001). Pervasive negative effects of rewards on intrinsic motivation: The myth continues. *The Behavior Analyst, 24,* 1–44.

Carpenter, T. P., Lindquist, M. M., Matthews, W., & Silver, E. A. (1983). Results of the third NAEP mathematics assessment: Secondary school. *The Mathematics Teacher, 76,* 652–659.

Carr, M., & Alexeev, N. (2011). Fluency, accuracy, and gender predict developmental trajectories of arithmetic strategies. *Journal of Educational Psychology, 103,* 617–631.

Carroll, E., Skinner, C. H., Turner, H., McCallum, E., & Woodland, S. (2006). Evaluating and comparing responsiveness to two interventions designed to enhance math-fact fluency. *School Psychology Forum, 1,* 28–45.

Case, L., Harris, K. R., & Graham, S. (1992). Improving the mathematical problem solving skills of students with learning disabilities: Self-regulated strategy development. *Journal of Special Education, 26,* 1–19.

Case, R., Griffin, S., & Kelly, W. (1999). Socioeconomic gradients in mathematical ability and their responsiveness to intervention during early childhood. In D. P. Keating & C. Hertzman (Eds.), *Developmental health and the wealth of nations: Social, biological, and educational dynamics* (pp. 125–149). New York: Guilford Press.

Cates, G. L., & Rhymer, K. N. (2003). Examining the relationship between mathematics anxiety and mathematics performance: A learning hierarchy perspective. *Journal of Behavioral Education, 12,* 23–34.

Chafouleas, S. M., Riley-Tillman, T. C., & Eckert, T. L. (2003). A comparison of school psychologists' acceptability, training, and use of norm-referenced, curriculum-based, and brief experimental analysis methods to assess reading. *School Psychology Review, 32,* 272–281.

Chang, K. E., Sung, Y. T., Chen, Y. L., & Huang, L. H. (2008). Learning multiplication through computer-assisted learning activities. *Computers in Human Behavior, 24,* 2904–2916. (*)

Chard, D. J., Clarke, B., Baker, S., Otterstedt, J., Braun, D., & Katz, R. (2005). Using measures of number sense to screen for difficulties in mathematics: Preliminary findings. *Assessment for Effective Intervention, 30,* 3–14.

Charles, R., Crown, W., Fennell, F., Caldwell, J. H., Cavanagh, M., Chancellor, D., et al. (2005). *Scott Foresman–Addison Wesley mathematics.* Glenview, IL: Pearson Scott Foresman.

Cheng, Z. (2012). Teaching young children decomposition strategies to solve addition problems: An experimental study. *Journal of Mathematical Behavior, 31,* 29–47.

Cheung, A. C., & Slavin, R. E. (2013). The effectiveness of educational technology applications for enhancing mathematics achievement in K–12 classrooms: A meta-analysis. *Educational Research Review, 9,* 88–113.

Christ, T. J. (2008). Best practices in problem analysis. In A. Thomas & J. Grimes (Eds.), *Best practices in school psychology V* (pp. 159–176). Bethesda, MD; National Association of School Psychologists.

Christ, T. J., Scullin, S., Tolbize, A., & Jiban, C. L. (2008). Implications of recent research: Curriculum-based measurement of math computation. *Assessment for Effective Intervention, 33*(4), 198–205.

Christmann, E. P., & Badgett, J. L. (2003). A meta-analytic comparison of the effects of computer-assisted instruction on elementary students' academic achievement. *Information Technology in Childhood Education Annual, 1,* 91–104.

Claessens, A., Duncan, G., & Engel, M. (2009). Kindergarten skills and fifth-grade achievement: Evidence from the ECLS-K. *Economics of Education Review, 28,* 415–427.

Claessens, A., Engel, M., & Curran, F. (2014). Academic content, student learning, and the persistence of preschool effects. *American Educational Research Journal, 51,* 403–434.

Clarke, B., Baker, S. K., Smolkowski, K., & Chard, D. J. (2008). An analysis of early numeracy curriculum-based measurement. *Remedial and Special Education, 29,* 46–57.

Clarke, B., Doabler, C. T., Smolkowski, K., Baker, S. K., Fien, H., & Strand Cary, M. (2016). Examining the efficacy of a tier 2 kindergarten mathematics intervention. *Journal of Learning Disabilities, 49*(2), 152–165.

Clarke, B., Doabler, C. T., Strand Cary, M., Kosty, D., Baker, S., Fien, H., et al. (2013). *Examining the efficacy of a tier 2 first grade mathematics intervention program* (Technical Report 1302). Eugene: University of Oregon, Center on Teaching and Learning.

Clarke, B., Doabler, C. T., Strand Cary, M., Kosty, D., Baker, S., Fien, H., & Smolkowski, K. (2014). Preliminary evaluation of a tier 2 mathematics intervention for first grade students: Using a theory of change to guide formative evaluation activities. *School Psychology Review, 43*(2), 160–178.

Clarke, B., & Shinn, M. R. (2004). A preliminary investigation into the identification and development of early mathematics curriculum-based measurement. *School Psychology Review, 33,* 234–248.

Clarke, B., Smolkowski, K., Baker, S. K., Fien, H., Doabler, C. T., & Chard, D. J. (2011). The impact of a comprehensive tier 1 core kindergarten program on the achievement of students at risk in mathematics. *Elementary School Journal, 111,* 561–584.

Clements, D. H. (1999). Teaching length measurement: Research challenges. *School Science and Mathematics, 99,* 5–11.

Clements, D. H. (2007). Curriculum research: Toward a framework for "research-based curricula." *Journal for Research in Mathematics Education, 38,* 35–70.

Clements, D. H., & Sarama, J. (2007). Effects of a preschool mathematics curriculum: Summative research on the Building Blocks project. *Journal for Research in Mathematics Education, 38,* 136–163.

Clements, D. H., & Sarama, J. (2008). Curriculum focal points: Pre-K to kindergarten. *Teaching Children Mathematics, 14,* 361–365.

Clements, D. H., & Sarama, J. (2011). Early childhood mathematics intervention. *Science, 333,* 968–970.

Clements, D. H., Sarama, J., Wolfe, C. B., & Spitler, M. E. (2013). Longitudinal evaluation of a scale-up model for teaching mathematics with trajectories and technologies: Persistence of effects in the year. *American Educational Research Journal, 50,* 812–850.

Codding, R. S., Archer, J., & Connell, J. (2010). A systematic replication and extension of using incremental rehearsal to improve multiplication skills: An investigation of generalization. *Journal of Behavioral Education, 19,* 93–105.

Codding, R. S., Baglici, S., Gottesman, D., Johnson, M., Schaffer Kert, A., & LeBeouf, P. (2009). Selecting interventions strategies: Using brief experimental analysis for mathematic problems. *Journal of Applied School Psychology, 25,* 146–168.

Codding, R. S., Burns, M. K., & Lukito, G. (2011). Meta-analysis of basic-fact fluency interventions: A component analysis. *Learning Disabilities Research and Practice, 26,* 36–47.

Codding, R. S., Chan-Iannetta, L., George, S., Ferreira, K., & Volpe, R. (2011). Early number skills: Examining the effects of class-wide interventions on kindergarten performance. *School Psychology Quarterly, 26,* 85–96.

Codding, R. S., Chan-Iannetta, L., Palmer, M., & Lukito, G. (2009). Examining a class-wide application of cover–copy–compare with and without goal setting to enhance mathematics fluency. *School Psychology Quarterly, 24,* 173–185.

Codding, R. S., & Connell, J. E., Jr. (2008). Preparing educators to use curriculum-based measurement. In T. J. Kowalski & T. J. Lasley, II (Eds.), *Handbook on data-based decision making in education* (pp. 136–152). New York: Routledge.

Codding, R. S., Feinberg, A. B., Pace, G. M., & Dunn, E. (2005). Effects of immediate performance feedback on implementation of behavior support plans. *Journal of Applied Behavior Analysis, 38,* 205–219.

Codding, R. S., Hilt-Panahon, A., Panahon, C., & Benson, J. (2009). Addressing mathematics computation problems: A review of simple and moderate intensity interventions. *Education and Treatment of Children, 32,* 279–312.

Codding, R. S., & Lane, K. L. (2015). A spotlight on treatment intensity: An important and often overlooked component of intervention inquiry. *Journal of Behavioral Education, 24,* 1–10.

Codding, R. S., Lewandowski, L., & Eckert, T. (2005). Examining the efficacy of performance feedback and goal setting interventions in children with ADHD: A comparison of two methods. *Journal of Evidence-Based Practices for Schools, 6*(1), 42–58.

Codding, R. S., & Martin, R. (2016). Tier 3: Intensive mathematics intervention strategies. In S. R. Jimerson, M. K. Burns, & A. M. VanDerHeyden (Eds.), *Handbook of response to intervention: The science and practice of multi-tiered systems of support* (2nd ed., pp. 375–388). New York: Springer Science.

Codding, R. S., Shiyko, M., Russo, M., Birch, S., Fanning, E., & Jaspen, D. (2007). Comparing mathematics interventions: Does initial level of fluency predict intervention effectiveness? *Journal of School Psychology, 45,* 603–617.

Codding, R. S., & VanDerHeyden, A. (2014, February). Treatment dose: Does session distribution matter? In R. Codding (Chair), *Mathematics intervention development and examination of intervention intensity.* Symposium presented at the annual conference of the National Association of School Psychologists, Washington, DC.

Cohen, J. D., Servan-Schreiber, D., & McClelland, J. L. (1992). A parallel distributed processing approach to automaticity. *American Journal of Psychology, 105,* 239–269.

Compton, D. L., Fuchs, L. S., Fuchs, D., Lambert, W., & Hamlett, C. (2012). The cognitive and academic profiles of reading and mathematics learning disabilities. *Journal of Learning Disabilities*, *45*, 79–95.

Cooke, N. L., Guzaukas, R., Pressley, J. S., & Kerr, K. (1993). Effects of using a rationale of new to review items during drill and practice: Three experiments. *Education and Treatment of Children*, *16*, 213–234.

Cooper, G., & Sweller, J. (1987). The effects of schema acquisition and rule automation on mathematical problem-solving transfer. *Journal of Educational Psychology*, *79*, 347–362.

Cooper, J., Heron, T., & Heward, W. (2007). *Applied behavior analysis* (2nd ed.). Old Tappan, NJ: Pearson Education.

Crowe, A. R. (2010). What's math got to do with it?: Numeracy and social studies education. *The Social Studies*, *101*(3), 105–110.

Cumming, J. J., & Elkins, J. (1999). Lack of automaticity in the basic addition facts as a characteristic of arithmetic learning problems and instructional needs. *Mathematical Cognition*, *5*, 149–180.

Daly, E. J., Hintze, J. M., & Hamler, K. R. (2000). Improving practice by taking steps towards technological improvements in academic intervention in the new millennium. *Psychology in the Schools*, *37*, 61–72.

Daly, E. J., Witt, J. C., Martens, B. K., & Dool, E. J. (1997). A model for conducting a functional analysis of academic performance problems. *School Psychology Review*, *26*, 554–574.

Daly, E. J., Wright, J. A., Kelley, S. Q., & Martens, B. K. (1997). Measures of early academic skills: Reliability and validity with a first grade sample. *School Psychology Quarterly*, *12*, 268–280.

Daly, E. J., III, Martens, B. K., Barnett, D., Witt, J. C., & Olson, S. C. (2007). Varying intervention delivery in response to intervention: Confronting and resolving challenges with measurement, instruction, and intensity. *School Psychology Review*, *36*, 562–581.

Deci, E. L., Koestner, R., & Ryan, R. M. (1999). A meta-analytic review of experiments examining the effects of extrinsic rewards on intrinsic motivation. *Psychological Bulletin*, *125*, 627–668.

Deci, E. L., Koestner, R., & Ryan, R. M. (2001). Extrinsic rewards and intrinsic motivation in education: Reconsidered once again. *Review of Educational Research*, *71*, 1–27.

Deci, E. L., & Ryan, R. M. (1985). *Intrinsic motivation and self-determination in human behavior*. New York: Plenum Press.

Dehaene, S. (2011). *The number sense: How the mind creates mathematics* (2nd ed.). New York: Oxford University Press.

Dehaene, S., Piazza, M., Pinel, P., & Cohen, L. (2005). Three parietal circuits for number processing. In J. I. D. Campbell (Ed.), *Handbook of mathematical cognition* (pp. 433–453). New York: Psychology Press.

de Koster, S., Kuiper, E., & Volman, M. (2012). Concept-guided development of ICT use in "traditional" and "innovative" primary schools: What types of ICT use do schools develop? *Journal of Computer Assisted Learning*, *28*, 454–464.

Dennis, M. S., Calhoon, M. B., Olson, C. L., & Williams, C. (2014). Using computation curriculum-based measurement probes for error pattern analysis. *Intervention in School and Clinic*, *49*, 281–289.

Deno, S. L. (1985). Curriculum-based measurement: The emerging alternative. *Exceptional Children*, *52*, 219–232.

Deno, S. L., & Mirkin, P. K. (1977). *Data-based program modification: A manual*. Reston, VA: Council for Exceptional Children.

DeSmedt, B., Holloway, I. D., & Ansari, D. (2011). Effects of problem size and arithmetic operation on brain activation in children with varying levels of arithmetical fluency. *NeuroImage*, *57*, 771–781.

Desoete, A., Roeyers, H., & De Clercq, A. (2003). Can off-line metacognition enhance mathematical problem solving? *Journal of Educational Psychology*, *95*, 188–200.

Deubel, P. (2002). Selecting curriculum-based software. *Learning and Leading with Technology*, *29*(5), 10–17.

Dewey, E. N., Rice, D. P., Wheeler, C. E., Kaminski, R. A., & Good, R. H. (2014). *2014–2015 DIBELSnet® Preliminary System-Wide Percentile Ranks for DIBELS® Math Early Release (Technical Report No. 18)*. Eugene, OR: Dynamic Measurement Group.

Diezmann, C. M., & McCosker, N. T. (2011). Reading students' representations. *Teaching Children Mathematics*, *18*, 162–169.

DiGennaro Reed, F. D., & Codding, R. S. (2014). Advancements in procedural fidelity assessment and intervention: Introduction to the special issue. *Journal of Behavioral Education*, *23*, 1–18.

Doabler, C. T., Cary, M. S., Jungjohann, K., Clarke, B., Fien, H., Baker, S., et al. (2012). Enhancing core mathematics instruction for students at high risk for mathematics disabilities. *Teaching Exceptional Children*, *44*, 48–57.

Doabler, C. T., & Fien, H. (2013). Explicit mathematics instruction: What teachers can do for teaching students with mathematics difficulties. *Intervention in School and Clinic*, *48*, 276–285.

Doabler, C. T., Fien, H., Nelson-Walker, N. J., &

Baker, S. K. (2012). Evaluating three elementary mathematics programs for presence of eight research-based instructional design principles. *Learning Disability Quarterly, 35*(4), 200–211.

Doabler, C. T., Nelson, N. J., Kosty, D. B., Fien, H., Baker, S. K., Smolkowski, K., et al. (2014). Examining teachers' use of evidence-based practices during core mathematics instruction. *Assessment for Effective Intervention, 39*, 99–111.

Doggett, R. A., Henington, C., & Johnson-Gros, K. N. (2006). *Math to Mastery: A direct instruction remedial math intervention designed to increase student fluency with basic math facts.* Unpublished manuscript, Mississippi State University.

Dowker, A. (2001). Numeracy recovery: A pilot scheme for early intervention with young children with numeracy difficulties. *Support for Learning, 16*, 6–10.

Dowker, A. (2005). Early identification and intervention for students with mathematics difficulties. *Journal of Learning Disabilities, 38*, 324–332.

Dowker, A. (2007). What can intervention tell us about the development of arithmetic? *Educational and Child Psychology, 24*, 64–82.

Dufrene B., Noell, G., Gilbertson, D., & Duhon, G. (2005). Monitoring implementation of reciprocal peer tutoring: Identifying and intervening with students who do not maintain accurate implementation. *School Psychology Review, 34*, 74–86.

Duhon, G. J., House, S., Hastings, K., Poncy, B., & Solomon, B. (2015). Adding immediate feedback to explicit timing: An option for enhancing treatment intensity to improve mathematics fluency. *Journal of Behavioral Education, 24*, 74–87.

Duhon, G. J., House, S. H., & Stinnett, T. A. (2012). Evaluating the generalization of math fact fluency gains across paper and computer performance modalities. *Journal of School Psychology, 50*, 335–345. (*)

Duhon, G. J., Noell, G. H., Witt, J. C., Freeland, J. T., Dufrene, B. A., & Gilbertson, D. N. (2004). Identifying academic skill and performance deficits: The experimental analysis of brief assessments of academic skills. *School Psychology Review, 33*, 429–443.

Duncan, G. J., Dowsett, C. J., Claessens, A., Magnuson, K., Huston, A. C., Klebanov, P., et al. (2007). School readiness and later achievement. *Developmental Psychology, 43*, 1428–1446.

DuPaul, G. J., & Eckert, T. L. (1998). Academic interventions for students with attention-deficit/hyperactivity disorder: A review of the literature. *Reading and Writing Quarterly: Overcoming Learning Difficulties, 14*(1), 59–82.

Dweck, C. S. (1999). *Self-theories: Their role in motivation, personality, and development.* Philadelphia: Taylor & Francis.

Dweck, C. S. (2008). *Mindsets: The new psychology of success.* New York: Ballantine Books.

Dyson, N., Jordan, N. C., Beliakoff, A., & Hassinger-Das, B. (2015). A kindergarten number-sense intervention with contrasting practice conditions for low-achieving children. *Journal for Research in Mathematics Education, 46*, 331–370.

Dyson, N. I., Jordan, N. C., & Glutting, J. (2013). A number sense intervention for low-income kindergartners at risk for mathematics difficulties. *Journal of Learning Disabilities, 46*, 166–181.

Ehrhardt, K. E., Barnett, D. W., Lentz, F. E., Jr., Stollar, S. A., & Reifin, L. H. (1996). Innovative methodology in ecological consultation: Use of scripts to promote treatment acceptability and integrity. *School Psychology Quarterly, 11*, 149–168.

Erchul, W. P., & Martens, B. K. (2010). *School consultation: Conceptual and empirical bases of practice* (3rd ed.). New York: Springer.

Fantuzzo, J. W., King, J. A., & Heller, L. R. (1992). Effects of reciprocal peer tutoring on mathematics and school adjustment: A component analysis. *Journal of Educational Psychology, 84*, 331–339.

Figarola, P. M., Gunter, P. L., Reffel, J. M., Worth, S. R., Hummel, J., & Gerber, B. L. (2008). Effects of self-graphing and goal setting on the math fact fluency of students with disabilities. *Behavior Analysis in Practice, 1*, 36–41.

Fitzgerald, G., Koury, K., & Mitchem, K. (2008). Research on computer-mediated instruction for students with high incidence disabilities. *Journal of Educational Computing Research, 38*, 201–233.

Fletcher-Flinn, C. M., & Gravatt, B. (1995). The efficacy of computer assisted instruction (CAI): A meta-analysis. *Journal of Educational Computing Research, 12*, 219–241.

Flores, M. M. (2009). Teaching subtraction with regrouping to students experiencing difficulty in mathematics. *Preventing School Failure: Alternative Education for Children and Youth, 53*(3), 145–152.

Flores, M. M. (2010). Using the concrete–representational–abstract sequence to teach subtraction with regrouping to students at risk for failure. *Remedial and Special Education, 31*, 195–207.

Flores, M. M., Hinton, V., & Strozier, S. D. (2014). Teaching subtraction and multiplication with regrouping using the concrete–representational–abstract sequence. *Learning Disabilities Research and Practice, 29*, 75–88.

Foegen, A., Jiban, C., & Deno, S. (2007). Progress

monitoring measures in mathematics. *Journal of Special Education, 41,* 121–139.

Ford, M. J., Poe, V., & Cox, J. (1993). Attending behaviors of ADHD children in math and reading using various types of software. *Journal of Computing in Childhood Education, 4,* 183–196.

Friedberg, H. J. (n.d.). Consistency management and cooperative discipline (CMCD). Retrieved from *http://cmcd.coe.uh.edu.*

Fuchs, L. S. (2003). Assessing intervention responsiveness: Conceptual and technical issues. *Learning Disabilities Research and Practice, 18,* 172–186.

Fuchs, L. S. (2005). Prevention research in mathematics: Improving outcomes, building identification models, and understanding disability. *Journal of Learning Disabilities, 38,* 350–352.

Fuchs, L. S., Compton, D. L., Fuchs, D., Hollenbeck, K. N., Hamlett, C. L., & Seethaler, P. M. (2011). Two-stage screening for math problem-solving difficulty using dynamic assessment of algebraic learning. *Journal of Learning Disabilities, 44,* 372–380.

Fuchs, L. S., Compton, D. L., Fuchs, D., Paulsen, K., Bryant, J. D., & Hamlett, C. L. (2005). The prevention, identification, and cognitive determinants of math difficulty. *Journal of Educational Psychology, 97*(3), 493–513.

Fuchs, L. S., & Deno, S. L. (1991). Paradigmatic distinctions between instructionally relevant measurement models. *Exceptional Children, 57,* 488–501.

Fuchs, L. S., & Fuchs, D. (2004). Determining adequate yearly progress from kindergarten through grade 6 with curriculum-based measurement. *Assessment for Effective Intervention, 29,* 25–37.

Fuchs, L. S., Fuchs, D., & Compton, D. L. (2012). The early prevention of mathematics difficulty: Its power and limitations. *Journal of Learning Disabilities, 43,* 257–269.

Fuchs, L. S., Fuchs, D., Compton, D. L., Bryant, J. D., Hamlett, C. L., & Seethaler, P. M. (2007). Mathematics screening and progress monitoring at first grade: Implications for responsiveness to intervention. *Council for Exceptional Children, 73,* 311–330.

Fuchs, L. S., Fuchs, D., Compton, D. L., Powell, S. R., Seethaler, P. M., Capizzi, A. M., et al. (2006). The cognitive correlates of third-grade skill in arithmetic, algorithmic computation, and arithmetic word problems. *Journal of Educational Psychology, 43,* 29–43.

Fuchs, L. S., Fuchs, D., Craddock, C., Hollenbeck, K. N., Hamlett, C. L., & Schatschneider, C. (2008). Effects of small-group tutoring with and without validated classroom instruction on at-risk students' math problem solving: Are two tiers of prevention better than one? *Journal of Educational Psychology, 100,* 491–509.

Fuchs, L. S., Fuchs, D., Finelli, R., Courey, S. J., & Hamlett, C. L. (2004). Expanding schema-based transfer instruction to help third graders solve real-life mathematical problems. *American Educational Research Journal, 41,* 419–445.

Fuchs, L. S., Fuchs, D., Hamlett, C. L., Katazaroff, M., & Dutka, S. (1997). Effects of task-focused goals on low-achieving students with and without learning disabilities. *American Educational Research Journal, 34,* 513–543.

Fuchs, L. S., Fuchs, D., Hamlett, C. L., Phillips, N. B., Karns, K., & Dutka, S. (1997). Enhancing students' helping behavior during peer-mediated instruction with conceptual mathematical explanations. *Elementary School Journal, 97,* 223–249.

Fuchs, L. S., Fuchs, D., Hamlett, C. L., Powell, S. R., Capizzi, A. M., & Seethaler, P. M. (2006). The effects of computer-assisted instruction on number combination skill in at-risk first graders. *Journal of Learning Disabilities, 39,* 467–475. (*)

Fuchs, L. S., Fuchs, D., Hamlett, C. L., & Stecker, P. M. (1990). The role of skills analysis in curriculum-based measurement in math. *School Psychology Review, 19,* 6–22.

Fuchs, L. S., Fuchs, D., & Hollenbeck, K. N. (2007). Extending responsiveness to intervention to mathematics at first and third grades. *Learning Disabilities Research and Practice, 22,* 13–24.

Fuchs, L. S., Fuchs, D., Karns, K., Hamlett, C. L., Katzaroff, M., & Dutka, S. (1997). Effects of task focused goals on low achieving students with and without learning disabilities. *American Educational Research Journal, 34,* 513–543.

Fuchs, L. S., Fuchs, D., Powell, S. R., Seethaler, P. M., Cirino, P. T., & Fletcher, J. M. (2008). Intensive intervention for students with mathematics disabilities: Seven principles for effective practice. *Learning Disability Quarterly, 31,* 79–92.

Fuchs, L. S., Fuchs, D., Prentice, K., Burch, M., Hamlett, C. L., Owen, R., et al. (2003a). Enhancing third-grade students' mathematical problem solving with self-regulated learning strategies. *Journal of Educational Psychology, 95*(2), 306–315.

Fuchs, L. S., Fuchs, D., Prentice, K., Burch, M., Hamlett, C. L., Owen, R., et al. (2003b). Explicitly teaching for transfer: Effects on third-grade students' mathematical problem solving. *Journal of Educational Psychology, 95,* 293–304.

Fuchs, L. S., Fuchs, D., Prentice, K., Hamlett, C. L., Finelli, R., & Courey, S. J. (2004). Enhancing mathematical problem solving among third-grade students with schema-based instruction. *Journal of Educational Psychology, 96*, 635–647.

Fuchs, L. S., Fuchs, D., & Speece, D. L. (2002). Treatment validity as a unifying construct for identifying learning disabilities. *Learning Disability Quarterly, 25*, 33–45.

Fuchs, L. S., Fuchs, D., & Zumeta, R. O. (2008). A curricular-sampling approach to progress monitoring: Mathematics concepts and applications. *Assessment for Effective Intervention, 33*(4), 225–233.

Fuchs, L. S., Geary, D. C., Compton, D. L., Fuchs, D., Hamlett, C. L., & Bryant, J. D. (2010). The contributions of numerosity and domain-general abilities to school readiness. *Child Development, 81*, 1520–1533.

Fuchs, L. S., Geary, D. C., Compton, D. L., Fuchs, D., Hamlett, C. L., Seethaler, P. M., et al. (2010). Do different types of school mathematics development depend on different constellations of numerical and general cognitive abilities? *Developmental Psychology, 46*, 1731–1746.

Fuchs, L. S., Geary, D. C., Fuchs, D., Compton, D. L., & Hamlett, C. L. (2014). Sources of individual differences in emerging competence with numeration understanding versus multi-digit calculation skill. *Journal of Educational Psychology, 106*(2), 482–498.

Fuchs, L. S., Hamlett, C. L., & Fuchs, D. (1999). *Monitoring basic skills progress: Basic math concepts and applications* [Computer software, manual, and blackline masters]. Austin, TX: PRO-ED.

Fuchs, L. S., Hamlett, C. L., & Powell, S. R. (2003). *Fact fluency assessment.* (Available from L. S. Fuchs, 328 Peabody, Vanderbilt University, Nashville, TN 37203)

Fuchs, L. S., Paulsen, K., & Fuchs, D. (n.d.). Number rockets: First grade small group tutoring. Retrieved from *http://vkc.mc.vanderbilt.edu/numberrockets*.

Fuchs, L. S., Powell, S. R., Cirino, P. T., Schumacher, R. F., Marrin, S., Hamlett, C. L., et al. (2014). Does calculation or word-problem instruction provide a stronger route to prealgebraic knowledge? *Journal of Educational Psychology, 106*, 990–1006.

Fuchs, L. S., Powell, S. R., Seethaler, P. M., Cirino, P. T., Fletcher, J. M., Fuchs, D., et al. (2009). Remediating number combination and word problem deficits among students with mathematics difficulties: A randomized control trial. *Journal of Educational Psychology, 101*(3), 561–576.

Fuchs, L. S., Powell, S. R., Seethaler, P. M., Fuchs, D., Hamlett, C. L., Cirino, P. T., et al. (2010). A framework for remediating number combination deficits. *Exceptional Children, 76*(2), 135–165.

Fuchs, L. S., Seethaler, P. M., Powell, S. R., Fuchs, D., Hamlett, C. L., & Fletcher, J. M. (2008). Effects of preventative tutoring on the mathematical problem solving of third-grade students with math and reading difficulties. *Exceptional Children, 74*, 155–173.

Fuson, K. C. (2009). *Math expressions.* Orlando, FL: Houghton Mifflin Harcourt.

Fuson, K. C., & Fuson, A. M. (1992). Instruction supporting children's counting on for addition and counting up for subtraction. *Journal for Research in Mathematics Education, 23*, 72–78.

Fuson, K. C., & Kwon, Y. (1992). Learning addition and subtraction: Effects of number word and other cultural tools. In J. Bideau, C. Meljac, & J. P. Fisher (Eds.), *Pathways to number* (pp. 351–374). Hillsdale, NJ: Erlbaum.

Geary, D. C. (2004). Mathematics and learning disabilities. *Journal of Learning Disabilities, 37*, 4–15.

Geary, D. C. (2007). An evolutionary perspective on learning disability in mathematics. *Developmental Neuropsychology, 32*, 471–519.

Geary, D. C. (2011a). Cognitive predictors of achievement growth in mathematics: A 5-year longitudinal study. *Developmental Psychology, 47*, 1539–1552.

Geary, D. C. (2011b). Consequences, characteristics, and causes of mathematical learning disabilities and persistent low achievement in mathematics. *Journal of Developmental and Behavioral Pediatrics, 33*, 250–263.

Geary, D. C. (2013). Early foundations for mathematics learning and their relations to learning disabilities. *Current Directions in Psychological Science, 22*, 23–27.

Geary, D. C., Bailey, D. H., & Hoard, M. K. (2009). Predicting mathematical achievement and mathematical learning disability with a simple screening tool: The number sets test. *Journal of Psychoeducational Assessment, 27*, 265–279.

Geary, D. C., Hoard, M. K., & Bailey, D. H. (2010). How SLD manifests in mathematics. In D. P. Flanagan & V. C. Alfonso (Eds.), *Essentials of specific learning disability identification* (pp. 43–64). Hoboken, NJ: Wiley.

Geary, D. C., Hoard, M. K., & Bailey, D. H. (2012). Fact retrieval deficits in low achieving children and children with mathematical learning disability. *Journal of Learning Disabilities, 45*, 291–307.

Geary, D. C., Hoard, M. K., Byrd-Craven, J., & Catherine DeSoto, M. (2004). Strategy choices in simple and complex addition: Contributions of working memory and counting knowledge for children with mathematical disability. *Journal of Experimental Child Psychology, 88,* 121–151.

Geary, D. C., Hoard, M. K., & Nugent, L. (2012). Independent contributions of the central executive, intelligence, and in-class attentive behavior to developmental change in the strategies used to solve addition problems. *Journal of Experimental Child Psychology, 113,* 49–65.

Gelman, R., & Gallistel, C. (1978). *The child's understanding of number.* Cambridge, MA: Harvard University Press.

Gersten, R., Beckmann, S., Clarke, B., Foegen, A., Marsh, L., Star, J. R., et al. (2009). *Assisting students struggling with mathematics: Response to intervention (RtI) for elementary and middle schools* (NCEE 2009-4060). Washington, DC: National Center for Education Evaluation and Regional Assistance, Institute of Education Sciences, U.S. Department of Education. Retrieved from *http://ies.ed.gov/ncee/wwc/publications/practiceguides.*

Gersten, R., & Chard, D. (1999). Number sense: Rethinking arithmetic instruction of students with mathematical disabilities. *Journal of Special Education, 33,* 18–28.

Gersten, R., Chard, D. J., Jayanthi, M., Baker, S. K., Morphy, P., & Flojo, J. (2009). Mathematics instruction for students with learning disabilities: A meta-analysis of instructional components. *Review of Educational Research, 79,* 1202–1242.

Gersten, R., Clarke, B. S., & Jordan, N. C. (2007). *Screening for mathematics difficulties in K–3 students.* Portsmouth, NH: RMC Research Corporation, Center on Instruction.

Gersten, R., Jordan, N. C., & Flojo, J. R. (2005). Early identification and interventions for students with mathematics difficulties. *Journal of Learning Disabilities, 38,* 293–304.

Gersten, R., & Newman-Gonchar, R. (2011). *Response to intervention in mathematics.* Baltimore: Brookes.

Gickling, E. E., & Havertape, S. (1981). *Curriculum-based assessment (CBA).* Minneapolis, MN: School Psychology Inservice Training Network.

Gickling, E. E., & Thompson, V. (1985). A personal view of curriculum-based assessment. *Exceptional Children, 52,* 205–218.

Gilbertson, D., Duhon, G., Witt, J. C., & Dufrene, B. (2008). Effects of academic response rates on time-on-task in the classroom for students at academic and behavioral risk. *Education and Treatment of Children, 31,* 153–165.

Gilbertson, D., Witt, J., Duhon, G., & Dufrene, B. (2008). Using brief assessments to select math fluency and on-task behavior interventions: An investigation of treatment utility. *Education and Treatment of Children, 31,* 167–181.

Ginsburg, H. P. (2009). The challenge of formative assessment in mathematics education: Children's minds, teachers' minds. *Human Development, 52,* 109–128.

Ginsburg-Block, M. D., Rohrbeck, C. A., & Fantuzzo, J. W. (2006). A meta-analytic review of social, self-concept, and behavioral outcomes of peer-assisted learning. *Journal of Educational Psychology, 98,* 732–749.

Goldman, S. R. (1989). Strategy instruction in mathematics. *Learning Disability Quarterly, 12,* 43–55.

Goodman, M., Finnegan, R., Mohadjer, L., Krenzke, T., & Hogan, J. (2013). *Literacy, numeracy, and problem solving in technology-rich environments among U.S. adults: Results from the Program for the International Assessment of Adult Competencies 2012—firstlLook* (NCES 2014-008). Washington, DC: National Center for Education Statistics. Retrieved from *http://nces.ed.gov/pubsearch.*

Grafman, J. M., & Cates, G. L. (2010). The differential effects of two self-managed math instruction procedures: Cover, copy, and compare versus copy, cover, and compare. *Psychology in the Schools, 47,* 153–165.

Gray, L., Thomas, N. T., & Lewis, L. (2010). *Teachers' use of educational technology in U.S. public schools: 2009* (NCES No. 2010040). Washington, DC: National Center for Education Statistics.

Greenwood, C. R., Delquadri, J., & Carta, J. J. (1997). *Together we can!: Classwide peer tutoring to improve basic academic skills.* Longmont, CO: Sopris West.

Greenwood, C. R., Terry, B., Utley, C. A., Montagna, D., & Walker, D. (1993). Achievement placement and services: Middle school benefits of Classwide Peer Tutoring used at the elementary school. *School Psychology Review, 22,* 497–516.

Grégoire, J., & Desoete, A. (2009). Mathematical disabilities: An underestimated topic? *Journal of Psychoeducational Assessment, 27,* 171–174.

Gresham, F. M. (1989). Assessment of treatment integrity in school consultation/prereferral intervention. *School Psychology Review, 18,* 37–50.

Gresham, F. M. (2007). Evolution of the response to intervention concept: Empirical foundations and recent developments. In S. Jimmerson, M. Burns,

& A. VanDerHeyden (Eds.), *The handbook of response to intervention: The science and practice of assessment and intervention* (pp. 10–24). New York: Springer.

Griffin, S. (2003). Laying the foundation for computational fluency in early childhood. *Teaching Children Mathematics, 9*, 306–309.

Griffin, S. (2004). Building number sense with SRA Number Worlds: A mathematics program for young children. *Early Childhood Research Quarterly, 19*, 173–180.

Griffin, S., & Case, R. (1997). Re-thinking the primary school math curriculum: An approach based on cognitive science. *Issues in Education, 3*, 1–49.

Griffin, S. A., Case, R., & Siegler, R. S. (1994). Rightstart: Providing the central conceptual prerequisites for first formal learning of arithmetic to students at risk for school failure. In K. McGilly (Ed.), *Classroom lessons: Integrating cognitive theory and classroom practice* (pp. 24–49). Cambridge, MA: MIT Press.

Gross, T. J., & Duhon, G. (2013). Evaluation of computer-assisted instruction for math accuracy intervention. *Journal of Applied School Psychology, 29*, 246–261.

Gross, T. J., Duhon, G. J., Hansen, B., Rowland, J. E., Schutte, G., & Williams, J. (2014). Effect of goal-line presentation and goal selection on first-grader subtraction fluency. *Journal of Experimental Education, 82*, 555–571.

Haegele, K., & Burns, M. K. (2015). The effect of modifying instructional set size based on the acquisition rate among students identified with a learning disability. *Journal of Behavioral Education, 24*, 33–50.

Hall, T. E., Hughes, C. A., & Filbert, M. (2000). Computer assisted instruction in reading for students with learning disabilities: A research synthesis. *Education and Treatment of Children, 23*, 173–193.

Hardman, M. L., McDonnell, J., & Welch, M. (1997). Perspectives on the future of IDEA. *Journal of the Association for Persons with Severe Handicaps, 22*, 61–77.

Haring, N. G., & Eaton, M. D. (1978). Systematic procedures: An instructional hierarchy. In N. G. Haring, T. C. Lovitt, M. D. Eaton, & C. L. Hansen (Eds.), *The fourth R: Research in the classroom* (pp. 23–40). Columbus, OH: Merrill.

Hasselbring, T. S., Goin, L. I., & Bransford, J. D. (1988). Developing math automaticity in learning handicapped children: The role of computerized drill and practice. *Focus on Exceptional Children, 20*, 1–7.

Hasselbring, T. S., Goin, L. I., & Sherwood, R. D. (1986). *The effects of computer-based drill and practice on automaticity* (Technical Report). Nashville, TN: Vanderbilt University, Learning Technology Center.

Hasselbring, T. S., Lott, A., & Zydney, J. (2005). *Technology-supported math instruction for students with disabilities: Two decades of research and development.* Washington, DC: American Institutes for Research. Available at *www. everydaymath.org/research/tech.pdf.*

Hattie, J. A. C. (2009). *Visible learning: A synthesis of 800 meta-analyses relating to achievement.* Oxon, UK: Routledge.

Hawkins, J., Skinner, C. H., & Oliver, R. (2005). The effects of task demands and additive interspersal ratios on fifth grade students' mathematics accuracy. *School Psychology Review, 34*, 543–555.

Hawkins, R., Musti-Rao, S., Hughes, C., Berry, L., & McGuire, S. (2009). Applying a randomized interdependent group contingency component to classwide peer tutoring for multiplication fact fluency. *Journal of Behavioral Education, 18*, 300–318.

Heinecke, W. F., Milman, N. B., Washington, L. A., & Blasi, L. (2001). New directions in the evaluation of the effectiveness of educational technology. *Computers in the Schools, 18*, 97–110.

Heller, L. R., & Fantuzzo, J. W. (1993). Reciprocal peer tutoring and parent partnership: Does parent involvement make a difference? *School Psychology Review, 22*, 517–534.

Hintze, J. M. (2007). *Conceptual and empirical issues related to developing a response-to-intervention framework.* Paper presented at the National Center on Student Progress Monitoring, Washington, DC. Retrieved from *http://studentprogress.org/doc/Hintze2008Conceptualand EmpiricalIssuesofRTI.doc.*

Hintze, J. M. (2008). Conceptual and empirical issues related to developing a response-to-intervention framework. *Journal of Evidence-Based Practice for Schools, 9*, 128–147.

Hintze, J. M., Christ, T. J., & Methe, S. A. (2006). Curriculum-based assessment. *Psychology in the Schools, 43*, 45–56.

Hoover, H. D., Hieronymus, A. N., Frisbie, D. A., & Dunbar, S. B. (1993). *Iowa test of basic skills.* Itasca, IL: Riverside.

Hosp, J. L. (2012). Formative evaluation: Developing a framework for using assessment data to plan instruction. *Focus on Exceptional Children, 44*, 1–10.

Hosp, J. L., & Ardoin, S. P. (2008). Assessment for

instructional planning. *Assessment for Effective Intervention, 33*, 69–77.

Hosp, M., Hosp, J., & Howell, K. (2007). *The ABCs of CBM: A practical guide to curriculum-based measurement.* New York: Guilford Press.

Howell, K. W., & Nolet, V. (1999). *Curriculum-based evaluation: Teaching and decision making* (3rd ed.). Belmont, CA: Wadsworth.

Hoza, B., Pelham, W. E., Waschbusch, D. A., Kipp, H., & Owens, J. S. (2001). Academic task persistence of normally achieving ADHD and control boys: Performance, self-evaluations, and attributions. *Journal of Consulting and Clinical Psychology, 69*, 271–283.

Hudson, P., Miller, S. P., & Butler, F. (2006). Adapting and merging explicit instruction within reform based mathematics classrooms. *American Secondary Education, 35*, 19–32.

Individuals with Disabilities Education Act Amendments of 1997. (1997). Retrieved from *http://thomas.loc.gov/home/thomas.php*.

Individuals with Disabilities Education Improvement Act, 20 U.S.C. § 1400 (2004).

International Society for Technology in Education. (2008). *Technology and student achievement: The indelible link* (Policy Brief). Washington, DC: International Society for Technology in Education. Retrieved March 15, 2015, from *www.k12hsn.org/files/research/Technology/ISTE_policy_brief_student_achievement.pdf*.

Intervention Central. (n.d.). Math work: Math worksheet generator. Retrieved from *www.interventioncentral.org/teacher-resources/math-work sheet-generator*.

Jitendra, A. K. (2007). *Solving math word problems: Teaching students with learning disabilities using schema-based instruction.* Austin, TX: PRO-ED.

Jitendra, A. K., DiPipi, C. M., & Perron-Jones, N. (2002). An exploratory study of schema-based word-problem-solving instruction for middle school students with learning disabilities: An emphasis on conceptual and procedural understanding. *Journal of Special Education, 36*, 23–38.

Jitendra, A. K., Griffin, C., Deatline-Buchman, A., & Sczesniak, E. (2007). Mathematical word problem solving in third grade classrooms. *Journal of Educational Research, 100*, 283–302.

Jitendra, A. K., & Hoff, K. (1996). The effects of schema-based instruction on mathematical word problem solving performance of students with learning disabilities. *Journal of Learning Disabilities, 29*, 422–431.

Jitendra, A. K., Rodriguez, M., Kanive, R., Huang, J., Church, C., Corroy, K. A., et al. (2013). Impact of small-group tutoring interventions on the mathematical problem solving and achievement of third-grade students with mathematics difficulties. *Learning Disability Quarterly, 36*, 21–35.

Jitendra, A. K., & Xin, Y. P. (1997). Mathematical word-problem-solving instruction for students with mild disabilities and students at risk for math failure: A research synthesis. *Journal of Special Education, 30*(4), 412–438.

Johns, G. A., Skinner, C. H., & Nail, G. L. (2000). Effects of interspersing briefer mathematics problems on assignment choices in students with learning disabilities. *Journal of Behavioral Education, 10*, 95–106.

Johnson, E. S., Jenkins, J. R., & Petscher, Y. (2010). Improving the accuracy of a direct route screening process. *Assessment for Effective Intervention, 35*, 131–140.

Johnson, K. R., & Layng, T. V. (1992). Breaking the structuralist barrier: Literacy and numeracy with fluency. *American Psychologist, 47*(11), 1475–1490.

Jonassen, D. H. (2003). Using cognitive tools to represent problems. *Journal of Research on Technology in Education, 35*, 362–381.

Jones, K., & Wickstrom, K. (2002). Done in sixty seconds: Further analysis of the brief assessment model for academic problems. *School Psychology Review, 31*, 554–568.

Jordan, N. C., & Dyson, N. (2014). *Number sense interventions.* Baltimore: Brookes.

Jordan, N. C., & Glutting, J. J. (2012). *Number Sense Screener* (Research ed.). Baltimore: Brookes.

Jordan, N. C., Glutting, J., Dyson, N., Hassinger-Das, B., & Irwin, C. (2012). Building kindergartners' number sense: A randomized controlled study. *Journal of Educational Psychology, 104*(3), 647–660.

Jordan, N. C., Glutting, J., & Ramineni, C. (2010). The importance of number sense to mathematics achievement in first and third grades. *Learning and Individual Differences, 20*, 82–88.

Jordan, N. C., Hanich, L. B., & Kaplan, D. (2003a). Arithmetic fact mastery in young children: A longitudinal investigation. *Journal of Experimental Child Psychology, 85*, 103–119.

Jordan, N. C., Hanich, L. B., & Kaplan, D. (2003b). A longitudinal study of mathematical competencies in children with specific mathematics difficulties versus children with comorbid mathematics and reading difficulties. *Child Development, 74*, 834–850.

Jordan, N. C., Kaplan, D., Locuniak, M. N., & Ramineni, C. (2007). Predicting first-grade math achievement from developmental number sense trajectories. *Learning Disabilities Research and Practice, 22,* 36–46.

Jordan, N. C., Kaplan, D., Ramineni, C., & Locuniak, M. N. (2008). Development of number combination skill in the early school years: When do fingers help? *Developmental Science, 11,* 662–668.

Jordan, N. C., Kaplan, D., Ramineni, C., & Locuniak, M. N. (2009). Early math matters: Kindergarten number and later mathematics outcomes. *Developmental Psychology, 45,* 850–867.

Joseph, L. M., Konrad, M., Cates, G., Vajcner, T., Eveleigh, E., & Fishley, K. M. (2012). A meta-analytic review of the cover–copy–compare and variations of this self-management procedure. *Psychology in the Schools, 49,* 122–136.

Joyce, B., & Showers, B. (2003). *Student achievement through staff development* (3rd ed.). Alexandria, VA: Association for Supervision and Curriculum Development.

Judge, S., & Watson, S. M. R. (2011). Longitudinal outcomes for mathematics achievement for students with learning disabilities. *Journal of Educational Research, 104,* 147–157.

Kalchman, M., Moss, J., & Case, R. (2001). Psychological models for the development of mathematical understanding: Rational numbers and functions. In S. Carver & D. Klahr (Eds.), *Cognition and instruction: Twenty-five years of progress* (pp. 1–38), Mahwah, NJ: Erlbaum.

Kebritchi, M., Hirumi, A., & Bai, H. (2010). The effects of modern mathematics computer games on mathematics achievement and class motivation. *Computers and Education, 55,* 427–443.

Kern, L., & Clemens, N. (2007). Antecedent strategies to promote appropriate classroom behavior. *Psychology in the Schools, 44,* 65–75.

Kilpatrick, J., Swafford, J., & Findell, B. (Eds.). (2001). *Adding it up: Helping children learn mathematics.* Washington, DC: National Academy Press. Retrieved from *www.nap.edu/catalog. php?record_id=9822.*

Kingston, N., & Nash, B. (2011). Formative assessment: A meta-analysis and a call for research. *Educational Measurement: Issues and Practice, 30,* 28–37.

Kleinert, W., Codding, R. S., Sheppard, V., Silva, M., & Gould, K. (2015, February). *Research synthesis on the taped problems and taped words interventions.* Poster presented at the annual meeting of the National Association of School Psychologists, Orlando, FL.

Kovaleski, J. F., Tucker, J. A., & Duffy, D. J. (1995).

School Reform through Instructional Support: The Pennsylvania Initiative (Part I) [Insert]. *Communiqué, 23*(8).

Kratochwill, T. R., & Shernoff, E. S. (2003). Evidence-based practice: Promoting evidence-based interventions in school psychology. *School Psychology Quarterly, 18,* 389–408.

Kratochwill, T. R., & Shernoff, E. S. (2004). Evidence-based practice: Promoting evidence-based interventions in school psychology. *School Psychology Review, 33,* 34–48.

Kroeger, S., & Kouche, B. (2006). Using peer assisted learning strategies to increase response to intervention in inclusive middle math settings. *Teaching Exceptional Children, 6,* 13.

Kroesbergen, E. H., & Van Luit, J. E. H. (2003). Mathematics interventions for children with special needs: A meta-analysis. *Remedial and Special Education, 24,* 97–114.

Kulik, C. L. C., & Kulik, J. A. (1991). Effectiveness of computer-based instruction: An updated analysis. *Computers in Human Behavior, 7,* 75–94.

Kulik, J. A., Kulik, C. L. C., & Bangert-Drowns, R. L. (1985). Effectiveness of computer-based education in elementary schools. *Computers in Human Behavior, 1,* 59–74.

Kunsch, C. A., Jitendra, A. K., & Sood, S. (2007). The effects of peer-mediated instruction in mathematics for students with learning problems: A research synthesis. *Learning Disabilities Research and Practice, 22,* 1–12.

Lackaye, T. D., & Margalit, M. (2006). Comparison of achievement, effort, and self-perceptions among students with learning disabilities and their peers from different achievement groups. *Journal of Learning Disabilities, 39,* 432–446.

Lago, R. M., & DiPerna, J. C. (2010). Number sense in kindergarten: A factor-analytic study of the construct. *School Psychology Review, 39,* 164–180.

Larson, N. (2008). *Saxon math.* Orlando, FL: Harcourt Achieve.

Laski, E. V., & Siegler, R. S. (2014). Learning from number board games: You learn what you encode. *Developmental Psychology, 50*(3), 853–864.

Le Corre, M., & Carey, S. (2007). One, two, three, four, nothing more: An investigation of the conceptual sources of the verbal counting principles. *Cognition, 105,* 395–438.

Le Corre, M., Van de Walle, G. A., Brannon, E., & Carey, S. (2006). Re-visiting the performance/ competence debate in the acquisition of counting as a representation of the positive integers. *Cognitive Psychology, 52,* 130–169.

Lee, C., & Tindal, G. A. (1994). Self-recording and

goal-setting: Effects on on-task and math productivity of low-achieving Korean elementary school students. *Journal of Behavioral Education, 4,* 459–479.

Lee, D. L., Lylo, B. J., Vostal, B. R., & Hua, Y. (2012). The effects of high-preference problems on the completion of non-preferred mathematics problems. *Journal of Applied Behavior Analysis, 45,* 223–228.

Lee, J. O. (2011). Reach teachers now to ensure common core success. *Kappan, 92*(6), 42–44.

Leh, J. M., & Jitendra, A. K. (2012). Effects of computer-mediated versus teacher-mediated instruction on the mathematical word problem-solving performance of third-grade students with mathematical difficulties. *Learning Disability Quarterly, 36,* 68–79.

Lembke, E. S., Hampton, D., & Beyers, S. J. (2012). Response to intervention in mathematics: Critical elements. *Psychology in the Schools, 49,* 257–272.

Li, Q., & Ma, X. (2010). A meta-analysis of the effects of computer technology on school students' mathematics learning. *Educational Psychology Review, 22,* 215–243.

Licht, B. G., & Kistner, J. A. (1986). Motivational problems of learning-disabled children: Individual differences and their implications for treatment. In J. K. Torgesen, & B. W. L. Wong (Eds.), *Psychological and educational perspectives on learning disabilities* (pp. 225–255). Orlando, FL: Academic Press.

Linnenbrink, E. A., & Pintrich, P. R. (2001). Motivation as an enabler for academic success. *School Psychology Review, 31,* 313–327.

Locuniak, M. N., & Jordan, N. C. (2008). Using kindergarten number sense to predict calculation fluency in second grade. *Journal of Learning Disabilities, 41,* 451–459.

Mancl, D. B., Miller, S. P., & Kennedy, M. (2012). Using the concrete–representational–abstract sequence with integrated strategy instruction to teach subtraction with regrouping to students with learning disabilities. *Learning Disabilities Research and Practice, 27,* 152–166.

Martens, B., & Eckert, T. (2007). The Instructional hierarchy as a model of stimulus control over student and teacher behavior: We're close but are we close enough? *Journal of Behavioral Education, 16*(1), 82–90.

Marzano, R. J., Pickering, D. J., & Pollock, J. E. (2001). *Classroom instruction that works: Research-based strategies for increasing student achievement.* Alexandria, VA: Association for Supervision and Curriculum Development.

Mautone, J. A., DuPaul, G. J., & Jitendra, A. K. (2005). The effects of computer-assisted instruction on the mathematics performance and classroom behavior of children with ADHD. *Journal of Attention Disorders, 9,* 301–312.

Mayfield, K. H., & Chase, P. N. (2002). The effects of cumulative practice on mathematics problem solving. *Journal of Applied Behavior Analysis, 35,* 105–123.

Mazzocco, M. M. M. (2007). Defining and differentiating mathematical learning disabilities and difficulties. In D. B. Berch & M. M. M. Mazzocco (Eds.), *Why is math so hard for some children?: The nature and origins of mathematics learning difficulties and disabilities* (pp. 29–47). Baltimore: Brookes.

Mazzocco, M. M. M., Devlin, K. T., & McKenney, J. L. (2008). Is it a fact?: Timed arithmetic performance of children with mathematical learning disabilities (MLD) varies as a function of how MLD is defined. *Developmental Neuropsychology, 33,* 318–344.

Mazzocco, M. M. M., & Thompson, R. (2005). Kindergarten predictors of math learning disability. *Learning Disabilities Research and Practice, 20,* 142–155.

McCallum, E., Skinner, C. H., & Hutchins, H. (2004). The taped-problems intervention: Increasing division fact fluency using a low-tech self-managed time-delay intervention. *Journal of Applied School Psychology, 20,* 129–147.

McCallum, E., Skinner, C. H., Turner, H., & Saecker, L. (2006). The taped-problems intervention: Increasing multiplication fact fluency using a low-tech, classwide, time-delay intervention. *School Psychology Review, 35,* 419–434.

McCleary, D. F., Aspiranti, K. B., Skinner, C. H., Foster, L. N., Luna, E., Murray, K., et al. (2011). Enhancing math fact fluency via taped problems in intact second- and fourth-grade classrooms. *Journal of Evidence-Based Practices for Schools, 12,* 179–201.

Meichenbaum, D., & Goodman, J. (1971). Training impulsive children to talk to themselves: A means of developing self-control. *Journal of Abnormal Psychology, 77,* 115–126.

Menesses, K. F., & Gresham, F. M. (2009). Relative efficacy of reciprocal and nonreciprocal peer tutoring for students at-risk for academic failure. *School Psychology Quarterly, 24,* 266–275.

Mercer, C. D., & Miller, S. P. (1992a). *Multiplication facts 0 to 81.* Lawrence, KS: Edge Enterprises.

Mercer, C. D., & Miller, S. P. (1992b). Teaching students with learning problems in math to acquire, understand, and apply basic math facts. *Remedial and Special Education, 13,* 19–35.

Methe, S., Kilgus, S., Neiman, C., & Riley-Tillman, T. C. (2012). Meta-analysis of interventions for basic mathematics computation in single-case research. *Journal of Behavioral Education, 21,* 230–253.

Miller, K. C., Skinner, C. H., Gibby, L., Galyon, C. E., & Meadows-Allen, S. (2011). Evaluating generalization of addition-fact fluency using the taped-problems procedure in a second-grade classroom. *Journal of Behavioral Education, 20,* 203–220.

Miller, S. P., & Hudson, P. J. (2007). Using evidence-based practices to build mathematics competence related to conceptual, procedural, and declarative knowledge. *Learning Disabilities Research and Practice, 22,* 47–57.

Miller, S. P., & Kaffar, B. J. (2011). Developing addition with regrouping competence among second graders with mathematics difficulties. *Investigations in Mathematics Learning, 4,* 24–49.

Miller, S. P., & Mercer, C. D. (1993a). Mnemonics: Enhancing the math performance of students with learning difficulties. *Intervention in School and Clinic, 29,* 78–82.

Miller, S. P., & Mercer, C. D. (1993b). Using data to learn about concrete–semi-concrete abstract instruction for students with math disabilities. *Learning Disabilities Research and Practice, 8,* 89–96.

Mong, M. D., Doggett, R. A., Mong, K. W., & Henington, C. (2012). An evaluation of the math to mastery intervention package with elementary school students in a school setting. *Journal of Evidence-Based Practices for Schools, 13,* 61–78.

Mong, M. D., & Mong, K. W. (2010). Efficacy of two math interventions for enhancing fluency with elementary students. *Journal of Behavioral Education, 19,* 273–288.

Mong, M. D., & Mong, K. W. (2012). The utility of brief experimental analysis and extended intervention analysis in selecting effective mathematics interventions. *Journal of Behavioral Education, 21,* 99–118.

Montague, M. (1997). Cognitive strategy instruction in mathematics for students with learning disabilities. In D. P. Rivera (Ed.), *Mathematics education for students with learning disabilities: Theory to practice* (pp. 177–200). Austin, TX: PRO-ED.

Montague, M. (2003). *Solve It!: A mathematical problem-solving instructional program.* Reston, VA: Exceptional Innovations.

Montague, M. (2007). Self-regulation and mathematics instruction. *Learning Disabilities Research and Practice, 22,* 75–83.

Montague, M. (2008a). *Implementing Solve It!: A professional development guide for facilitators.* Reston, VA: Exceptional Innovations.

Montague, M. (2008b). Self-regulation strategies to improve mathematical problem solving for students with learning disabilities. *Learning Disability Quarterly, 31,* 37–44.

Montague, M., Enders, C., & Dietz, S. (2011). The effects of cognitive strategy instruction on math problem solving of middle school students with learning disabilities. *Learning Disability Quarterly, 35,* 1–11.

Montarello, S., & Martens, B. K. (2005). Effects of interspersed brief problems on students' endurance at completing math work. *Journal of Behavioral Education, 14,* 249–266.

Morgan, P. L., Farkas, G., & Wu, Q. (2009). Five-year growth trajectories of kindergarten children with learning difficulties in mathematics. *Journal of Learning Disabilities, 42,* 306–321.

Morgan, P. L., & Sideridis, G. D. (2006). Contrasting the effectiveness of fluency interventions for students with or at-risk for learning disabilities: A multilevel random coefficient modeling meta-analysis. *Learning Disabilities Research and Practice, 21,* 191–210.

Morisano, D., & Shore, B. M. (2010). Can personal goal setting tap the potential of the gifted underachiever? *Roeper Review, 32,* 249–258.

Murayama, K., Pekrun, R., Lichtenfeld, S., & vom Hofe, R. (2013). Predicting long-term growth in students' mathematics achievement: The unique contributions of motivation and cognitive strategies. *Child Development, 84*(4), 1475–1490.

Murphy, M. M., Mazzocco, M. M., Hanich, L. B., & Early, M. C. (2007). Cognitive characteristics of children with mathematics learning disability (MLD) vary as a function of the cutoff criterion used to define MLD. *Journal of Learning Disabilities, 40,* 458–478.

National Center for Education Statistics. (2013). National assessment of educational progress: Mathematics. Retrieved from *www.nationsreportcard. gov/reading_math_2013.*

National Center for Education Statistics. (2015). National assessment of educational progress: Mathematics. Retrieved from *www.nationsreportcard. gov/reading_math_2015.*

National Center on Intensive Interventions. (n.d.). Academic progress monitoring: GOM. Retrieved from *www.intensiveintervention.org/chart/ progress-monitoring.*

National Council of Teachers of Mathematics. (2006). *Curriculum focal points for prekindergarten through grade 8 mathematics: A quest for coherence.* Reston, VA: The National Council of Teachers of Mathematics, Inc.

National Governors Association Center for Best

Practices & Council of Chief State School Officers. (2010). *Common core state standards for mathematics.* Washington, DC: Author. Retrieved from *www.corestandards.org/Math.*

National Mathematics Advisory Panel. (2008). *Foundations for success: The final report of the National Mathematics Advisory Panel.* Washington, DC: U.S. Department of Education. Retrieved from *www2.ed.gov/about/bdscomm/list/math-panel/report/final-report.pdf.*

Nelson, P. M., Burns, M. K., Kanive, R., & Ysseldyke, J. E. (2013). Comparison of a math fact rehearsal and a mnemonic strategy approach for improving math fact fluency. *Journal of School Psychology, 51,* 659–667. (*)

Niemiec, R. P., & Walberg, H. J. (1985). Computers and achievement in the elementary schools. *Journal of Educational Computing Research, 1,* 435–440.

Noell, G. H. (2008). Research examining the relationships among consultation process, treatment integrity, and outcomes. In W. P. Erchul & S. M. Sheridan (Eds.), *Handbook of research in school consultation: Empirical foundations for the field* (pp. 323–342). Mahwah, NJ: Erlbaum.

Noell, G. H., Freeland, J. T., Witt, J. C., & Gansle, K. A. (2001). Using brief assessments to identify effective interventions for individual students. *Journal of School Psychology, 39,* 335–355.

O'Connell, S., & SanGiovanni, J. (2011). *Mastering the basic math facts in addition and subtraction.* Portsmouth, NH: Heinemann.

Ota, K. R., & DuPaul, G. J. (2002). Task engagement and mathematics performance in children with attention-deficit hyperactivity disorder: Effects of supplemental computer instruction. *School Psychology Quarterly, 17,* 242–257.

Owens, J. & Hoza, B. (2003). The role of inattention and hyperactivity/impulsivity in the positive illusory bias. *Journal of Consulting and Clinical Psychology, 4,* 680–691.

Parkhurst, J., Skinner, C. H., Yaw, J., Poncy, B., Adcock, W., & Luna, E. (2010). Efficient class-wide remediation: Using technology to identify idiosyncratic math facts for additional automaticity drills. *International Journal of Behavioral Consultation and Therapy, 6,* 111–123.

Parsons, S., & Bynner, J. (1997). Numeracy and employment. *Education and Training, 39,* 43–51.

Patton, J. R., Cronin, M. E., Bassett, D. S., & Koppel, A. E. (1997). A life skills approach to mathematics instruction: Preparing students with learning disabilities for the real-life math demands of adulthood. *Journal of Learning Disabilities, 30,* 178–187.

Peterson, S. K., Mercer, C. D., & O'Shea, L. (1988). Teaching learning disabled children place value using the concrete to abstract sequence. *Learning Disabilities Research, 4,* 52–56.

Pintrich, P. R., & de Groot, E. (1990). Motivational and self-regulated learning components of classroom academic performance. *Journal of Educational Psychology, 82,* 66–78.

Pintrich, P. R., & Schunk, D. H. (2002). *Motivation in education: Theory, research, and applications* (2nd ed.). Upper Saddle River, NJ: Merrill.

Poncy, B. C., Duhon, G. J., Lee, S. B., & Key, A. (2010). Evaluation of techniques to promote generalization with basic math fact skills. *Journal of Behavioral Education, 19,* 76–92.

Poncy, B. C., Fontelle, S. F., IV, & Skinner, C. H. (2013). Using detect, practice, and repair (DPR) to differentiate and individualize math fact instruction in a class-wide setting. *Journal of Behavioral Education, 22,* 211–228.

Poncy, B. C., McCallum, E., & Schmitt, A. J. (2010). A comparison of behavioral and constructivist interventions for increasing math-fact fluency in a second-grade classroom. *Psychology in the Schools, 47,* 917–930.

Poncy, B. C., & Skinner, C. H. (2011). Combining class-wide cover, copy, and compare (CCC) with an interdependent group contingency to enhance addition-fact fluency in a first-grade classroom. *Journal of Applied School Psychology, 27,* 1–20.

Poncy, B. C., Skinner, C. H., & Axtell, P. K. (2010). An investigation of detect, practice, and repair (DPR) to remedy math fact deficits in third-grade students. *Psychology in the Schools, 47,* 342–353.

Poncy, B. C., Skinner, C. H., & Jaspers, K. E. (2007). Evaluating and comparing interventions designed to enhance math fact accuracy and fluency: Cover, copy, and compare versus taped problems. *Journal of Behavioral Education, 16,* 27–37.

Poncy, B. C., Skinner, C. H., & McCallum, E. (2012). A comparison of class-wide taped problems and cover, copy, and compare for enhancing mathematics fluency. *Psychology in the Schools, 49,* 744–755.

Poncy, B. C., Skinner, C. H., & O'Mara, T. (2006). Detect, practice, and repair: The effects of a class-wide intervention on elementary students' math fact fluency. *Journal of Evidence Based Practices for Schools, 7,* 47–68.

Poncy, B. C., Solomon, B., Duhon, G., Skinner, C., Moore, K., & Simons, S. (2015). An analysis of learning rate and curricular scope: Caution when choosing academic interventions based on aggregated outcomes. *School Psychology Review, 44,* 289–305.

Porter, A., McMaken, J., Hwang, J., & Yang, R. (2011). Common core standards: The new U.S. intended curriculum. *Educational Researcher, 40*(3), 103–116.

Porter, A. C., Polikoff, M. S., & Smithson, J. (2009). Is there a de facto national intended curriculum?: Evidence from state content standards. *Educational Evaluation and Policy Analysis, 31,* 238–268.

Powell, S. R. (2011). Solving word problems using schemas: A review of the literature. *Learning Disabilities Research and Practice, 26,* 94–108.

Powell, S. R., & Fuchs, L. S. (2014). Does early algebraic reasoning differ as a function of students' difficulty with calculations versus word problems? *Learning Disabilities Research and Practice, 29,* 106–116.

Powell, S. R., Fuchs, L. S., & Fuchs, D. (2013). Reaching the mountaintop: Addressing the common core standards in mathematics for students with mathematics difficulties. *Learning Disabilities Research and Practice, 28,* 38–48.

Powell, S. R., Fuchs, L. S., Fuchs, D., Cirino, P. T., & Fletcher, J. M. (2009). Effects of fact retrieval tutoring on third-grade students with math difficulties with and without reading difficulties. *Learning Disabilities Research and Practice, 24,* 1–11.

Price, G. R., Mazzocco, M. M., & Ansari, D. (2013). Why mental arithmetic counts: Brain activation during single digit arithmetic predicts high-school math scores. *Journal of Neuroscience, 33,* 156–163.

Raghubar, K. P., Cirino, P., Barnes, M. A., Ewing-Cobbs, L., Fletcher, J., & Fuchs, L. (2009). Errors in multi-digit arithmetic and behavioral inattention in children with math difficulties. *Journal of Learning Disabilities, 42,* 356–371.

Ramani, G. B., Hitti, A., & Siegler, R. S. (2012). Taking it to the classroom: Number board games as a small group learning activity. *Journal of Educational Psychology, 104,* 661–672.

Ramani, G. B., & Siegler, R. S. (2008). Promoting broad and stable improvements in low-income children's numerical knowledge through playing number board games. *Child Development, 79,* 375–394.

Räsänen, P., Salminen, J., Wilson, A. J., Aunio, P., & Dehaene, S. (2009). Computer-assisted intervention for children with low numeracy skills. *Cognitive Development, 24,* 450–472.

Reinke, W. M., Herman, K. C., Petras, H., & Ialongo, N. S. (2008). Empirically derived subtypes of child academic and behavior problems: Co-occurrence and distal outcomes. *Journal of Abnormal Child Psychology, 36,* 759–770.

Resnick, R. M., Sanislo, G., & Oda, S. (2010). *The complete K–12 report: Market facts and segment analyses.* Rockaway Park, NY: Education Market Research.

Reynolds, J. L. (2010). *The effects of computerized instruction and systematic presentation and review of math fact acquisition and fluency* (doctoral dissertation). Retrieved from ProQuest Dissertations & Theses Global (Order No. 3440726). (*)

Rhymer, K. N., Henington, C., Skinner, C. H., & Looby, E. J. (1999). The effects of explicit timing on mathematics performance in second-grade Caucasian and African American students. *School Psychology Quarterly, 14,* 397–407.

Rhymer, K. N., & Morgan, S. K. (2005). Comparison of the explicit timing and interspersal interventions: Analysis of problem completion rates, student preference, and teacher acceptability. *Journal of Behavioral Education, 14,* 283–303.

Rhymer, K. N., Skinner, C. H., Henington, C., D'Reaux, R. A., & Sims, S. (1998). Effects of explicit timing on mathematics problem completion rates in African-American third grade elementary students. *Journal of Applied Behavior Analysis, 31,* 673–677.

Rhymer, K. N., Skinner, C. H., Jackson, S., McNeill, S., Smith, T., & Jackson, B. (2002). The 1-minute explicit timing intervention: The influence of mathematics problem difficulty. *Journal of Instructional Psychology, 29,* 305–311.

Riccomini, P. J., & Witzel, B. S. (2010). *Response to intervention in math.* Thousand Oaks, CA: Corwin Press.

Rinne, L. F., & Mazzocco, M. M. M. (2014). Knowing right from wrong in mental arithmetic judgments: Calibration of confidence predicts the development of accuracy. *PLoS ONE, 9,* e98663.

Rivera, D. M., & Bryant, B. R. (1992). Mathematics instruction for students with special needs. *Intervention in School and Clinic, 28,* 71–86.

Robinson, D. R., Schofield, J. W., & Steers-Wentzell, K. L. (2005). Peer and cross-age tutoring in math: Outcomes and their design implications. *Educational Psychology Review, 17,* 327–362.

Rohrbeck, C. A., Ginsburg-Block, M. D., Fantuzzo, J. W., & Miller, T. R. (2003). Peer-assisted learning interventions with elementary school students: A meta-analytic review. *Journal of Educational Psychology, 95,* 240–257.

Rohrer, D., & Taylor, K. (2006). The effects of overlearning and distributed practice on the retention of mathematics knowledge. *Applied Cognitive Psychology, 20,* 1209–1224.

Rosenzweig, C., Krawec, J., & Montague, M. (2011). Metacognitive strategy use of eighth-grade students with and without learning disabilities during mathematical problem solving: A think-aloud analysis. *Journal of Learning Disabilities, 44,* 508–520.

Russell, R. L., & Ginsburg, H. P. (1984). Cognitive analysis of children's mathematical difficulties. *Cognition and Instruction, 1,* 217–244.

Russell, S. J. (2012). CCSSM: Keeping teaching and learning strong. *Teaching Children Mathematics, 19,* 50–56.

Russell, S. J., Economopolous, K., Cochran, K., Murray, M., Hollister, A., Bastable, V., et al. (2008). *Investigations in number, data, and space* (2nd ed.). Glenview, IL: Pearson Scott Foresman.

Ryan, R. M., & Deci, E. L. (2000). Intrinsic and extrinsic motivations: Classic definitions and new directions. *Contemporary Educational Psychology, 25,* 54–67.

Salvia, J. S., Ysseldyke, J. E., & Bolt, S. (2010). *Assessment in special and inclusive education.* (11th ed.). Boston: Wadsworth/Cengage.

Sanetti, L. M. H., & Collier-Meek, M. A. (2014). Increasing the rigor of treatment integrity assessment: An empirical comparison of direct observation and permanent product review methods. *Journal of Behavioral Education, 23,* 60–88.

Sanetti, L. M. H., & Kratochwill, T. R. (2009). Toward developing a science of treatment integrity: Introduction to the special series. *School Psychology Review, 38,* 445–459.

Sarama, J., & Clements, D. H. (2004). Building blocks for early childhood mathematics. *Early Childhood Research Quarterly, 19,* 181–189.

Sarama, J., & Clements, D. H. (2006). Mathematics in kindergarten. *Young Children, 61,* 38–41.

Sarama, J., & Clements, D. H. (2009). Concrete computer manipulatives in mathematics education. *Child Development Perspectives, 3,* 145–150.

Sarnecka, B. W., & Carey, S. (2008). How counting represents number: What children must learn and when they learn it. *Cognition, 108,* 662–674.

Sayeski, K. L., & Paulsen, K. J. (2010). Mathematics reform curricula and special education: Identifying intersections and implications for practice. *Intervention in School and Clinic, 46,* 13–21.

Schmidt, W. H., Cogan L. S., Houang, R. T., & McKnight, C. C. (2011). Content coverage differences across districts/states: A persisting challenge for U.S. education policy. *American Journal of Education, 117,* 399–427.

Schmidt, W. H., & Houang, R. T. (2012). Curricular coherence and the common core state standards for mathematics. *Educational Researcher, 41,* 294–308.

Schmidt, W., Houang, R., & Cogan, L. (2002, Summer). A coherent curriculum: The case of mathematics. *American Educator,* pp. 1–18.

Schmidt, W. H., Wang, H. C., & McKnight, C. C. (2005). Curriculum coherence: An examination of US mathematics and science content standards from an international perspective. *Journal of Curriculum Studies, 37*(5), 525–559.

Schnorr, J. M. (1989). Practicing math facts on the computer. *Teacher Education and Special Education, 12,* 65–69.

Schoppek, W., & Tulis, M. (2010). Enhancing arithmetic and word-problem solving skills efficiently by individualized computer-assisted practice. *Journal of Educational Research, 103,* 239–252.

Schunk, D. H. (1985a). Participation in goal setting: Effects on self-efficacy and skills of learning disabled children. *Journal of Special Education, 19,* 307–317.

Schunk, D. H. (1985b). Self-efficacy and classroom learning. *Psychology in the Schools, 22,* 208–223.

Schunk, D. H. (1996). Goal and self-evaluative influences during children's cognitive skill learning. *American Educational Research Journal, 33,* 359–382.

Schunk, D. H., & Cox, P. D. (1986). Strategy training and attributional feedback with learning disabled students. *Journal of Educational Psychology, 78,* 201–209.

Schunk, D. H., & Zimmerman, B. J. (Eds.). (1998). *Self-regulated learning: From teaching to self-reflective practice.* New York: Guilford Press.

Schunk, D. H., & Zimmerman, B. J. (Eds.). (2008). *Motivation and self-regulated learning: Theory, research, and applications.* New York: Erlbaum.

Schutte, G. M., Duhon, G. J., Solomon, B. G., Poncy, B. C., Moore, K., & Story, B. (2015). A comparative analysis of massed vs. distributed practice on basic math fact fluency growth rates. *Journal of School Psychology, 53,* 149–159.

Seidel, T., & Shavelson, R. J. (2007). Teaching effectiveness research in the past decade: The role of theory and research design in disentangling meta-analysis results. *Review of Educational Research, 77,* 454–499.

Seo, Y. J., & Bryant, D. (2009). Analysis of studies of the effects of computer-assisted instruction on the mathematics performance of students with learning disabilities. *Computers and Education, 53,* 913–928.

Seo, Y. J., & Bryant, D. (2012). Multimedia CAI program for students with mathematics difficulties. *Remedial and Special Education, 33,* 217–225.

Shalev, R. S., Manor, O., & Gross-Tsur, V. (2005). Developmental dyscalculia: A prospective six-year follow-up. *Developmental Medicine and Child Neurology, 47,* 121–125.

Shapiro, E. S. (2011). *Academic skills problems: Direct assessment and intervention.* New York: Guilford Press.

Shapiro, E. S., & Gebhardt, S. N. (2012). Comparing computer-adaptive and curriculum-based measurement methods of assessment. *School Psychology Review, 41,* 295–305.

Shiah, R. (1994). *The effects of computer-assisted instruction on the mathematical problem-solving of students with learning disabilities* (doctoral dissertation). Retrieved from ProQuest Dissertations & Theses Global (Order No. 9501770).

Shin, M., & Bryant, D. P. (2015). A synthesis of mathematical and cognitive performances of students with mathematics learning disabilities. *Journal of Learning Disabilities, 48,* 96–112.

Shinn, M. R. (Ed.). (1989). *Curriculum-based measurement: Assessing special children.* New York: Guilford Press.

Siegler, R. S. (1988). Individual differences in strategy choices: Good students, not-so-good students, and perfectionists. *Child Development, 59,* 833–851.

Siegler, R. S., & Booth, J. L. (2004). Development of numerical estimation in young children. *Child Development, 75,* 428–444.

Siegler, R. S., & Pyke, A. A. (2013). Developmental and individual differences in understanding of fractions. *Developmental Psychology, 49,* 1994–2004.

Siegler, R. S., & Ramani, G. B. (2008). Playing linear numerical board games promote low-income children's numerical development. *Developmental Science, 11,* 655–661.

Siegler, R. S., & Ramani, G. B. (2009). Playing linear number board games—but not circular ones—improves low-income preschoolers' numerical understanding. *Journal of Educational Psychology, 101,* 545–560.

Silberglitt, B., & Hintze, J. M. (2005). Formative assessment using CBM-R cut scores to track progress toward success on state-mandated achievement tests: A comparison of methods. *Journal of Psychoeducational Assessment, 23,* 304–325.

Simonsen, B., Fairbanks, S., Briesch, A., Myers, D., & Sugai, G. (2008). Evidence-based practices in classroom management: Considerations for research to practice. *Education and Treatment of Children, 31,* 351–380.

Skinner, C. H. (1998). Preventing academic skills deficits. In T. S. Watson & F. Gresham (Eds.), *Handbook of child behavior therapy: Ecological considerations in assessment, treatment, and evaluation* (pp. 61–83). New York: Plenum Press.

Skinner, C. H., Belfiore, P. J., Mace, H. W., Williams, S., & Johns, G. A. (1997). Altering response topography to increase response efficiency and learning rates. *School Psychology Quarterly, 12,* 54–64.

Skinner, C. H., Fletcher, P. A., & Henington, C. (1996). Increasing learning rates by increasing student response rates: A summary of research. *School Psychology Quarterly, 11,* 313.

Skinner, C. H., Fletcher, P. A., Wildmon, M., & Belfiore, P. J. (1996). Improving assignment preference through interspersing additional problems: Brief versus easy problems. *Journal of Behavioral Education, 6,* 427–436.

Skinner, C. H., Hurst, K. L., Teeple, D. F., & Meadow, S. O. (2002). Increasing on-task behavior during mathematics independent seat-work in students with emotional disturbance in interspersing additional brief problems. *Psychology in the Schools, 39,* 647–659.

Skinner, C. H., McLaughlin, T. F., & Logan, P. (1997). Cover, copy, and compare: A self-managed academic intervention effective across skills, students, and settings. *Journal of Behavioral Education, 7,* 295–306.

Slattow, G. (1977). *Demonstration of the PLATO IV computer-based education system.* Final report, computer-based Education Research Laboratory, University of Illinois.

Slavin, R. E., & Lake, C. (2008). Effective programs in elementary mathematics: An evidence-based synthesis. *Review of Educational Research, 78,* 427–515.

Slavin, R. E., Lake, C., & Groff, C. (2009). Effective programs in middle and high school mathematics: A best-evidence synthesis. *Review of Educational Research, 79*(2), 839–911.

Smith, C. L. (2010). *Examining the effectiveness of peer-tutoring and computer-aided instruction for mastery of multiplication facts* (doctoral dissertation). Retrieved from ProQuest Dissertations & Theses Global (Order No. 3405891). (*)

Spectrum K–12 School Solutions. (2011). Response to intervention adoption survey 2011. Retrieved from *www.spectrumk12.com/rti/the_rti_corner/rti_adoption_report*.

Stecker, P. M., & Fuchs, L. S. (2000). Effecting superior achievement using curriculum-based measurement: The importance of individual progress monitoring. *Learning Disabilities Research and Practice, 15,* 128–134.

Stein, M., Kinder, D., Silbert, J., & Carnine, D. W. (2006). *Designing effective mathematics instruction: A direct instruction approach* (4th ed.). Columbus, OH: Merrill Prentice Hall.

Stein, M., Kinder, D., Zapp, K., & Feuerborn, L. (2010). Promoting positive math outcomes. In M. R. Shinn & H. W. Walker (Eds.), *Interventions for achievement and behavior problems in a three-tier model including RTI* (pp. 527–551). Bethesda, MD: National Association of School Psychologists.

Stickney, E. M., Sharp, L. B., & Kenyon, A. S. (2012). Technology-enhanced assessment of math fact automaticity: Patterns of performance for low- and typically achieving students. *Assessment for Effective Intervention, 37,* 84–94.

Stokes, T. F., & Baer, D. M. (1977). An implicit technology of generalization. *Journal of Applied Behavior Analysis, 10,* 349–367.

Styers, M. K., & Baird-Wilkerson, S. (2011). *A final report for the evaluation of Pearson's focusMATH program.* Charlottesville, VA: Magnolia Consulting.

Suppes, P. (1979). Current trends in computer-assisted instruction. *Advances in Computers, 18,* 173–229.

Swain, K. (2005). CBM with goal setting: Impacting students' understanding of reading goals. *Journal of Instructional Psychology, 32,* 259–265.

Swanson, H. L. (2006). Cross-sectional and incremental changes in working memory and mathematical problem solving. *Journal of Educational Psychology, 98,* 265–281.

Swanson, H. L. (2009). Science-supported math instruction for children with math difficulties: Converting a meta-analysis to practice. In S. Rosenfield, V. Berninger, S. Rosenfield, & V. Berninger (Eds.), *Implementing evidence-based academic interventions in school settings* (pp. 85–106). New York: Oxford University Press.

Swanson, H. L., & Sachse-Lee, C. (2000). A meta-analysis of single-subject design intervention research for students with learning disabilities. *Journal of Learning Disabilities, 33,* 114–136.

Symonds, P. M., & Chase, D. H. (1992). Practice vs. motivation. *Journal of Educational Psychology, 84,* 282–289.

Tabassam, W., & Grainger, J. (2002). Self-concept, attribution style and self-efficacy beliefs of students with learning disabilities with and without attention deficit hyperactivity disorder. *Learning Disability Quarterly, 25,* 141–151.

Tamim, R. M., Bernard, R. M., Borokhovski, E., Abrami, P. C., & Schmid, R. F. (2011). What forty years of research says about the impact of technology on learning a second-order meta-analysis and validation study. *Review of Educational Research, 81,* 4–28.

Taylor, R. P. (2003). The computer in school: Tutor, tool, tutee. *Contemporary Issues in Technology and Teacher Education, 3,* 240–252.

Thanheiser, E. (2012). Understanding multi-digit whole numbers: The role of knowledge components, connections, and context in understanding regrouping 3+-digit numbers. *Journal of Mathematical Behavior, 31,* 220–234.

Thompson, C. A. (2013). Poor quantitative skills of newly insured may affect ability to manage medications. *American Journal of Health-System Pharmacy, 70,* 1464–1475.

Throndsen, I. (2010). Self-regulated learning of basic arithmetic skills: A longitudinal study. *British Journal of Educational Psychology, 81,* 558–578.

Torlaković, E. (2011). Academy of MATH® Efficacy Report: Westwood Elementary School. Retrieved from *www.intensiveintervention.org/chart/academic-intervention-chart/13677.*

Tournaki, N. (2003). The differential effects of teaching addition through strategy instruction versus drill and practice to students with and without learning disabilities. *Journal of Learning Disabilities, 36,* 449–458.

van Garderen, D. (2007). Teaching students with LD to use diagrams to solve mathematical word problems. *Journal of Learning Disabilities, 40,* 540–563.

van Garderen, D., & Scheuermann, A. M. (2014). Diagramming word problems: A strategic approach for instruction. *Intervention in School and Clinic, 50,* 282–290.

van Garderen, D., Scheuermann, A., & Jackson, C. (2012). Examining how students with diverse abilities use diagrams to solve mathematics word problems. *Learning Disability Quarterly, 36,* 145–160.

Van Houten, R., & Thompson, C. (1976). The effects of explicit timing on math performance. *Journal of Applied Behavior Analysis, 9,* 227–230.

VanDerHeyden, A., Codding, R. S., & Martin, R. (2014, February). Relative value of common screening measures in mathematics. In M. Burns (Chair), *Assessment to intervention for math: Putting theory into practice.* Symposium presented at the annual conference of the National Association of School Psychologists, Washington, DC.

VanDerHeyden, A., McLaughlin, T., Algina, K., & Snyder, P. (2012). Randomized evaluation of a supplemental grade-wide mathematics intervention. *American Educational Research Journal, 49*, 1251–1284.

VanDerHeyden, A. M. (2014). Best practices in can't do/won't do academic assessment. In P. Harrison & A. Thomas (Eds.), *Best practices in school psychology: Data-based and collaborative decision making* (pp. 305–316). Bethesda, MD: National Association of School Psychologists.

VanDerHeyden, A. M., & Burns, M. K. (2005). Using curriculum-based assessment and curriculum-based measurement to guide elementary mathematics instruction: Effect on individual and group accountability scores. *Assessment for Effective Intervention, 30*, 15–31.

VanDerHeyden, A. M., & Burns, M. K. (2009). Performance indicators in math: Implications for brief experimental analysis of academic performance. *Journal of Behavioral Education, 18*, 71–91.

VanDerHeyden, A. M., Witt, J. C., & Barnett, D. A. (2005). The emergence and possible futures of response to intervention. *Journal of Psychoeducational Assessment, 23*, 339–361.

VanDerHeyden, A. M., Witt, J. C., & Gilbertson, D. (2007). A multi-year evaluation of the effects of a response to intervention (RTI) model on identification of children for special education. *Journal of School Psychology, 45*, 225–256.

VanDerHeyden, A. M., Witt, J. C., & Naquin, G. (2003). Development and validation of a process for screening referrals to special education. *School Psychology Review, 32*, 204–227.

Walles, R. L. (2008). *The road to mathematics in elementary school: Social and cognitive influences on performance and response to intervention* (doctoral dissertation). Retrieved from ProQuest Dissertations & Theses Global (Order No. 3315496). (*)

Wang, H., & Woodworth, K. (2011). *A randomized controlled trial of two online mathematics curricula.* Evanston, IL: Society for Research on Educational Effectiveness.

Watson, S. M. R., & Gable, R. A. (2012). Unraveling the complex nature of mathematics learning disability: Implications for research and practice. *Learning Disability Quarterly, 36*, 178–187.

Weinert, F. E., Schrader, F. W., & Helmke, A. (1989). Quality of instruction and achievement outcomes. *International Journal of Educational Research, 13*, 895–914.

Wesson, C. L. (1991). Curriculum-based measurement and two models of follow-up consultation. *Exceptional Children, 57*, 246–256.

What Works Clearinghouse. (2013). *Procedures and standards handbook (Version 3.0).* Washington,

DC: National Center for Education Evaluation and Regional Assistance, Institute of Education Sciences, U.S. Department of Education.

Wilkins, J. L. M. (2010). Modeling quantitative literacy. *Educational and Psychological Measurement, 70*, 267–290.

Wilson, A. J., Dehaene, S., Dubois, O., & Fayol, M. (2009). Effects of an adaptive game intervention on accessing number sense in low-socioeconomic-status kindergarten children. *Mind, Brain, and Education, 3*, 224–234.

Wilson, A. J., Dehaene, S., Pinel, P., Revkin, S. K., Cohen, L., & Cohen, D. (2006, May 30). Principles underlying the design of "The Number Race," an adaptive computer game for remediation of dyscalculia. *Behavioral and Brain Functions, 2*, 19.

Wilson, A. J., Revkin, S. K., Cohen, D., Cohen, L., & Dehaene, S. (2006, May 30). An open trial assessment of "The Number Race," an adaptive computer game for remediation of dyscalculia. *Behavioral and Brain Functions, 2*, 20.

Windingstad, S., Skinner, C. H., Rowland, E., Cardin, E., & Fearrington, J. (2009). Extending research on a class-wide, math fluency building intervention: Applying taped-problems in a second-grade classroom. *Journal of Applied School Psychology, 25*, 364–381.

Witt, J. C., Daly, E. M., & Noell, G. (2000). *Functional assessments: A step-by-step guide to solving academic and behavior problems.* Longmont, CO: Sopris West.

Woodward, J. (2006). Developing automaticity in basic multiplication facts: Integrating strategy instruction with time practice drills. *Learning Disability Quarterly, 29*, 269–289.

Woodward, J., Beckmann, S., Driscoll, M., Franke, M., Herzig, P., Jitendra, A., et al. (2012). *Improving mathematical problem solving in grades 4 through 8: A practice guide* (NCEE 2012-4055). Washington, DC: National Center for Education Evaluation and Regional Assistance, Institute of Education Sciences, U.S. Department of Education. Retrieved from *http://ies.ed.gov/ncee/wwc/publications_reviews.aspx#pubsearch.*

Woodward, J., & Howard, L. (1994). The misconceptions of youth: Errors and their mathematical meaning. *Exceptional Children, 61*, 126–136.

Wright, J. (2011). Response-to-intervention school readiness survey. Retrieved from *www.jimwrightonline.com/php/rti/rti_wire.php.*

Wu, H. (1999). Basic skills versus conceptual understanding: A bogus dichotomy in mathematics education. *American Educator, 23*, 14–19, 50–52.

Wu, H. (2011). *Understanding numbers in elementary school mathematics.* Providence, RI: American Mathematical Society.

Wynn, K. (1992). Children's acquisition of the number words and the counting system. *Cognitive Psychology, 24,* 220–251.

Xin, Y. P. (2008). The effect of schema-based instruction in solving mathematics word problems: An emphasis on pre-algebraic conceptualization of multiplicative relations. *Journal for Research in Mathematics Education, 39,* 526–551.

Xin, Y. P., & Jitendra, A. K. (1999). The effects of instruction in solving mathematical word problems for students with learning problems: A meta-analysis. *Journal of Special Education, 32,* 40–78.

Yeaton, W. H., & Sechrest, L. (1981). Critical dimensions in the choice and maintenance of successful treatments: Strength, integrity, and effectiveness. *Journal of Consulting and Clinical Psychology, 49,* 156–167.

Yell, M. L., Shriner, J. G., & Katsiyannis, A. (2006). The Individual with Disabilities Education Improvement Act of 2004: Implications for special and general educators, administrators, and teacher trainers. *Focus on Exceptional Children, 39,* 1–24.

Ysseldyke, J. E., Thill, T., Pohl, J., & Bolt, D. (2005). Using MathFacts in a Flash to enhance computational fluency. *Journal of Evidence-Based Practices for Schools, 6,* 59–89.

Zhang, D., & Xin, Y. P. (2012). A follow-up meta-analysis for word-problem-solving interventions for students with mathematics difficulties. *Journal of Educational Research, 105,* 303–318.

Zheng, X., Flynn, L. J., & Swanson, H. L. (2012). Experimental intervention studies on word problem solving and math disabilities: A selective analysis of the literature. *Learning Disability Quarterly, 36,* 97–111.

Zimmerman, B. J. (2002). Becoming a self-regulated learner: An overview. *Theory into Practice, 41,* 64–70.

Zimmerman, B. J., & Campillo, M. (2003). Motivating self-regulated problem solvers. In J. E. Davidson & R. Sternberg (Eds.), *The nature of problem solving* (pp. 233–262). New York: Cambridge University Press.

Zimmerman, B. J., & Martinez-Pons, M. (1988). Construct validation of a strategy model of student self-regulated learning. *Journal of Educational Psychology, 80,* 284–290.

Index

Note: *f* following a page number indicates a figure; *t* indicates a table.